MY TEENAGE WEREWOLF

MY
TEENAGE
WEREWOLF

A MOTHER, A DAUGHTER,
A JOURNEY THROUGH THE
THICKET OF ADOLESCENCE

LAUREN KESSLER

VIKING

VIKING
Published by the Penguin Group
Penguin Group (USA) Inc., 375 Hudson Street, New York, New York 10014, U.S.A.
Penguin Group (Canada), 90 Eglinton Avenue East, Suite 700, Toronto,
Ontario, Canada M4P 2Y3 (a division of Pearson Penguin Canada Inc.)
Penguin Books Ltd, 80 Strand, London WC2R 0RL, England
Penguin Ireland, 25 St. Stephen's Green, Dublin 2, Ireland (a division of Penguin Books Ltd)
Penguin Books Australia Ltd, 250 Camberwell Road, Camberwell, Victoria 3124, Australia
(a division of Pearson Australia Group Pty Ltd)
Penguin Books India Pvt Ltd, 11 Community Centre, Panchsheel Park,
New Delhi—110 017, India
Penguin Group (NZ), 67 Apollo Drive, Rosedale, North Shore 0632, New Zealand
(a division of Pearson New Zealand Ltd)
Penguin Books (South Africa) (Pty) Ltd, 24 Sturdee Avenue, Rosebank,
Johannesburg 2196, South Africa

Penguin Books Ltd, Registered Offices: 80 Strand, London WC2R 0RL, England

First published in 2010 by Viking Penguin, a member of Penguin Group (USA) Inc.

1 3 5 7 9 10 8 6 4 2

LIBRARY OF CONGRESS CATALOGING-IN-PUBLICATION DATA
Kessler, Lauren.
My teenage werewolf : a mother, a daughter, a journey into the wilds of adolescence /
Lauren Kessler.
p. cm.
ISBN 978-0-670-02169-7
1. Teenage girls. 2. Mothers and daughters. I. Title.
HQ798.K475 2010
306.874'30973—dc22   2009037524

Printed in the United States of America

*Penguin is committed to publishing works of quality and integrity.
In that spirit, we are proud to offer this book to our readers;
however, the story, the experiences, and the words
are the author's alone.*

To Lizzie, of course

AUTHOR'S NOTE

This is a work of nonfiction. Every character in this book is a real person. There are no composites or creations. I have changed the names of the kids (except for Lizzie, who wanted her real name used) to protect their privacy, but I have not changed any other details about them. Every scene in the book happened. I witnessed (sometimes participated in, or very occasionally debriefed the participants about) all of them. Every bit of dialogue, every conversation was spoken. I recorded it all as faithfully as I could.

Any liberties I have taken are liberties of interpretation, not fact. I spent this year and a half immersed in teen/tween girl culture and my daughter's life, filtering what I saw—as all writers, nonfiction or otherwise, do—through my own eyes, my own sensibilities. I mean to tell truths both factual and emotional.

MY TEENAGE WEREWOLF

ONE

Lizzie comes home from school, walking down the long access road from the street where the bus drops her off. She makes her way to the side door of our house. She's wearing (for the fourth day in a row) a particularly unflattering pair of brown corduroy jeans that sag at the knees and butt, a gray Oregon Girls Rock T-shirt (three days for that item), and a pair of blown-out Skechers. On her back is a twenty-pound pack that includes, among other things, several dozen broken pencils, two or three sack lunches that she thinks I don't know she hasn't eaten, and a science book so heavy it makes you wonder if there really is that much science a seventh-grader needs to know. She drops everything on the floor of the foyer, kicks off her shoes, and starts to walk down the hall past my writing room. She knows I'm in there. I'm always in there, but she doesn't stop.

"Hi!" I call out. "So, how was school?" I ask before she completely disappears from view. She turns her head and gives me a look. There may be nothing quite so withering as the look an almost teenaged daughter can give her mother. What is it, exactly, that look? Exasperation, annoyance, disgust? And that's on a good day. Sometimes it's pure, unadulterated antipathy. She sighs dramatically and mutters something under her breath. I don't want to know what she says. I can tell where this afternoon is headed.

"So, how was school?" I repeat. I hear the false, purposeful brightness in my voice, and, of course, so does she. Why am I doing this? It's like baiting a bear. She's edged back into view, standing in the doorway to my room. Her hand is on her hip, her head cocked to one side, her eyes focused on a point about six inches above my head. I know this posture. I stood in front of my own mother like this countless times. The stance communicates two of the sacred tenets of teen girlhood: boredom and defiance. The message is unmistakable. I choose to ignore it.

"School?" I prompt her.

"You're always asking me about school," she says accusingly. "Stop asking me about school."

"Well," I say sweetly, "that's how you spend seven hours five days a week, so naturally I . . ." She interrupts me.

"I hate school," she says.

"You don't really hate school," I say.

"I hate it."

"No, you don't."

"Oh yes I do."

"Oh no you don't."

I'm listening to this conversation as if I were not the one enmeshed in it, and I don't believe what I'm hearing. She's twelve and in a crappy mood. What's my excuse? It's a cliché that adults revert to being children when we visit our own parents. I wonder if I'm the only mother out there who reverts to being a teenager when faced with her own (almost) teen.

I'm suddenly reminded of a bit of nasty dialog the writer Gay Talese caught between a famous director (Joshua Logan) and a famous Broadway actress (Claudia McNeil) in one of his iconic pieces of new journalism. The conversation begins with Logan critiquing McNeil's stage performance and devolves into this:

"You're a shocking rude woman!"

"Yes, Mr. Logan."

"You're being a beast."

"Yes, Mr. Logan."

"Yes, Miss Beast."

"Yes, Mr. Logan."

"Yes, Miss Beast."

I remember reading this, years ago, having no clue who Logan and

McNeil were—their heydays were before my time—but being completely immersed in their mutual hostility. It comes as a shock—and a wake-up call—that this is sometimes the story of me and my daughter: completely immersed in mutual hostility.

But it wasn't always like this.

There was for us a golden era, a magic decade of peace, love, and understanding that is common in the early years of the mother-daughter relationship. It's like you get a free pass for the first decade or so. You don't even have to work up a sweat. These are the years when Mommy is a saint and a genius, beautiful and beneficent, the font of everything cool and fun. I remember the scores of Wednesday afternoons my daughter Lizzie and I spent together when she was in elementary school. Wednesday was early-release day. I would pick her up at school at one p.m., and we would go roller-skating or bowling or spend an hour at a downtown tearoom sipping hot chocolate from bone china cups and nibbling on the world's fanciest PB&Js. We did projects—making candles, friendship bracelets, tie-dye. We made Valentine's Day cards by carefully ironing sheets of waxed paper between which we had sandwiched the shavings of red and pink crayons. (Thank you, Martha Stewart.) We rode bicycles. We hung out at pet shops, oohing and aahing at puppies and letting ferrets crawl up our arms. If this sounds a bit precious, it was—but in the unironic sense of the word: special, beloved. She actually looked forward to these times. There was no sense of obligation or dread—Oh god, I have to go do something with my mom again. No rolling of eyes, no looking at me as if I were the enemy or, less dramatically, as if I were the least interesting object in view.

Back in those halcyon days—which were, I am sure, less uniformly glorious than I am choosing to remember—Lizzie pitched fits, as the old expression goes, but the anger was superficial and transient. The battles were contained and low risk (yes, you can watch an extra half hour of TV; no, you can't have cookies for breakfast); the damage, minimal; the resolutions, quick. When it was over, she would sit on my lap. At night, I would curl up next to her on top of the covers of her bed—the four-poster bed that had been mine as a child—and rub her back until I heard her breathing deepen. In the morning, I would wake her with a kiss. She was warm and smelled like a loaf of fresh bread.

I remember those easy days as clearly as if they were yesterday. Wait a minute, they *were* yesterday.

Yesterday we spent an hour talking preteen nonsense—who has a crush on whom, whose school locker has the weirdest decorations—and drinking hot chocolates at Starbucks. We walked arm in arm back to the car. She put in a Lucinda Williams CD, and we drummed together on the dashboard. But hold on. Yesterday was also when, just a half hour after we got home from our happy adventure, World War III broke out over the issue of eating fish for dinner. Her mood blackened the evening, as it often does. My husband, Tom, and I sniped at each other. Lizzie shot me the signature look, stomped upstairs, slammed her door, cranked up the music in her room, and then later refused a good-night kiss.

Who is this girl I live with, this twelve-year-old, this daughter I wanted so badly and now don't know how to connect with? And who do I turn into when we lock horns, as we do most days, on . . . well, on just about everything. We fight about taking showers, choosing appropriate clothing (flip-flops in December?), food and nutrition (she recognizes only two food groups: cheese and deep-fried), table manners, chores, homework, screen time. We fight over everything, and nothing. Most mornings we eye each other warily, waiting to see who will cast the first stone—neither of us free of sin, both of us well armed.

It doesn't help at all to discover that our stormy relationship is so common as to be prosaic, that the descent from mother-goddess to mother-demon is a predictable, well-documented narrative, as predictable as the descent from sweet little girl to moody, mercurial teenager. The years after a daughter reaches puberty are renowned for their drama and tumult. Psychologists, psychoanalysts, sociologists, social learning theorists, and a boatload of feminist scholars are all over this. It is, many argue, the most significant of all intergenerational connections, the earliest and most profound bond. There is no relationship quite as primal, as vitally important, or as deeply conflicted. Mother-daughter identities are enmeshed and interwoven, yet need to be individual and distinct. There is no other relationship that veers so sharply between intimacy and distance, between love and hate.

I've been dabbling in some of the research, slogging through lingo like "conflictual femininities" and "compulsory differentiation," "emotional incest" and "unconscious internalization processes." I've been introduced to mothers who won't let go of their daughters ("toxic entanglement"), and daughters who won't let go of their mothers ("intrafamilial codependency"); mothers who view daughters as rivals, and daughters who view mothers as object lessons in how not to live their lives; mothers who view daughters as brats, and daughters who view mothers as bitches.

Daughters spend their whole lives figuring out how to differentiate themselves from their mothers. (I guess this is why we adult daughters, so many years later, still live in fear of turning out to be just like our mothers.) It appears that particularly intense mother-daughter bonds can inhibit the daughter from establishing her own identity. But particularly weak ones can inhibit the daughter from learning how to be female. There's a strong sense of damned if you do, damned if you don't running through the research.

With all this attention to the relationship that everyone seems to agree is at the core of being female, I wrack my brain trying to think of important, classic mother-daughter relationships. I'd like to learn something from them if I can. I come up with only one, Persephone and Demeter. You remember the story: Daughter is abducted, and loving mother is so distraught that she abandons her goddess responsibilities, and the earth goes to hell in a hand basket, or, as one literary critic put it, oh so literarily, "The springs of fertility ran dry, vegetation languished and animals ceased to multiply." I suppose that puts Lizzie and me in perspective. As distraught as I am about the distance that has opened up between us, I am not likely to visit eternal winter on the earth.

I look in vain for other examples that are not evil stepmother makes daughter's life a living hell (Snow White, Cinderella, Joan Crawford). One of my friends, an English professor with a charming, huggable seven-year-old daughter whom I wish I could kidnap, tells me to stop looking. I won't find many mother-daughter relationships explored in classic literature, she says.

I devolve to popular culture, and here I find all kinds of examples of feisty, interesting daughters—with no mothers: Nancy Drew (dead mother); Margie from *My Little Margie*, the 1950s sitcom I saw in endless campy reruns when I was a kid (dead mother); *Veronica Mars*, a show Lizzie and I have watched together (MIA alcoholic mother); Lyra in *The Golden Compass* (her mother isn't dead, but Lyra comes of age thinking she is). What a great way to finesse the issue of how the young women in question achieve their independence, how they negotiate their separate female identity—and how the mothers survive it all.

Okay, so there's the *Gilmore Girls*—another series Lizzie and I have watched together—with a feisty daughter and a mother who is actually alive. But, as Lizzie was quick to point out to me (multiple times and with unrepressed glee), the Gilmore daughter is not as much in need of mothering as is her own mother. Daughter Rory handles just about everything in her teen life better than her mother did. No wonder Lizzie loved this series—and I had trouble watching it.

What other mothers and daughters do we see out there? The Shirley MacLaine and Debra Winger characters in *Terms of Endearment*? Ouch. Sharon and Kelly Osbourne? Joan and Melissa Rivers? Double ouch.

There may be few finely drawn portraits of the mother-daughter dynamic, but there is plenty of advice about it, especially the conflicting kind. Give the girl room! Step back! That's the conventional wisdom and the recommendations from those who endorse what's known as traditional development theory. Move closer! Stay connected! That's what others are saying, psychologists and therapists among them. Connection, not separation, will keep girls strong and whole. Some experts offer lists of fifty fun things you can do with your teens. Others warn you against "smotherhood."

And so, the road I am traveling—that every mother of an about-to-be or full-fledged teen is traveling—is both well trod and mysterious. It's a mapped road, but there is significant disagreement about how to navigate it. It's a mapped road, but even so, the twists and turns take us by surprise. Yes, it's all happened before, but it's never happened to *us* before.

There are those who believe the mother-teen daughter relationship is "just a phase," that if you can shut up and grit your teeth, it will be over in a few years. This, I think, is the prevailing opinion. I hear it from mothers of twenty-somethings when I tell them my tale of woe. They nod in solemn agreement as I offer the gory details of my life with Lizzie, the daily drama, the random acts of meanness, the horrific shopping trips. And then they smile serenely and pat my shoulder. "That's how it used to be with me and my daughter," they say consolingly. "But now we're really close." Or, "Now we're best friends." Or, "Now we talk on the phone every day." The transformative miracle, according to these beatific mothers? Time. I'd like to believe that, but my own history as a daughter belies the "heals all wounds" conviction.

Even among the grin-and-bear-it folks I think there is impetus to do *something* other than just wait it out. After all, these years can be a particularly unpleasant phase that may do familial harm if left to play itself out in real time. If the dinner table is a battlefield every night, everyone gets wounded sooner or later. There will be collateral damage. The younger kids, treated to daily lessons in attitude, will soon turn around and practice that attitude on you; the better-behaved kids, disgusted with the sister who makes everything such a big deal, resent you for letting her occupy so much of your time and attention. Meanwhile, the husband, the father, tethered between wife and daughter, two of the three most important women in his life (let's not forget *his* mother), is playing way out of his league. He hates the nonstop drama. He doesn't understand the turmoil that domestic life has turned into. He sees his wife in one of her least flattering roles, and doesn't like what he sees. They clash over issues neither of them knew they had.

And even if it is just a phase, there is a school of thought that says it is an *extraordinarily important* phase that deserves as much attention as you can give it. Don't wait it out. Wade into it—because this particular moment in this all-important relationship can affect every subsequent intimate bond in a young woman's life. It is here, in the heat and the heart of the mother-daughter dance, that the girl develops the interpersonal skills she will need to stay close (yet separate) from others. It is here she will stretch and strengthen the emotional muscles that she will need to flex later as she makes healthy connections with friends, lovers, and mates. At school, if a relationship goes sour, if a friend who used to be close now all of a sudden shuns her—or, in the soap opera that is middle school, stabs her in the back—she can take a deep breath, cry a few tears, and move on. At home, if a relationship goes sour, she can't move on. She has to deal. They both, daughter and mother, have to deal. And that's good. I mean, theoretically, that's good. In real life, it's hell.

If those reasons were not enough, I have my own motivation for wanting—*needing*—to make this relationship between me and Lizzie work. She is the third and last of my children, and I am simply not ready yet to get out of the sweaty, body-contact-sport phase of being a mother. I am not ready to step back. My older son has started college; his younger brother will be out of the house in a year. I know that a mother is a mother forever, but my days of heavy lifting with these two are over. They are who they are. Although my older son consults me when he needs a copyeditor for his term papers, and my younger son occasionally asks for my opinion on music or literature or girlfriends, they no longer need me in that intense, everyday way kids who are not yet grown need their mothers. I am glad they don't need me that way. I want them to be strong and independent.

But I can't help myself: I am in mourning for the old days, not the days of diapers but the days of being part of everything they did, of calming their fears and taking away their hurts, of teaching them to read and ride bikes, to swim, to dance. I miss the high-energy craziness of the mornings, with three kids going to three different schools at three different times. I miss everyone converging on home at 3:30, filings to the magnet, birds to the nest. I miss being a full-time family of five. It was hard and often stressful back then. I remember that too. There was always too much to do: Boy Scouts and music lessons, playdates and play rehearsals, fencing club, unmissable band concerts, choir concerts, school plays, community service projects, sleepovers, homework times three, school conferences times three. When you're in the thick of it, it seems as if it will never end. And then it does. I see now how quickly. I know that Lizzie's trashed-out room, the one with the post-Katrina décor—clothes, CDs, books, homework, candy wrappers, used Kleenex, loose change everywhere—the one that smells of old socks and cheap perfume, the one I rant about (or, when I muster the self-control, merely stew about), that room will soon be empty.

We are now a family of three and a half, the half being my younger son who sleeps here, occasionally eats here but has a rich, busy academic-work-social life that is his own. Next year we will be a family of three. This motherhood thing, which I was not convinced was for me in the first place, now has me firmly in its grip. I want—and need—these last years to be satisfying and enriching, to be fun. For a few more years (two? three?) I want to feel that essential connection between mother and child. That child, the remaining child, is Lizzie.

And, of course, underlying the dynamics of the family I helped make are the dynamics of the family I was born into. Those of us who had difficult relationships with our own mothers, those of us who were hell on wheels as teens—we're often told that it serves us right, the comment veiled with humor that only partially masks the lack of sympathy. We're being paid back for our sins. What goes around comes around. Maybe that's true. I don't know. What I do know is that it's not helpful or insightful or comforting in any way. The truth is, I was an estranged daughter of a distant mother. We never came back together after my teen years. We were never again close. And I don't want the same fate for me and my daughter. I don't want to mess up now, to become, in turn, the distant mother of an estranged daughter. Or, as the author of one book about surviving a daughter's teen years put it: Ten years from now, I don't want my adult daughter to be screening her calls so as to avoid taking mine.

I am not a candidate for smotherhood. I understand, really I do, that my daughter—all our daughters—needs to pull away. I understand the power, the necessity, of rebellion, small and large, quiet and noisy. I was a rebellious teen. I understand that my daughter needs to find her own identity and that sometimes that means pushing me so hard it hurts. I get that this is all part of the process of becoming an individual. If I could be guaranteed that this was only a developmental stage, I would not fret about what we're going through. But the turmoil between my mother and me was not a developmental stage. The rift that opened up between us when I was twelve or thirteen defined our relationship for the next thirty years. For us, this wasn't a phase; this was the beginning of the rest of our lives together—or rather, the rest of our lives apart.

TWO

izzie was four months old when my mother came west. "Came west" sounds like a bold, cross-country trek undertaken by a pioneer or, in this context, the eagerly anticipated visit of a doting East Coast grandmother. But when my mother came west, she was in the middle stages of Alzheimer's. She was by then a befuddled woman in diapers who had forgotten she was a grandmother, forgotten she had a daughter, forgotten me. I had persuaded my father to send her to me—he was weary from a several-year stint as a 24/7 at-home caregiver—and I had found a place for her in a safe, relatively homey memory care facility near my house. For the next five months I visited her there almost every day, often bringing Lizzie with me, a sweet, swaddled bundle in her baby carrier, sometimes bringing my sons as well, who were eight and six at the time. I fed my mother, or walked her to the bathroom and tried to get her to brush her teeth, or sat uncomfortably in the chair in her room watching her sleep, her body stiff and twitchy. Meanwhile, the boys played with the LEGOs I brought along, and Lizzie slept in her carrier. When she awoke, she looked around with her big gray-blue eyes, interested in everything, understanding nothing, content. She was an easy baby, a pleasure. My mother acknowledged her only once during those months of visits, peering at her with suspicion, then distaste. I wondered at the time if she thought I was the baby I held in my arms. I still wonder.

In those last years of my mother's life, and particularly in those months she was in the nearby care facility, I was aware of existing in a world of painful ironies that bordered on melodrama: My baby daughter happily babbling on the road to language while my mother traveled, grim-faced, in the opposite direction. My daughter hungry to know the world, sparked by stimuli, curious to see, to touch, to taste; my mother disconnected, distant, lost. My daughter learning, my mother forgetting. Lizzie kept me buoyant and alive during those very hard months. At home, I could replace the mental image of my mother's haggard, expressionless face with the reality of my beautiful daughter, her skin midway between peachy and tawny, her impish, toothless smile, her ears perfectly fashioned little shells, sticking out just a bit too much, the flaw that made her even more beautiful. She liked to lie on a fleece blanket on the family room floor in a patch of sunlight that came through the French doors. I would play music for her: Vivaldi, the Supremes. I would massage her tiny feet, the soft soles of which had yet to touch the floor. Everything was ahead of her.

It was my third time as a mother, and I thought that maybe I was finally going to get it right. I had been a crazed mother with my first child, knowing nothing, fearing everything. My husband and I were jumpy and skittish, which made our son as jumpy and skittish as we were, which made us more jumpy and skittish. My husband kept a log of our son's sleep-wake cycles and then plotted the data, in two colors, on oversized graph paper. The math soothed us. When our second son was born a little more than two years later, I was overwhelmed with the twoness of everything: two in diapers, two in baby seats, two lifted in and out of cribs, two to bathe, to dress, to take to the doctor, two naps at two different times, a two-career household trying to get by with as little outside help as possible. It wasn't until the boys were three and five that I felt comfortable in my life again. Or felt that I had one.

So I was determined to enjoy Lizzie's babyhood and toddler years in a way I wasn't able to with my sons, and she made it easy. She was mellow and even-tempered. She didn't get ear infections. She ate most anything. She fit right into the family, and the family fit around her. The boys were old enough to be helpful yet young enough to be playmates. They ran errands, zipping upstairs for washcloths or clean diapers, spooning applesauce or sweet potato puree into her little mouth while I got dinner ready. They built elaborate towers of wooden blocks just so she could, with an imperial swipe of an arm, topple them. They devised an evening entertainment known as The Dance Party, where they turned off all the lights in the living room, turned up the music, and bopped around in front of her, clicking flashlights on and off to create a strobe effect. She dissolved in giggles every time. Later, when she was old enough, they transported her, piggyback, up the ladder to the tree house my husband had built, where the plots of their elaborate fantasy games always opened with her, a queen, being attacked by what she called "the baah" and the boys defending her with sticks and pinecones. When they weren't doting over her, they ignored her completely, forgetting her existence for hours, sometimes days at a time while they tended to their own boy things. It was perfect.

Lizzie heralded a new era: I was no longer the only female in the house. I could now shop for all that great little girl stuff I had lusted after in catalogs and kids' stores during those long boy-only years when I glumly purchased anything I could find that did not feature the logo of an NFL team. Now I could buy adorable knit hats with crocheted roses on top and onesies dotted with tiny purples irises and little green velvet dresses that would bring tears to your eyes. I could hunt for booties that looked like Mary Janes and find reproduction Raggedy Ann dolls. I could send away a lock of her hair so that a company in Denver would craft an almost eerie "just-like-me doll created to look like the special child in your life," complete with exorbitantly priced matching clothes for her and the doll (including, I admit it, twin lockets). Yes, I know this is hopelessly gender stereotypical. Even then I saw the political incorrectness of it all. But I couldn't help myself. I had a girl! Here was my chance, at last, to braid hair, to play Polly Pockets. Here was my chance to do everything right, to be the kind of mother to a daughter my mother hadn't been to me: accessible, accepting, and lovable.

It's not that my own childhood was monstrous. No one stuffed me in a closet and fed me dog food when I was a kid. No sinister, alcoholic uncle fondled me on the swing set. My parents were not quirky homeless people who made us camp out in ramshackle houses with no plumbing. Ours was a perfectly ordinary, suburban, middle-middle class, two-parent, two-child family, none of whose members had criminal records. The edgiest thing that happened during my interminable childhood was that my California aunt got divorced, creating a cross-continental scandal. It was the first divorce ever on either side of the family.

But I remember realizing, as a child, that there was something missing in our family, an emotional component, a warm, beating heart. And I remember the moment I realized this. It was a Sunday night—we almost always ate out on Sundays to give my mother a break from cooking—and we were eating at a local restaurant that my father loved because of the make-your-own-sundae dessert (a lazy Susan with silver bowls of vanilla ice cream, real whipped cream, crushed pecans, and three kinds of syrup), and my mother loved because of the Haitian waiters with whom she could speak French. I was a little younger than Lizzie is now, maybe ten. My brother was a toddler. The four of us were sitting around the table, silent as we usually were, fiddling with silverware, folding and unfolding napkins, staring off into space. My brother was undoubtedly busy making potions (salt, pepper, packets of sugar) in a drinking glass.

Suddenly, there was an explosion of laughter at the next table. I looked over and saw a family like us, two parents, two kids, but not like us at all. They were all talking and grinning and elbowing each other and chucking each other on the arm. What were they talking about? What were they so damned happy about? I realized that I didn't have a clue. My own family never laughed like that. I don't know where the insight came from, but it hit me head-on: *That* over *there*, *that* family was what families were supposed to be like. Other families actively enjoyed each other's company. Other families actually seemed to like each other.

Why we didn't was a mystery to me then. Now I think it was because my parents didn't like themselves, or each other, very much. They were not happy people, and they were not happily married people. Both of them, for their own reasons, made themselves unknowable, impenetrable. Growing up, I knew almost nothing about my mother beyond the person she was in my presence: a great cook, a talented seamstress; my Brownie and Girl Scout troop leader; a PTA president. I never thought about—or asked about—what she did when I was at school, or during those eight weeks every summer I was away at camp. I never thought about who she might have been before I came on the scene. And she never told me. Years later, when I forged a close relationship with my California aunt, the Divorced One, she filled me in: My mother had, in fact, lived a pretty interesting early life. She had skipped both fifth and eighth grades and graduated from high school at fifteen. She studied costume design, worked as a draftsman, had a career, shared an apartment with a girl from Connecticut. She'd fallen in love with a Frenchman.

The relationship we had in my childhood was never warm, and it became downright icy in my teen years. By the time I was the age Lizzie is now, it seemed to me that everything I wanted, everything I liked, everything I was, clashed with her. Most of it was trivial: I loved my long hair. She said it looked like a mattress and often threatened to sneak into my room at night and cut it off. I was not interested in clothes—Levi's and a T-shirt were just fine with me. My mother, however, had gotten a degree in clothes design from Pratt Institute and was the kind of woman who wore heels and sweater sets to the A&P. I was a fearless kid, very physical, encouraged and tutored in athletics by my father. My idea of a good time was sledding down hills in Bethpage State Park at breakneck speed. She was an indoor person whose idea of a good time was doing the *New York Times* crossword puzzle with a glass of vodka by her side.

We hardly talked about anything of consequence. I never told her that I had fallen madly in love, at twelve, with a boy at summer camp. I never told her that some of the kids in eighth grade teased me unmercifully for having a big vocabulary and how much that hurt. I never told her that I had a crush on my history teacher, that I lived in fear of losing my best friend, that I thought this kid Brian was gay. I never told her when I got my period. Maybe because she never talked about herself, I didn't talk about myself. Maybe because I wanted her approval, I didn't tell her anything that I thought might get in the way. Or maybe I was just a moody, taciturn teen who wanted to create as much distance between me and my mother as possible. Whatever the dynamic, whatever the reason, we were strangers to each other.

We were, however, *polite* strangers. I am pretty sure that I had just as much Attitude with a capital A as Lizzie has now, but I didn't show it the way she does. I didn't mouth off. I didn't talk back. I didn't slam doors. That kind of behavior was unthinkable in my parents' house. I did a lot of eye rolling and sighing. I wrote antiparental screeds in my diary. I spent a lot of time alone in my room. Other girls, my friends, also had dicey relationships with their mothers—that was all part of being a teen, right?—but one by one, it seemed, they found their way back to each other. I remember one of my old high school friends telling me, ten years after our graduation, that she and her mother were now "best friends." She might just as well have told me that she and her mother had recently returned from a trip to Jupiter. That's how alien the concept was to me.

For me and my mother, the emotional distance remained, intensified by geographical distance when I moved first to the Midwest for college, then west to make my life. And it stayed that way, when all through my twenties I persisted in those things that provoked my mother's most fervent disapproval—remaining unmarried and steadfastly refusing to return to the East Coast to take that job at the *New York Times* she was convinced was just waiting for me. In my thirties—when I did marry, find gainful employment, and start to produce grandchildren—it stayed that way still. The distance no longer had anything to do with rebellion (mine) or disapproval (hers). It was ingrained. It was who we were and how we operated.

I thought about this, from time to time, as my own family grew. As the years went by, I began to see my parents as people, the way only an adult child can. I began to understand my mother's unhappiness, her trapped spirit. I thought about how I should make an effort to close the gap between me and my mother now that I too was a mother. I should show some empathy. If familial bonds didn't bind us, maybe the bonds of womanhood or motherhood would. And so, there were some visits back and forth, some newsy letters, gifts sent and received, the occasional phone call. I tried. But not my hardest, not nearly my hardest. I already had such a full life. And the gulf between us seemed so vast, so unswimmable, that even though I went through the motions, I could not really imagine bridging it. The reconciliation never happened. And then it was too late. Alzheimer's put her beyond reach.

Now, as my own daughter is perched to enter her teens, I'm cringing—which may very well be the normal posture for mothers of girls confronted with the all-of-a-sudden, all-too-close lures of sex, drugs, salacious

Web sites, nasty-girl cliques, junk food, black bras under flimsy white T-shirts, and awkwardly inserted tampons that are sure to result in toxic shock. Cringe-wise, that would be more than enough. But my concern goes deeper. I am cringing because my daughter and I are becoming strangers, and I realize that I am in danger of repeating family history, of raising a daughter who is as alienated from me as I was from my mother.

Despite—or maybe it's *because of*—my distant relationship with my mother, I have long labored under the Lifetime TV image of the mother-daughter bond. My daughter Lizzie and I would stroll through life, arms intertwined. We'd share secrets. We'd shop, take a pottery class together, join a mother-daughter book group, get side-by-side pedicures, cry together at the movies. We would have, in short, the opposite of the strained and aloof relationship I had with my mother.

And so this is the challenge I give myself: to not repeat history. To figure out who this girl I live with is and how to create a lasting, loving bond between us. Yes, with a soon-to-be teenager. Yes, in the midst of this already difficult and contentious time. I can't wait out the teen years believing that what happens now will be magically reversed later. My own past tells me that this is not something that will work itself out unless I work at it. I give myself the next eighteen months—from the middle of seventh grade, where Lizzie is now, to the beginning of high school, when she will be launched fully into her teen years. I will make this work, or go down fighting.

THREE

Okay. I've decided to *do* something about this stormy relationship I have with my daughter, about this rift opening up between us. But what, exactly, am I going to do? It makes sense, first, to consider how I have been doing. Which is not well.

On some days I've tried to ignore the situation, repeating the "it's just a phase" mantra and pretending that I believe everything will work itself out. But even if things do improve eventually, I don't know how I am going to weather the next five or six years, or how my family will weather it, or how my family will weather me weathering it.

Other days I've jumped into the fray, reacting in anger, which I know is just hurt turned inside out. I've shouted. I've used the scalpel of sarcasm— such an unfair weapon against a twelve-year-old, but sometimes, shamefully, one takes any advantage available. I've matched Lizzie's coldness with my own, scaring myself as I realize how much this mirrors my mother's approach during my teen years. I've cried in secret—out of necessity, not strategy. I tried, lump in throat, talking to my husband, who is a kind, sympathetic man and a terrific father. But there's the rub: He's a father. He truly doesn't get this mother-daughter thing. He had a charmed relationship with his own charming mother—as boys often do. The fourth child, the first and only boy, he was known in the household (and, one hopes, nowhere else) as Kingy Boy. Enough said.

I have got to stop thinking like a beleaguered, frightened, panicky mother and start thinking like the person I am when I am not a beleaguered, frightened, panicky mother—and that would be an overeducated bookworm, a veteran researcher, a tireless investigator of topics, issues, and problems. I will research my way out of this! I will do what I know best and love most: I will read.

After dropping Lizzie at school the next morning, following an argument about breakfast, which she doesn't want to eat, and a tiff over her fashion-statement attire ("I'm wearing a colored bra, and I want the world to see it"), I sit down at my computer and start the search. At www .amazon.com I type in "mother-daughter," and, although I know that this is The Relationship of All Relationships, I am still astonished to find 104,365 entries. If I read at the rate of a book a day, it will take me 285 years and nine months to get through the list. "Teen daughter," "mothering a teen daughter," and other such iterations scale the numbers back to a manageable two thousand or so. Reading through that list would take me a mere five and a half years, by which time Lizzie would be seventeen going on eighteen, and I would be . . . I try to imagine: Medicated? In therapy?

I spend the next two weeks staring at my computer screen going from entry to entry, book to book, reading summaries and descriptions, scanning tables of contents, checking out reviews and readers' comments. This literature on teens and on parenting a teen daughter is, unlike much in our economy, a growth industry. Advice books are written by, it seems, one out of every three practicing child psychologists, a battalion of educators, a phalanx of feminists, and who knows who else. This discovery is both comforting (I am clearly not alone in my misery) and scary (if there were an Answer, a Cure, a way out, there wouldn't be this many competing titles). How, I wonder, did mothers manage to bungle through it all when this literature did not exist—as in the first 199,950 years of *Homo sapien* history?

One of the first books to catch my eye is *Raising a Godly Daughter in an Ungodly World*. I am drawn to its bold and optimistic declaration in light of a study I've just read about a national survey of thirty-four hundred teens that found that evangelicals were more sexually active (and had a higher rate of STDs and pregnancy) than teens affiliated with any other major religion. It seems that abstinence is not, as some may have hoped, next to godliness. At any rate, a godly daughter is not what I'm after right now. I'd be delighted with a *civil* daughter. Or a daughter who has not "gone wild" like the teens described in *Daughters Gone Wild, Dads Gone Crazy* (the next title that grabs me, a look at girls who practice any number of ungodly behaviors suffered by teen girls: depression, anxiety, eating disorders, cutting, running away and living on the streets, drugs, alcohol).

I can't stop reading about these books, my impulse analogous to the driver who slows to a crawl to check out the horrific accident by the side of the road. After two days of this, I am feeling—ungenerously—much better. My empathy for the poor parents who have to go through this is trumped by my elation that I have (so far) been spared their fate. Compared to these kids, Lizzie is, if not godly, then at least angelic. I am living a charmed life, and I didn't even know it.

Buoyed by this new concept of my dysfunction-free daughter and our idyllic life, I feel distinctly and unusually optimistic as I drive Lizzie into town one Saturday morning. I am transporting her to a Patriot Act protest her history teacher has organized—on his own time, of course. "Habeas corpus," Lizzie says, when I ask her what the demonstration will be about.

"And what's that mean?" I ask. I am curious to know how much she knows about this pretty sophisticated issue, how well her history teacher has explained what the kids will be protesting.

"Forget it, Mom. Okay?" Her tone is testy.

It occurs to me that she hears my question not as an expression of curiosity but rather as parental interrogation.

"Can you just drive me to the place?"

I let the comment go. I am, in fact, happy to drive her to the federal building downtown, whether she knows what she's protesting or not. I want her to have the experience of joining a group of right-minded rabble-rousers. I want her to hold up a sign and chant a slogan and feel that giddy feeling of power I once felt: Yes, I can change this. I can right a wrong. I can make a difference. To me, this is good, healthy rebellion, and I'm all for it. I park the car, and as we go on foot to look for her group, I try to engage her in conversation. She speeds up her gait and pulls ahead of me, and I am left talking to myself. I speed up. She looks over her shoulder and speeds up some more, keeping the gap wide.

"Why are you following me?" she yells, as if I were some scary stranger. This is not going well. I feel my earlier optimism waning quickly.

Her group is gathered at the next street corner holding sloppily scrawled signs—my favorite is Honk for Habeas Corpus—waving at drivers and talking on cell phones to friends about how they are holding signs and waving at drivers. One of the girls I wish Lizzie was friends with, a smart, spirited kid whose mother has told me that her daughter wants more than anything else to be a writer, gives Lizzie her sign. She also lets Lizzie wear her cap with a Feminist in the Making button pinned on the front. I give Lizzie a thumbs-up and, surprisingly, she responds with a big smile. For the next half hour I watch from the sidelines, pleased and proud, as my daughter stands up for a principle the importance of which she doesn't yet understand, or even care about. No matter. The drivers are slowing down to read the signs. They are honking and waving. The kids are chanting and smiling. Something is happening, and it is good.

My optimism meter is now registering in the positive zone. The thought occurs to me that I can be every bit as mercurial as my daughter, that this teen tango we're dancing does, in fact, take two. Now I do something that, even as I do it, I know is stupid—but that's what optimism does to you. I move in to take advantage of this moment, to capitalize on the good vibes. Now is the time to tell her a story about my own protest past, to forge a connection, to impress on her that I too was a teen once, that I too stood on a street corner and held a sign and felt important and powerful. I make it short. She listens with what might almost be interpreted as interest. Then, just as I'm finishing, while the last word still hangs in the air, she puts down her sign.

"Can I have some money for dessert?" she asks sweetly.

I look at my watch. It's almost noon.

"You can have money for lunch," I say. "We can talk about dessert after."

"Forget it," she says, turning away. She is using that nasty, dismissive tone she reserves for me only. "I'm, like, *not hungry* anymore." And she starts walking down the street, this time not glancing once over her shoulder to see if I follow. Of course, I follow, albeit unsteady on my feet. These sudden mood shifts—hers and now mine—make me dizzy, almost nauseated. If someone exhibited this sort of erratic behavior, these wild, severe changes in disposition at any time other than the teen years, she would surely be institutionalized.

On Monday, Lizzie deposited at school, I come home, brew a pot of tea, and set myself up for a long day of reading. It is a relief to get back to my research, away from the reality of living with a teen and off to the safer, kinder, saner world of reading books about living with a teen. Besides being safer, kinder, and saner, this world between the covers is also, according to the raft of clever titles I am finding, apparently a whole lot more amusing. *Loving Your Teenage Daughter (Whether She Likes It or Not)*, *How to Hug a Porcupine*, *Driven to Distraction*, or—one of my favorites—*The Agony and the Agony*—the titles normalize what feels like the least normal of times.

A few days later, the FedEx guy delivers a big box of books, and my reading begins in earnest. I've chosen a selection of top sellers that have gone to multiple printings, advice books that readers say have been particularly helpful. Because Lizzie just recently shunned me in public, I begin with the aptly titled *When We're in Public, Pretend You Don't Know Me*. The author, a former TV writer, knows how to write zippy prose. And she's funny. My favorite part of the book is the "Teen Talk Translation Table." It looks like this:

WHAT SHE SAYS	WHAT SHE MEANS
I hate you.	I am very confused about what's happening to me and my body.
I hate you.	I'm bored and I want to get a rise out of you.
I hate you.	I'm embarrassed by what I just did and can't admit it.
I hate you.	I know some day I'll appreciate you, but right now this is the only fun I get.
I hate you.	I'm mad at the world and you are the closest target.

WHAT SHE SAYS	WHAT SHE MEANS
I hate you.	I want to be alone.
I hate you.	This is the best way I know to hurt you.
I hate you.	I'm scared and I really need a hug, but I'm too proud to say so.
I hate you.	I hate you.

I'm sitting at the kitchen table late one afternoon that same week, reading this and laughing. Lizzie is upstairs, supposedly doing homework. I call her to take a look. It is, for reasons unknown—reasons I wish I *did* know—a good afternoon, a calm afternoon, an afternoon during which not a nasty word has been said. She galumphs down the stairs, gives me a smile, grabs the book, and reads the teen translation table. Then she starts laughing. "So, which one is what *you* think?" I ask.

She looks at me earnestly. "Well, first of all, I have never said I hate you!"

"Right," I say. "But you have said some pretty evil things." As it is a good afternoon, a calm afternoon, I can say this without risking all-out war.

"True," she says, giving me another winning smile. "It's like, I know some day I'll appreciate whatever it is you're telling me, but at the moment I hear it, I just don't want to hear it." This sounds like serious sucking up to me. I'm enjoying it, but I don't think she's being entirely honest. I don't say anything, but I give her that squinty look that says I don't quite believe her.

"Okay, okay," she says, her mood still (mysteriously) buoyant. "It's like, I'm mad or tired or something's wrong, and you're right there. You're the closest target, like the book says." This sounds more honest.

"Anything else sound right to you?" She looks down at the book again, studying the choices.

"Nope." I let out what I hope is not an audible sigh. I am enormously relieved that she didn't choose "This is the best way I know to hurt you," because oftentimes I interpret her rudeness as a direct barb, an arrow aimed with specific intent at my mother heart. It would be wonderful if this were not her motivation. Or at least not all the time. We smile at each other. What a lot of smiling is going on this afternoon. Lizzie walks out of the kitchen, then stops and turns, dramatically, at the doorway. She gives me a fierce look.

"I hate you!" she screams. "I hate you hate you hate you!" She starts laughing. "There," she says in a schoolmarmish voice, "I am so glad we could have this little moment together."

I silently thank Susan Borowitz, the author of *When We're in Public*, for providing said moment. Then, with a light heart, I go back to reading. The main point of the book is that there are three types of mothers: the Clueless Mom, who doesn't get the fact that she actually has a teenaged daughter (and continues to treat her like a child); the Best Pal Mom, who acts (dresses, talks) like a friend rather than a parent; and, what the author deems to be the ideal mom, the Uncool Mom, a realist with a sense of humor, tough but understanding, a setter of limits who nevertheless respects her daughter's growing autonomy. She is "uncool" because she is not a fad-follower. She doesn't care what others think. She is true to herself—and to her daughter.

I am certainly not a Clueless Mom. Although I mourn the end of Lizzie's childhood, I am not trying to hold her back. Not that I could. And I am definitely not a Best Pal Mom. I don't have—never did have—the legs for miniskirts, and I don't want to relive my teen years in any shape or form. Once was quite enough.

But the bar is set pretty high for the Uncool Mom, and I don't think I measure up. This Uncool Mom always manages to be rational and reasonable, evaluating all situations, however trying, with both wisdom and warmth. She doesn't gird her loins for battle. Mothering, she knows, is a challenge, not a war zone. Although the author doesn't make this point, it's clear that the Uncool Mom, doesn't, as I do, run upstairs and cry in the closet when her daughter snipes at her. The more I read about this sanctified creature, the worse I feel about my own mothering skills.

In a chapter on school, the author lists ten ways to know if you are too involved in your daughter's homework (and, by implication, her life). It's a funny list, but when I see that I can check off six of the items right away, I stop laughing. I am guilty of, among other sins, being more interested than she is in the research she has to do for projects, saving every one of her papers, projects, and tests, and caring more than she does about her grades. I really hadn't thought of it this way. I had just considered myself attentive to her schoolwork, a parent who expressed interest and concern about academics. But the book says my behavior falls way short of Uncoolness.

When I read the chapter on beauty and body, my spirits rise. I think maybe I might be on the right track here. Not surprisingly, the chapter focuses on body image—from weight to zits to clothing—but it is really about communication and honesty, about being able to connect with your daughter in the midst of tumultuous physical, biological changes. As I read, I remember something that happened about a week ago.

Lizzie and I were both naked standing in front of the big mirror in my bathroom. Just the fact that we were doing this, I realize, is pretty amazing. I don't think I ever saw my mother naked, and I certainly never let her see me unclothed after the age of maybe eight. But I'm of the opinion that you get one "freebie" with each kid, one great thing you don't have to work for. A gift. With Jackson, eldest son, it was toilet training: He trained himself at eleven months. With Zane it was food: An open-minded, experimental omnivore, he has always been a delight to cook for, a delight to take to a restaurant. With Lizzie it is her no-nonsense lack of modesty.

When she was just beginning to "develop" two and a half years ago, I was astonished and thrilled that she allowed me—*invited* me—to check out her changing body. She used to call me into the bathroom when she was showering. "Don't you think I need a bra now?" she would ask, pointing at her not-quite-flat chest proudly. She kept me fully informed about the sprouting of underarm and pubic hair. She kept her bedroom door open when she was dressing. I've quizzed her about this on more than one occasion. I want to know where this forthrightness comes from, how she manages to be so comfortable with her body at a time when girls are usually so terribly uncomfortable. Maybe it has something to do with being athletic, which she is, and being at ease in her own skin.

But I was an athlete too, and I didn't stand next to my mother comparing butts when I was twelve. Or ever. Lizzie has never come up with an answer other than "It's just who I am," and I believe her. I am recalling this intimate scene, thinking what a great mom I am—maybe even approaching Uncool status—when I remember the rest of what happened. We're talking about our thighs. We're turning around to stare at our butts. And we're laughing. But I am also critiquing my body with the harshness one reserves for oneself, with the same merciless judgments I've levied for years. Words that, even as I say them, I know should not be uttered aloud in the presence of an almost-teen daughter. I mean, that's not advice I need to read in a book. That's common sense. Yet the difficult relationship I have with my body—that so many of us have with our bodies, regardless of size or shape—is deeply ingrained, encapsulated somewhere in my psyche and virtually immune to common sense. When I look at myself, I see faults and flaws. It's as simple, and as complex, as that. What I realize too late, what I realize while Lizzie and I are laughing about one of the several self-deprecating remarks I've made, is that I could be doing real harm here. I could very well be passing along the lessons of the body my mother taught me: dissatisfaction, the constant need for self-improvement, the equation of self-worth with thigh circumference. We're joking, but it's no laughing matter.

This is big—bigger for me than for her, I think. She is the one who is comfortable in her body. I am the one who is not. And I want to keep it that way—her comfort, that is, not my neurosis. The best thing I can do, I tell myself after I have made one joke too many, after I really *hear* what I'm saying, is to shut up about my own insecurities. I can choose not to pass along this lesson, and I have to consciously, purposefully make that choice. At the very least, the issue is front and center on my radar screen.

This *When We're in Public* book, like so many of the other advice books I've looked at, pays scant attention to the idea that who we are as mothers might have something to do with who we were as daughters and how we ourselves were mothered. There are offhand remarks in these books about "sounding just like your mother" when you utter phrases like "because I said so," but that's the extent of it. Isn't there anyone, any pithy best-selling adviser who understands the complexities of this relationship, gets how tangled it is, how deep?

• • •

Two days later, Lizzie and I have the following conversation. I am taking the family out for dinner to celebrate a bit of good news. The restaurant isn't fancy, but it's a nice place: tablecloths, waitstaff who introduce themselves, items other than chicken fingers on the menu. Lizzie comes down the stairs in the stained, bagged-out jeans she's worn all week and a none-too-clean T-shirt.

Upon reflection, I realize that the Uncool Mom would think hard—not to mention rationally—about whether this was a battle worth fighting. I? At that moment, I don't think at all. My reaction is immediate. And knee-jerk.

"You're wearing *that*?" I say. We both know this is an accusation, not a question.

"Yeah," she says, planting her feet. "So what?"

"What do you mean 'so what?' This *is* an occasion. What you've got on is inappropriate."

"Whatever."

"Whatever? What does *that* mean?" If there is another more infuriating word, I don't know what it is.

"*I'm* wearing this . . . not you, so why do *you* care?" Lizzie is not giving an inch. I would admire her spirit if I were not so pissed off.

"But I'm *with* you. And this is a nice place."

"Fine. Then I'll stay home." And she storms upstairs to her room and slams the door.

Fifteen minutes pass, during which she plays excessively loud music in her room and I seethe and then force myself to practice yoga breathing. Finally, I yell up the stairs, "We're going!" and she comes down and we all go to dinner. In my mind, I claim a partial victory: She gave in and came to dinner. On the other hand, she managed to go out wearing those ratty clothes. Two points for her. I think of it this way—who wins and who loses—as if our daily life were a game, a very *serious* game, a game I want to win. Only problem: She wants to win too.

Oddly, eerily, when I go back to my pile of best sellers the next day, the book on top is *You're Wearing That?* The author, linguist Deborah Tannen, points out what every mother and every daughter know: What we say to each other means much more than what we say to each other. Or, to put it in more elevated terms: The subtext of our conversations is generally more important than the text. The "meta-message," to use Tannen's word, trumps the literal message just about every time. To test this theory, I go up to Lizzie's room later that afternoon where she is lying on her unmade bed reading a manga book while listening to Bon Jovi at a volume that will, I know from experience, later cause her a ten or fifteen decibel hearing loss. I ask her if she remembers the fight we had the other night about what she was wearing to go to the restaurant.

"Yeah?" she says warily.

I tell her I'd like to know what she was thinking when I said what I said.

"I don't mean what I *actually* said," I explain. "It's like, what you think I meant, what other message did you think I was sending out? Understand?" She says she does. So I ask her what she was thinking to herself when I said 'You're wearing that?'" She doesn't hesitate more than a second before she replies.

"I thought, 'Why is she always criticizing me?' and 'Why can't she just let me be me?'" Yikes.

What Lizzie expresses is just what Deborah Tannen says in her book, almost to the word. I have two simultaneous, equally strong reactions: 1. My daughter is as smart as a Berkeley PhD full professor linguist! 2. I could *really* screw up this mother-daughter thing if I don't start paying better attention. There's a fundamental tension built into the mother-daughter relationship, Tannen says, that goes like this: The person a daughter most wants to have think that she is perfect is the person most likely to see her faults. That's the daughter's internal dynamic. The mother's is this: It is a mother's job to give guidance based on her greater experience. But any advice or suggestion offered implies criticism—because someone who is perfect does not need advice or suggestions.

Talk, Tannen says and everyone with an XY knows, plays a larger, more complex role in female relationships than in male relationships, which means that mothers and daughters live—and negotiate—their relationships through conversation. What it comes down to is the power of mothers to send "meta-messages" of either caring or criticism (which can often be the same thing—the mother saying something because she cares, the daughter hearing it as censure), and the often equally potent power of daughters to withhold talk. This last insight really strikes me. When Lizzie glares at me in stony silence, when she literally slams the door in my face, she is not only expressing her anger—which is how I've heretofore interpreted these actions—but also, I now see, flexing her power, the only real power she has in this conversational game, the power not to play. The problem is, in the heat of the moment, when her anger washes over me, when I feel hurt and disrespected and angry myself, will I be able to come back to this insight? That's a lot to expect.

It feels like too much to expect. I *do* understand what Tannen and the others are talking about. I *am* reading, and I am thinking about what I read. But it's like I'm one of those students who reads the textbook and thinks she's got a handle on the material right up until the test—which she blows. At least, I tell myself, I am aware of what I'm doing, even if I can't yet stop myself from doing it. That's progress, isn't it?

Happily, not all the insights I'm gaining from Tannen's book reflect the troubled state of our relationship. As with Borowitz's book, some actually reinforce what is right between Lizzie and me. For example, Tannen makes the point that when mothers and daughters share seemingly insignificant details about their lives this is actually a sign of closeness and caring. Although Lizzie is not much interested in the insignificant (or, for that matter, significant) details of my life—what self-respecting teen would be?—she does come home from school (on a good day) to tell me about Nattie's belly button piercing and what Aidan said to Scott about Dana and who is now sharing lockers with whom and what vivid new color Annie's hair is. I have listened to lengthy exegeses on eye shadow, rambling tales of misbehavior on the school bus, and comparative commentary on bean burritos. I vow to stop thinking of this as mere prattle and start appreciating it as an indication of intimacy.

I work through various other books in my pile until I come to the drolly titled *Get Out of My Life, but First Could You Drive Me and Cheryl to the Mall?* by the same author who brought us *Why Did You Have to Get a Divorce? And When Can I Get a Hamster?* This is an author who's obviously been around a lot of teens. It turns out that this book is the only one of my top selections written by a man (a clinical psychologist), and despite the flippant title, it turns out to be the most staid book I've read so far. The mother-daughter relationship, he says, is about two things:

management and communication. This sounds kind of like a business to me. All the mother has to do is make rules and stick to them, like a boss. Is this a fourth kind of mom: Executive Mom? I don't see this in my future, or Lizzie's.

The book is full of case studies and studded with conversational tidbits between parents and daughters that, while fabricated, ring true. Lizzie walks into the room just as I am reading this: "[My daughter] actually told me that she wished that I had put her in a foster home when she was a baby, rather than grow up with me as a mother." I read this aloud to Lizzie.

"Ouch," she says. Then she goes into the kitchen and makes me a cup of tea.

The best book of the lot turns out to be *I'm Not Mad, I Just Hate You!* From the jocular title and cartoonish cover, I expect some take-away messages worthy of bumper stickers, but instead, the little dialogs in the book allow me to look at some of the interactions between Lizzie and me in a different way. For example, there's this:

DAUGHTER: It's unfair that I can't go out tonight!
MOTHER: I told you. You cannot go out the night before a test.
DAUGHTER: You're so mean! I hate your guts!

(hours later)

DAUGHTER: Mom, what's for dinner?
MOTHER: There's sandwich meat in the fridge.
DAUGHTER: You're not making me stuffed shells? You said you would.
MOTHER: You expect me to spend hours preparing your favorite dinner? You just told me that you hated me.
DAUGHTER: God. You know I didn't mean it. I hate it when you overreact.

This is classic around our house. First she insults me, then she accuses me of overreacting. Or, she wounds me, forgets about it a minute later, and I walk around in pain the rest of the day. I am fascinated by these heated exchanges chronicled in the book. Reading them is like watching a movie (a *home* movie). The remove, the spectator position, allows me to see fights like this for what they are, or rather, for what they are not. They are not unique to Lizzie and me. They are not (maybe, I hope) indications of a deep and permanent rift in our relationship. They are not proof that, like my mother and I, Lizzie and I will never be close. They wound, but maybe, maybe, these wounds are not life threatening.

Ultimately, *I'm Not Mad* is so thoughtful and so thorough that its multitudinous suggestions for "surviving and thriving during your daughter's teenage years"—the subtitle—are exhausting. There are detailed scenarios, multi-itemed options, and complex strategies that require one to be mindful, insightful, and, in the thick of the action, emotionally stable, reasonable, rational, and, well, sane. This does not sound like any mother of a teen daughter I've ever met. And it certainly doesn't sound like me.

I've got other issues with all these books I've been reading, bigger ones: First, they all, at their core, treat these thorny mother-daughter problems as part of a developmental phase—the difficult and trying teen years. But my deepest fear is that what is happening with Lizzie and me is not a passing phase but rather a direction our relationship is headed, a clear path to a permanently icy terrain. Second, they are all about strategy, about everyday—and, it sometimes seems to me, superficial—ways of confronting the problems I'm facing. I don't want conversational gambits and behavioral tweaks. I want answers. I want to understand what's going on with her and between us. I am not going to ignore the advice and strategies offered by these books, but I am going to have to look elsewhere for guidance. I am going to look deeper. I hear that there's pretty interesting research being done on the teen brain. Maybe if I understood what was going on inside Lizzie's head—I mean literally inside her cranium—I might get a better handle on this mercurial girl I live with.

FOUR

I t's a raw, rainy, late fall evening, the kind of night you want to stay at home curled up on the couch wrapped in polar fleece watching a month's worth of TiVoed *Entourage* while making your way through an enormous bowl of popcorn. (Yes, my fantasies are that specific.) Instead, I force myself out of the house, into the car, and down the hill three miles to Lizzie's middle school to attend a program titled "Understanding Your Teen's Brain." I expect to see maybe a dozen people in the gym. These evening programs always draw poorly—most parents work full time and, unless it's an awards program featuring their kid, they just don't come out after dinner—and the rotten weather won't help. So when I walk into the room a few minutes late, I'm astonished to see more than seventy people sitting on folding chairs. I don't recognize any faces, but I do recognize the *look* on most of the faces. It is the same look on my face: parent under siege slogging through early teen years, a kind of shell shock, a mix of anxiety, desperation, and fatigue.

The man standing in front of us is Bob Sylwester, a well-published retired professor and one of the country's foremost lecturers on brain research applied to education. But tonight, at least, he doesn't look like a man who has crisscrossed the country delivering more than fourteen hundred such presentations. He looks like someone's grandfather—portly, rumpled, and somewhat flummoxed by the technology of the cordless mic he's just been handed.

"I know, I know," he says, with no setup, no introduction. He is holding the mic a little too close to his mouth, and his voice booms and fuzzes. "You had this child, this wonderful child. She was so nice. He was so compliant. Life was so sweet. And then . . ." He pauses to look out over the expectant faces. "And then, one day—like maybe *yesterday*—you looked over at this thirteen-year-old kid and you said to yourself, 'Did I actually spawn that?'" There is relief in the laughter that fills the room. The man knows his audience.

For the next ninety minutes he takes us on a bumpy ride through the teen brain, a voyage that is one part layman's neuroscience, two parts homespun advice. He's got kids. His kids have kids. He's lived with and around teens for a long time, and he's not down for the count. I listen with rapt attention. I take copious notes. Then I rush home, go online, and order a half dozen teen brain books. I am determined to try to understand what's going on inside Lizzie's head. Could all this Sturm und Drang we're living through be caused by that three-pound lump of clay in her skull? One can only hope.

Three days later, I am hunkered down with yet another pile of books, which range from a deeply researched and pleasantly written volume by the medical science and health editor of the *New York Times* (*The Primal Teen*) to an overly perky, keeping-sane-in-the-classroom strategy manual for teachers (*Secrets of the Teenage Brain*). The first thing that catches my eye—it's in the introductory pages of yet another of my new acquisitions, *Yes, Your Teen Is Crazy!*—is this "conversation" between a psychiatrist and the parent of the patient being seen by said psychiatrist:

> **DR:** She is suffering from a transient psychosis with an inter-mittent rage disorder, punctuated by episodic radical mood swings . . . but her prognosis is good for a full recovery.
> **PARENT:** What does that mean?
> **DR:** She's 13.

Another book begins this way: "Teenagers may indeed be a bit crazy. But . . . they are crazy by design."

I am relieved, at least a *little* relieved, to read these opening salvos because sometimes it does feel as if I were living with someone who suffers from severe mental illness. In fact, I said this out loud yesterday to a friend of mine who is fortunate enough to not yet have a teenager in the house. She looked at me with alarm (and, I think, pity) when I ranted about mood shifts so unexpected, so complete, so dramatic that they left me breathless and dizzy—and sometimes questioning my own sanity.

This afternoon I am sitting at the kitchen table reading another from my pile, *Why Do They Act That Way?*, when Lizzie comes bounding down the steps, beaming. She is wearing a T-shirt she designed by ripping apart and resewing two old T-shirts, a new pair of jeans, and a pair of Vans we just bought at the store an hour ago. She twirls around, modeling for me, sashaying her hips, pouting her lips.

"Don't I look hot?" she says. Hot? My twelve-year-old daughter? I take a breath.

"You look just *fabulous*," I say, trying to sound like a British fashion photographer.

"What do you think of this shirt?"

I tell her it's amazing, creative, colorful, a work of art. She winks at me and disappears back upstairs. I continue reading and am just parsing the sentence that begins "Your volatile teenager . . ." when I hear her shout from upstairs, "These shoes really suck! I hate them!" I hear a loud noise. It's the shoes, the ones we just bought, tumbling down the stairs. "And these jeans," she yells, "they make my ass look big. I am never, *ever* going to wear them!"

Okay then.

I can't think of a thing to say other than "Are you fucking kidding me?" which I understand, even in my agitated state, is not an appropriate response. I keep quiet, and I keep reading. Maybe if I focus on the page long enough my frustration will dissipate. A few minutes later, she comes downstairs and makes her way into the kitchen, where she peers at me to see if maybe I'm in a coma or something. There must be a reason I didn't shout back up at her.

"We never should have bought these shoes!" she says, glaring at me. "I hate these shoes!" She is baiting me. I want to remind her that we made

a special trip to go look for these shoes, that we spent an hour shopping for them, that they were *her* choice, and that she thought they were
perfect then and just fine ten minutes ago. I don't say any of it. It's not
that I've suddenly, miraculously reached some new level of understanding or enlightenment. I'm angry. My buttons (especially the one that says
"if you don't appreciate all the things I do for you, please press here")
have been pushed. But the situation is so perfectly matched to what I'm
reading that even *I* see the humor. I say all the things I want to say, but I
say them in my mind, not out loud. Out loud I say, managing a small
smile, "I'm just reading about the unexpected drama of living with a
teen." She sniffs.

"Whatever." Then she stomps back upstairs.

I wish I could report that the next day she wore the shoes. It would
be great if unpredictable mood swings were, well, predictable, like a
metronome swinging back and forth. For every action there is an equal
and opposite reaction. But, apparently, just because she loves something
one minute and hates it the next doesn't mean she'll love it again a minute later. Which is to say: She never wears the shoes. (Months later, the
cat throws up on them, and I toss them in the garbage.)

The answer to why teens are so often impulsive, moody, and judgment
impaired used to be a three parter: bad company, raging hormones, and,
the ultimate culprit, lousy parents. In *West Side Story*—Lizzie and I both
adore the musical and have watched it together on DVD dozens of
times—a group of ill-behaved, trouble-seeking teens (gang members à
la mid-1950s) sing to the local cop that their mothers are all junkies,
and their fathers are all drunks. That's why—"Golly Moses"—they're all
punks.

When these punks are brought before a judge, he proclaims them
"psychologically disturbed" and sends them to a headshrinker who decides they are, instead, "sociologically" sick.

But as I'm discovering in my reading, twenty-first-century neuroscientists
would say teen miscreants are neither. There's another explanation. Teens—
not the modern equivalent of *West Side Story* gangstas but rather the millions of ordinary, run-of-the-mill, back-talking, door-slamming teens—are

at the mercy of their still "under construction" brains. These brains are apparently undergoing a massive overhaul during the teen years. Researchers are now discovering that the actual *structure* of the brain is changing from ages twelve to twenty or thereabouts, and that this change is so profound it rivals the other, far more well-known period of brain development, early childhood.

Remember that amazing spurt of development when our little darlings learned to walk and talk and not poop in their pants? That was a mental and behavioral revolution of the first order. That was also the good part. The bad part was the screaming tantrums, the willful disobedience, the blatant, uncontrollable bad behavior known as the Terrible Twos. Now researchers are saying the teen brain is in a similar state of growth and flux as the toddler brain, and we need to recognize that this later set of changes is behind what might be called the Terrible Teens.

The news out of top labs from Brown to Berkeley and everywhere in between is that the teen brain is not what we once thought it was: a finished product, a fully functional organ that went through its one monumental change in early childhood. Instead, it is a work in progress, unfinished, incompletely wired, not yet up to speed, not yet open for the business of wise and measured living. Teen brains are in the midst of wild, even frantic activity marked by an intense overproduction of the branches at the ends of brain cells—a process called "blossoming" or, even more sweetly, known as "exuberance"—which is followed by a period of drastic pruning or sculpting of those branches. Like any construction site, it's a real mess up there.

Given that these changes are so big and involve so many different parts of the brain, I'm wondering why neuroscientists are just now chiming in with this evidence. Why didn't we know this before? The explanation is a little creepy. Most of what was known about brains until quite recently came from autopsies. Teens—young drivers and violent gang members notwithstanding—just don't die that often. Without actual brains to study, scientists assumed much about the teen brain. Like the body that carried it around, the body that began to *look* like an adult body, it was thought that the teen brain was mature.

It wasn't until the advent of noninvasive brain imaging (MRIs, PET scans, and the like) that researchers could study sufficient numbers of teen brains to understand what was going on inside them. Now they have access to as many teen brains as there are parents who will give their informed consent. So what, exactly, is it that they see? If Lizzie is not slamming doors in my face because she hates me or has taken as her personal mission making my life miserable, if it's her crazy about-to-be teen brain that's the culprit, what up there in her cranium is making her act this way?

Two words, say the researchers: prefrontal cortex.

The prefrontal cortex, or frontal lobes, is the seat of moral reasoning, rational decision making, emotional control, and impulse restraint. This is the "cop" part of the brain that, if functioning well, would stop a person from talking back, lashing out, slamming doors—doing something stupid or impulsive (or both) that will later be regretted.

As I delve into the literature of neuroscience, I keep coming across the same disturbing little historical anecdote about an unfortunate guy named Phineas Gage. Gage was a hard-working, honest, forthright, reliable, respectful construction foreman laying railroad tracks in Vermont when, one day in 1848, an explosion propelled a four-and-a-half-foot metal rod straight through his head. It entered below his left cheekbone and exited the top of his head. The front part of his brain, the frontal lobes, was instantly destroyed. Astonishingly, he survived. In fact, he never lost consciousness. What he did lose was his agreeable personality. Phineas Gage, postaccident, was moody, belligerent, contentious, and impulsive. Kind of like . . . a teenager. All of the books I am reading tell this story not just because this case was the beginning of understanding how specific areas of the brain affect self, but because it dramatically illustrates the singular power of the frontal lobes.

Although teens at least *have* frontal lobes, unlike the poor Mr. Gage, this part of their brain is not yet fully operational or completely wired. (In fact, the new research suggests that the frontal lobes are the last part of the brain to reach maturity, often not until a person is in her early twenties.) What this means is that sometimes other parts of the teen brain are used to process information that should be dealt with up front. And what *that* means is that teens sometimes use their "lizard brain"—the primal, fight-or-flight emotional core of the brain—to read their own emotions and respond to the emotions of others. When this happens, their reactions are quick and powerful, a "gut" reaction from the gut of the brain instead of a more thoughtful, even-handed reaction from the brain's policeman.

I am fascinated by this "lizard brain" thing. Lizzie's nickname at day camp a few years back was "Lizzie Lizard," and the more I read about what is officially known as the amygdala, the more I see that Lizzie is the owner of a particularly healthy specimen. I read that this is the "trigger happy" part of the brain, the part that prompts a "zero to sixty angry response." Yes, that's my girl. I read that through the teen years there will be a gradual shift from processing emotions in the lizard amygdala to processing them in the wise and reasonable frontal lobes. I can hardly wait.

But something else has to happen to get the frontal lobes front and center. The nerves—the branches of brain cells that are in the midst of blossoming and being pruned back—need to be effectively insulated. This insulation comes in the form of thin blankets of fat laid down around the nerves, protective sheaths that help keep the brain's electrical signals on clear pathways, that decrease interference and static, that speed along the signals, especially the ones that connect quick reactions to contextual thought. The insulation is called myelin, and the process of myelination is—you guessed it—still very much developing in the teen brain. Some studies show a 100 percent jump in myelin in the teen years. And what do you suppose is the last part of the brain to myelinate? The frontal lobes. I'm thinking it's a wonder that *any* teen is capable of committing a rational act.

What I've been reading about so far is the brain's mechanical and electrical systems. But there's a whole other thing going on up there: chemistry—as in hormones, those amazing chemical triggers and internal messengers that we have long accused of toying with the sanity of teenagers and women of a certain age. Although explanations for the weird workings of the teen brain are far more sophisticated than they used to be, hormones are still a big player and—no surprise—there's hormonal havoc up there. Of course, my first thought about hormones and teens is s-e-x, so I am interested to learn about the power of a hormone completely unrelated to sex. It is called melatonin, and it might have a lot to do with moodiness, crankiness, and those nightly "this is your bedtime" arguments that rock our household.

Lizzie can come home from school tired, bedraggled, and unable to do anything (like, for example, homework) other than veg on the couch; she can just barely summon the energy to set the table; she can slump sullen and sleepy eyed while we eat, but when 9:30 bedtime rolls around, she is a ball of energy. She has things to do, arrangements to make, phone calls to return, toenails to paint, eyebrows to tweeze, change to count. The flurry of activity is extraordinary. As the witching hour approaches, I give her the ten-minute warning, the five-minute warning, the countdown. Then come the minute-apart reminders. Then the nagging, followed by the usual threats, which fall on deaf ears, sometimes because she's upstairs in her room with Bon Jovi blasting on her headphones and actually can't hear me; other times because she (I imagine) wills herself into auditory impairment. Whatever the scene, she is often at her perkiest at ten p.m. and almost always at her attitudinal nadir at seven a.m. Now I know why: melatonin.

Melatonin is the chemical that tells our brain that it's time to get sleepy. It both chemically induces drowsiness and lowers the body's temperature readying it for sleep. It's the hormone that gets out of whack when we fly across too many time zones. It turns out that, for still mysterious reasons, melatonin is released up to two hours later in teen brains than in adult brains. This delay means Lizzie—and every other wide-awake-at-midnight teen out there—doesn't get the signal to go to sleep when they should. Staying up later wouldn't be that much of a problem (other than the bedtime battleground, that is) if it were not for the fact—newly discovered—that teens actually need a good hour and a half *more* sleep than adults need. School districts have not yet awoken to this fact. Perhaps they too are on melatonin delay. That is unfortunate because, say the researchers, the late-to-bed, forced-to-rise-early teen is officially, chronically sleep deprived. And, as we all know from personal experience, sleep deprivation means we are grouchy, testy, moody, and short-tempered. We're easily frustrated. We have less control over our emotions. We experience stress more often and more intensely (courtesy of the hormone cortisol, released when we don't get enough sleep).

Does this sound like anyone you know? It sounds like someone I know, and she's clomping down the stairs right now. It's 7:45 in the morning. I've already woken her twice, neither of which experience was pleasant for either of us. She comes into my writing room to tell me that she has no clean underwear and cannot find her homework. Also, that she hates every brand of cereal (that would be six) currently in the pantry. And why didn't I wake her up earlier because now she has to rush to take a shower, and her hair won't dry sufficiently to use the hair straightener wand (never mind that her hair is already straight). It's another melatonin-delayed, cortisol-rich morning.

Of course, the big kahuna of hormones, girl-wise, is estrogen. It's the one—along with that other famous puberty trigger, testosterone—that has been implicated in the "raging hormone" explanation of teen behavior. These are the chemicals that supposedly turn our sweet, innocent children into (if boys) sex-obsessed masturbators or (if girls) hip-swaying siren sluts. Actually, the role they play is far more complicated and more powerful than originally thought. For starters, researchers used to think that estrogen (and testosterone) acted only on parts of the brain linked to sex behavior. Not true. Newer brain studies have found estrogen (testosterone, progesterone) receptors sprinkled throughout the brain in various far flung regions associated with cognition, emotion, movement, and memory. Also, we now know that these hormones do not act alone. They are part of a complex feedback system that includes the triggering of powerful neurotransmitters that interact with each hormone and greatly affect mood.

Here's what I (barely) understand from my reading about this choreography of chemicals: Estrogen tweaks, and can play nasty games with, three distinct brain compounds—norepinephrine, dopamine, and serotonin. Norepinephrine is a brain stimulant, the energizer that kicks in when we need it—or sometimes when we don't—so that when faced with danger (real or imagined) we either have the strength to stay and do battle or the zip to get the hell out of there. Oddly, or perhaps if one were cynical, *aptly*, given its fight-or-flight reputation, norepinephrine is now thought by some researchers to contribute to the giddy, heart-pounding love high that is part of being a have-a-crush-or-be-crushed teen girl.

The second compound, dopamine, is known as the feel-good hormone, the pleasure chemical that can intensify experiences and make the world seem bigger, brighter, and better. Estrogen amps up dopamine, thus the wildly heightened experiences of teenage girlhood. Estrogen itself is wildly fluctuating at this age (varying as much as 650 to 4,900 percent in a given month), and so dopamine rises and falls as well, resulting in the many command performances of the Drama Queen. Just to make life even more interesting, the third brain compound, serotonin, a mood stabilizer, automatically decreases as dopamine increases, thus ensuring the histrionics and the sudden and spectacular mood swings that have been giving me whiplash for the past year.

And then, of course, there's the main job of estrogen: transforming girls into women (biologically, that is). Estrogen promotes the development of those secondary sexual characteristics (breasts, hips) that terrify us mothers of twelve-year-olds. It triggers the onset of what one recent Tampax ad so endearingly called "your monthly gift from Mother Nature." It also puts a brake on height growth and signals the female body to reduce muscle mass. This particular dance of the hormones, complex, confusing, and harrowing already, is further complicated by the fact that while the age of puberty has gone down during the past century, the brain continues to develop at its own leisurely pace. That means girls are *looking* like women earlier, but their brains are not helping them *act* like women any earlier. The teen years, now more than ever before, are a period of disconnect between brain and body.

Who knew that it was so tough to be a teen? I mean, most of us who've passed through those portals would rather forget the journey. Most of us suffered in our own acutely painful ways. But had we known about the firestorms and chemical warfare going on inside our heads, we possibly would have been even more morose, more testy, more self-pitying than we already were. With that in mind, I don't think I'll tell Lizzie about this research. Or rather, I will tell her selectively, as suits my purpose. I will tell her—and probably tonight—about her melatonin delay and how she needs much more sleep than she's getting. But I don't think I'll tell her about her under-construction prefrontal cortex—and not just because she will heave a sigh, roll her eyes, and leave the room before I manage to finish the first exquisitely educational sentence. It's because I don't want her to get the sense that all bad, rude, or disruptive behavior is out of her control, that she has no responsibility in the matter, that discoveries in neuroscience excuse her for being mean and nasty and hurtful to her mother. And I don't believe it either. Biology does not explain all behavior. Humans are far more complex than that.

I'm struggling with what to do with all this information myself. On the one hand, I find the new research on the teen brain to be overwhelming. Fascinating but overwhelming. It's been more than enough to try to deal with and adjust to the obvious *physical* changes she is going through. Now to realize that, hidden from view, inside her skull, massive structural changes are taking place and secret chemical and electrical storms are raging—that's almost too much. And yet, I am also somewhat relieved. Her unpredictable, sometimes outrageous behavior is, the research is telling me, "normal," the result of a healthy brain going through the changes it needs to go through.

Still, there's conflict in my own brain about what all this means to Lizzie and me. I imagine this new information ping-ponging between my frontal lobes—where I think rationally about it all, reasoning that this is a necessary developmental stage—and my lizard brain—where all those "gut reaction" buttons she so expertly pushes are apparently located. My frontal lobes tell me to be calm and understanding, to be a grown up, for goodness' sake. But then my lizard brain jumps in, loud and insistent, like a squalling infant. It tells me I'm hurt and angry. It speeds a signal to my solar plexus, making me feel as if I'd been kicked in the stomach when Lizzie disses or dismisses me. It sends little messages to my tear ducts.

I may be incapable of reacting to what feels like repeated stabs to the heart with "It's just her underdeveloped, poorly wired prefrontal cortex talking." It may not be possible to always, or even often, maintain my equilibrium in the midst of instability. I mean, I've got my own hormonal dance going too. Is it possible to be the warm, open mother I want so much to be while still somehow protecting myself from the barbs and arrows that Lizzie—knowingly or unknowingly, biologically determined or otherwise—sends my way every day?

● ● ●

It's close to 11:30 when I finally make my way upstairs to go to bed. It's a Tuesday, a school night, and Lizzie said her good nights almost two hours ago. But when I switch off the hall lamp, I see a strip of light under her bedroom door. She's still awake. Ah yes: Melatonin delay at work. I understand. But my new knowledge of brain chemistry doesn't change the fact that it is well past her bedtime and that, even if she falls asleep this minute, she will get barely seven hours of shut-eye tonight. I rein in the impulse to barge in and manage to knock instead. No answer. I knock a little louder. Still no answer. Good, I think, she is asleep in there. She just nodded off with the light on. I open the door quietly. There she is, fully awake, lying on her stomach on top of the covers, reading. She looks up briefly, annoyed.

"I knocked," I say. She ignores me, goes back to her book. "Do you know what time it is?" She doesn't answer. Her eyes are glued to the page. I stayed up all hours reading when I was her age—but I read under the covers with a flashlight so my mother wouldn't catch me. "It is two hours past your bedtime," I say. "Two hours." Her sigh is so forceful that the expelled air could flutter the curtains. She throws the book down on the floor and glares at me.

"I thought you were, like, real hot on me reading. Well . . . *I'm reading*," she says. Her defiance is worthy of a warlord.

"Well, yeah, but not at . . ."

She reaches over and switches off the bedside lamp before I can finish the sentence. I am left standing there in the dark, speechless. Where is that frontal lobe of mine when it's needed? My analytical brain, the part that has been sponging up all the scientific research, should be telling me to *chill*, that there is a perfectly reasonable neurobiological reason for her insolence. Instead: Enter lizard brain. "I cannot believe how rude you are!" I yell before I can stop myself. I grab the book and storm out. At least I resist the urge to slam the door.

Why is it so hard being the mother of a teen daughter, of *this* teen daughter, I ask myself for the zillionth time. I have yet to get the answers, or at least the guidance, I need. The cheery self-help advice manuals directed at clueless and exasperated mothers, the dozens, scores, of books out there (many of which I have now read) are, disappointingly, of little help.

The neuroscience I've been delving into makes sense. I'm glad I invested all the time reading the books and looking up those studies in journals. But I remain unsatisfied with the explanations, and it's not just because it all seems clinical and mechanistic in the face of real human drama. It's because I have already been through the middle school years, twice, with my two sons, and never encountered what I'm experiencing now. If the "brain under construction" explanation is true, why didn't the immature, poorly wired brains of my two sons result in just as much tumult a few years ago? The research clearly states that teen boys' brains are as muddled and chaotic as teen girls' brains—in fact, there's some evidence that boy brains are even *slower* to wire up than girls'—yet neither of my two sons acted out like this, and my relationship with them during their middle school years was not stormy.

FIVE

My sons were not perfect. I remember my oldest going through an oblivious-to-all-responsibilities period. And I remember a particularly rough patch at the end of sixth grade when my younger son sunk into a deep funk, the kind of silent, sad-eyed moodiness that would, if observed by a stranger, prompt that person to say, "He looks like he just lost his best friend." In fact, he *had* lost his best friend. His buddy since second grade had suddenly moved across the country, leaving my son bereft. The mood lasted so long that I wondered if we ought to consider therapy. But even in the worst of times, he was a dutiful, respectful kid. And, as hard as it was to live through, I could see and understand that there was a reason for his moodiness.

When I look back on those incredibly full and hectic days with my two sons in middle school, I realize that I didn't know how good I had it. When I rushed to make sack lunches in the morning while prepping breakfast, I didn't think, Gee, it's so great that the boys like just about any breakfast cereal I put in front of them. It's wonderful that I can pack lunches without conferring and consulting, bargaining, debating, cajoling. It's lovely that every morning is not an endless negotiation. It just never occurred to me that what I was experiencing was anything but normal, just as it never occurred to me to think, I have a great relationship with my sons. We didn't "have a relationship"—we just *were*.

I remember, wistfully, the three-week, seventy-five-hundred-mile land cruise we took, my two boys and I, when we traversed the continent on the diagonal, northwest to southeast and back, in a twenty-four-foot rented RV. My older son was a year younger than Lizzie is now, old enough to be decent company but young enough to still listen to me, at least some of the time. In truth, he listened to me, as did his two-year-younger brother, a lot more than Lizzie ever has.

In the RV, the mornings were full of talk and silence: I'd be driving, the boys would be taking their turns sitting up front by my side, sometimes dreamy, wordless, other times deep in monologues full of mind-numbing details about computer games and wars waged with little pewter action figures. At noon we would stop at some local park, where the boys would explore the terrain and play tag and fight off the insects while I busied myself in the tiny kitchen heating up cans of Chef Boyardee ravioli and slicing apples. I watched them from the window and listened to their voices, loud and confident.

That trip, special as it was, was just part of how we were—how we are—with each other: at ease, comfortable. No drama. Comedy, yes; drama, no. We talk movies and music and politics. We talk tech. (They talk, that is, I listen, generally with little comprehension.) We even—if I push the subject—talk girlfriends. They can be grouchy and short-tempered, but neither of them has ever turned off a light while I was talking to them, stomped out of a room midconversation, slammed a door in my face, or told me icily to "chill."

Being a mother to boys is a whole different ball game. Of course, there's the push-pull of adult-child, parent-teen. But with boys and mothers, there is no gender overlay, no way that this male child sees you as his personal future. He knows that, whatever else happens in his life, he will not someday be a mom. He feels no psychological necessity to simultaneously identify with and reject you. With a son, you, the mother, the female, don't stand in his path, and so you don't have to be mowed over.

I know that there are all sorts of unsavory psychological tangles to the mother-son relationship: "smothered" sons who are never able to achieve true adulthood; sons who grow up to seek a mother rather than a wife; sons who want to marry their mothers (thank you, Oedipus); sons who want to kill their mothers (thank you, Norman Bates). But I also think that a son can love a mother in an almost thoughtless, uncomplicated way. At least that's what it feels like to me, having just gone through two sets of teen years with sons. Whatever the differing dynamics of mothering sons and mothering daughters, this much I know: Being the mother of sons prepared me not a whit for being the mother of a daughter.

And being the father of a teen girl also, I think, provides little insight into the mother-daughter dance. My husband, for example, has a mystifyingly—and annoyingly—calm and comfortable relationship with Lizzie, and so he just doesn't get what's happening between the two of us. "What is it with you?" he asks, shaking his head after witnessing one of our many skirmishes. "Why can't you two just get along?" he will plead when Lizzie and I snipe at each other during dinner. They don't fight. He isn't on her, as I am, for the sludge pile of dirty clothes and soggy towels in her room or for eating nothing all day and then bingeing when she comes home from school. It's not that he doesn't care. He does. He will say something about egregious or errant behavior (neither of the two previous examples would qualify as far as he's concerned), but its all text and no subtext. He doesn't see himself in her, doesn't see his own childhood being played out in her life. He sees her at a remove: a girl. She is what she is. They go off to Blockbuster in search of the latest anime movie. They have lunch at Wendy's. They play Halo or cribbage. Simple. Uncomplicated.

My father-daughter relationship (unlike my husband and daughter's) was not stellar—but it was simple and straightforward. My father, a stubborn, often irascible man, pulled no punches. You knew where you stood with him, and where you stood was usually in the doghouse. He disliked a lot of things, including people who sneezed, people who left the lights on in a room after they left, people who sat around and read all day, all auto mechanics, most drivers (especially women), and anyone who rang our doorbell. He was not an easy guy to live with. Still, he took me out almost every Sunday of my life, from age five to eighteen. In the spring and fall, we played tennis. In the winter, we went roller-skating or ice-skating or snow sledded down the big hill at Bethpage State Park. We went horseback riding. We bowled. We stopped at Carvel on the way home, where we both ordered large swirling chocolate cones. (Among my father's dislikes were people who ordered vanilla ice cream.) We played catch in the backyard. He taught me how to throw a spiral pass. If this sounds too good to be true, it's because I left out the part about his being short-tempered and mean, unfailingly contentious and doggedly critical. But, as with my husband and daughter, it was all text and no subtext. Unlike my hard-to-read mother, my father made it clear what he wanted from me: high performance (academic, athletic), unquestioning obedience, and genuflection—not necessarily in that order. When he didn't get all three, he was not a happy camper and made sure I wasn't either. But however tough or embattled our relationship was, it was both transparent and predictable, and so, oddly, stress free.

Some mothers too have lovely, smooth, intimate, stress-free relationships with their teen daughters. Okay. I know of *one* mother who does.

Sarah is my exercise and running partner. We meet three mornings a week to run the trails or work out at the gym we both belong to. We talk nonstop when we run, covering topics from the mundane (we are both shoeaholics) to the arcane (hermaphrodites in colonial America—Sarah is a women's historian by trade). But most days, at least some of the time, we talk (that is, she talks, I listen) about her daughter, Leah, her amazing, flawless, high-achieving daughter, who gives her not a moment's worry, who never makes her cry (except tears of joy, that is). This is a daughter who wakes up early on Saturday morning to clean her room. This is a daughter who finishes her homework before it's due—and then redoes it because she's not quite satisfied. This is a daughter who apologizes (apologizes!) for being in a bad mood. They are in a mother-daughter reading group. They go to plays. They shop together.

One morning, on the way home from a run with Sarah, I stop at the grocery store, where, in the produce aisle, I encounter Diane, a mutual friend of Sarah's and mine. She wants to know what I'm working on. "Teen girls," I tell her. "And the whole turbulent, confusing mother-daughter thing." She nods sagely. "Well," I add, "unless you happen to be the mother of Leah." Diane rolls her eyes.

"Ah, yes," she says, "the perfect child. And you can't even hate her because she's not stuck-up or arrogant. I mean, she really *is* perfect."

"I know, I know."

"My child is not so perfect," Diane says, with careful understatement. Her "child" is thirty.

"Mine either." We both laugh.

"We ought to form a support group for friends of Sarah who need to commiserate about their imperfect daughters after hearing about Leah's latest accomplishments," Diane says. It's a joke, of course, but I can think of at least four women who would join immediately. Two mornings later, Sarah tells me that Leah has been named "Best Junior Girl." I'm ready to start a hotline.

My friend Sarah also—and not surprisingly—has an enviable relationship with her own mother. And she did not come late to this, as some daughters do, after a troubled adolescence or a tempestuous teenhood or a few kick-out-the-jams college years. She has *always* been close to her mother. Last week I pulled up alongside her car in our rendezvous parking lot. She was waiting for me, sitting with the window open talking on her cell phone to her mother. "When are you coming out to visit, Mommy?" I heard her ask. "Oh, that's great!" I heard her reply to whatever her mother answered. There were tears in my eyes. She calls her mother *Mommy*, I thought, which maybe is a little weird for a forty-seven-year-old woman, but it is also just plain wonderful. And she *wants* her mother to visit. (I never did. The psychic costs far outweighed the benefits.) She *delights* in her mother's visits. I know this from direct observation. I have seen them side by side on treadmills at the gym during her mother's frequent forays west. She comes west every time Leah is starring in a play, or soloing at a concert or singing with the jazz band, or doing any number of the other amazing, talented things she does.

I long to see the chink in this gleaming and undented mother-daughter-granddaughter armor—and hate myself for the thought.

And thus, I feel particularly guilty, as if I were somehow personally responsible for the information, when an acquaintance who is also a Jungian-influenced therapist informs me that tempestuous mother-daughter relationships are the healthiest kind. I have corralled her in my favorite espresso hangout and just finished venting about the latest domestic skirmish. That's how bad things get sometimes. I stop casual acquaintances midlatte to vent.

She takes a deep breath and tells the story of a mother and daughter who were very close, did everything together, shared confidences. Then the daughter starting cutting herself. She had all these feelings toward her mother, like "get out of my face" kind of feelings that she couldn't express. So she expressed them on her own wrists. "You *want* a feisty girl," my friend says, patting my arm. "Where there are no sparks, there's something wrong," she says. "It's dangerous to get along all the time. It's stifling to the girl's evolving sense of self. Suffocating, really." Hmmm. I wonder what the other members of the soon-to-be-forming Jealous of Sarah and Leah Support Group would think about this?

Probably not much. The truth is, Leah gives no indication of being a suffocated, repressed, or otherwise suffering kid. Just the opposite: She is friendly, cheerful, vivacious, and curve-breakingly well adjusted. My Jungian friend would say—in fact, *did* say when I alluded to the apparently conflict-free but seemingly emotionally healthy Sarah-Leah duo—that "the other shoe will fall someday." The therapist is absolutely convinced that a break, a significant emotional break, *must* happen between mother and daughter for their mutual psychological health. Maybe the other shoe will fall for Sarah and Leah. Or maybe not. Perhaps these two are genuinely blessed in some mysterious way that trained therapists and battle-scarred mothers will never understand.

One thing I do understand: I want a feisty girl. I want a girl who stands up for herself and makes her own way—and is comfortable doing so in my company. I want a girl unlike the girl I was. My relationship with my own mother was not, in fact, stormy. If I were to put a meteorological tag to it, I'd call it chilly. The lack of turbulence wasn't because I was a naturally compliant child. "A real handful" is how my favorite grandmother described me when I was Lizzie's age. I was stubborn. I wanted independence in the worst way. I didn't want to do anything—be seen anywhere—with my mother. But—and here's the big difference—I towed the line at home. I cleaned my room, made my bed, did my chores, ate what was on my plate, wore the clothes my mother deemed appropriate. I did my homework. I studied for tests. I excelled in school. If you didn't sneak a peek beneath the surface, I guess I looked a lot like Sarah's perfect daughter, Leah. I was the captain of this and the editor of that, the leader, the one who got the awards. My noncompliance played out off the radar. I smoked cigarettes. I stole loose change from the bottom of my mother's purse to buy the candy she wouldn't dream of letting me have. I lied about where I was going and with whom. This is all pretty tame compared to what I could have been doing (binge drinking, servicing the JV football squad). But the point is, I misbehaved quietly and covertly. The face I presented at home belonged to the flawless, high achiever. Although I challenged my parents' authority by my secret behavior, and although I often felt angry and contentious, I never picked a fight and I never talked back. *Ever.* Why was that? I set this out for my therapist acquaintance.

Her response is quick, so quick that I realize I must have just presented her with a textbook case. Too bad I never read that textbook. "Maybe you felt your parents' love was contingent on your being a good little girl," she says as gently as she can.

Bingo. That is *exactly* what I thought. And the better I was, the more I achieved, the more they would love me. Only it didn't—and doesn't—work that way, a lesson I might consider applying to other relationships in my life, if only I were smart enough to do so. There's a startling corollary to this, though: If Lizzie feels free to act out, to talk back, to be nasty, to offend me, maybe that means she feels secure in my love. Maybe her attitude, her disrespect, is a *good* thing.

It takes me a day or two to unpack this.

It could be, it occurs to me, that one of the paths to a better relationship with Lizzie is not my trying to change her behavior—that's not going to happen—but my changing the way I think about her behavior. Feisty is good. Talking back is healthy. This could be my new mantra. I can try it, at least. But there may be a bigger insight here if I can let myself come to it, let myself at least entertain its possibility: Lizzie with her "healthy" acting out is very different from the perform-for-love kid I was. Doesn't that mean that I, as her mother, am in fact very different from my own mother? I've been so afraid of being my mother, of reliving our relationship through my relationship with Lizzie. But wait. Lizzie feels free to rebel—often in obnoxious ways. That must mean I grant her that freedom by communicating, somehow, my unconditional love. And that must mean I am *not* my mother. My head hurts from all this. But in a good way.

Away from the immediate heat of our relationship—like when she's at school—I think to myself that I might even *enjoy* the wild energy her rilesome nature brings to my life if it weren't so evident that so much of the time the pain she causes me is anything but inadvertent.

A week later, on an early morning run with Sarah, I am filling her in on Lizzie's bad behavior at dinner the night before. I had made a dinner that featured two of her publicly known and acknowledged favorites. I had had a tough day at the word factory, followed by a hurried late after- noon trip into town to the grocery store, followed by more than an hour of cooking from scratch. Lizzie took two bites, spit the second one out into a napkin, and marched over to the sink with her plateful of food. Maybe she was paying me back for some comment I made earlier that day, or last week, or who knows when, about her trashed-out room or a poor showing on a math test. Who knows? I was probably culpable in some way. A discussion ensued. This discussion did not end well.

"If it were Leah, you know what I'd do?" Sarah asks.

"Leah would never do this," I say, unnecessarily.

"Well, yeah, but if she did . . . I would just make it about me. I'd just say: 'I spent a lot of time on this dinner, and you'll hurt my feelings if you don't at least try to enjoy some of it.'" I have to smile.

"But don't you see?" I say. "The point *was* to hurt my feelings."

At my espresso hangout, where I manage to run into everyone I know and everyone who knows everyone I know, I run into the sister of a friend of mine. She is the mother of two girls, seventeen and nineteen, and has the battle scars—or the red-rimmed eyes—to prove it. We are trading horror stories while waiting for our shots to be pulled. She tells me that she has recently taken up meditation. "I had to find a place of peace," she says. I can hear the weariness in her voice. She tells me she was spending a lot of time "cowering in the closet"—literally in the walk-in closet in her bedroom—crying after interactions with her daugh- ters. I tell her that I've put in some closet time myself. "You know," she says, shaking her head, "all my life people have been nice to me. Before my daughters, I'd never met anyone who purposely set out to hurt me."

After this encounter, it seems I can't run an errand, go to the movies, or take a trip without stumbling upon a beleaguered mother of a teenage daughter. The landscape is littered with them. I hear about a thirteen-year-old honor roll student who ran away to hook up with a boy she met on the Internet. Her mother has a detective searching the streets of Seattle. I hear about a twelve-year-old who has started to sneak out of the house at night and, when confronted, went at her mother with closed fists. In line at the grocery store, I eavesdrop on two mothers talking about their daughters. One, a fourteen-year-old, is threatening to drop out of school. The other, in treatment for anorexia, has started cutting herself. On a plane to Denver, I sit next to a lovely woman who shows me a photo of her smiling fifteen-year-old daughter. "She has screaming fits," the woman tells me, a catch in her voice. "She bought a lock and put it on her bedroom door." I listen with terror and fascination, like I'm hearing tales of Katrina victims or returning Iraq War soldiers. The narratives are powerful, poignant, and scary. Every story is different, but every story is the same.

Much later, more than a year later, Lizzie shows me an entry from a diary she started to keep at the time. There are only five short entries, all written when she was, as she put it, "twelve going on thirteen." The second entry begins:

> My dad is really nice to me and my mom is a little mean to me so I am a little mean back. I do that a lot.

SIX

Lizzie has a plan, she tells me a few days later. We will stop first for coffee—white chocolate decaf mocha for her—and then go on to Borders where she wants to buy a new anime book. This late afternoon excursion is entirely her idea, and I am, of course, thrilled. To have her initiate a mother-daughter outing—even if said mother is mainly along to play chauffeur and banker—lifts my spirits.

The coffee interlude goes well. The baristas at our favorite spot all know Lizzie and greet her warmly. We get our drinks and sit at a little table in companionable silence, alternately eavesdropping on the amorous conversation of a twenty-something couple at the next table and listening to the ambient music, which happens to be the new Coldplay CD. At the bookstore, we both go our separate ways, I to peruse the biography section, she to the manga and anime shelves. Twenty minutes later, ready to go, I walk the aisles looking for Lizzie. I find her back by the café.

"I've got my book," I say. "Where's yours? Let's buy them and get out of here."

"I don't have a book," she says, her tone flat.

"Couldn't find one you like?" She starts to walk away. "Couldn't find one you like?" I repeat.

"No. Mom. I. Couldn't." Her voice is too loud for the store, and she's enunciating each word, making each word its own sentence, as if she were talking to a very stupid person. I decide to ignore this.

"So can I help?"

"No. Mom. You. Can't."

I'm really confused now.

"We came here because you wanted to," I say. "You wanted a new book. Let's just get you a new book."

"I'll be in the car," she says, walking away. I jog after her.

"But we came here for *you*," I say again. "Let's get a new book."

"You get it," she says, and keeps walking. Huh? What did I miss here? I blink back some tears—disappointment, frustration, anger—as I stand in line to pay for my book. Then I follow her out to the parking lot.

I may be inching closer to what's going on in my own head, unpacking just a little of the baggage I carry as a mother (and a daughter), but I continue to be baffled by Lizzie. Did I say something to set her off? Was there some shift in the air current between us that I didn't pick up? What happened? Something other than the frontal lobe wiring issue must be happening inside her head. But what? If I could figure out what makes her tick—and especially what makes her tick when I tock—maybe together we could build the kind of relationship I dream of having, maybe I could stop crying in the closet (or the bookstore) and start enjoying these last years of intimate motherhood.

A few days later, a fat envelope arrives in our mailbox. It's a questionnaire for Lizzie from our pediatrician. A cover letter explains that the survey is part of an ongoing statewide assessment of teen mental, physical, and emotional health. Anonymity is promised in suitably high-minded language at the top of the six-page form. I leaf through it and find that it asks many of those questions anxious mothers want the answers to and don't get: Have you tried alcohol? Do you know kids who smoke marijuana? Are you happy with the way you look? Do you ever think about hurting yourself? Do you often feel unhappy? It is to be filled out by the girl in private, placed in a sealed envelope and handed to the doctor at the next scheduled appointment. Lizzie has received one in the mail because she has a scheduled sports physical next week. She's not thrilled about filling it out—it has the whiff of homework about it—but I force the issue, shooing her upstairs with the form and a freshly sharpened pencil.

I want to see what her responses are. I *really* want to see what her responses are. In fact, I momentarily contemplate steaming open the envelope later that night, when she's asleep. But I know I won't do it. However clueless I might be about other aspects of my daughter's life, I do get the privacy thing. This was a huge issue for me as a teen. I wanted to keep everything—every thought, every experience other than the I-got-an-A-on-the-bio-test-today kind of experience—hidden from my mother. It wasn't even that I had evil thoughts (I did, sometimes) or risky experiences (ditto). It was that I wanted to be separate and unknowable, unbreachable, unreachable. I was hell-bent on forging a separate identity and, in retrospect, I didn't want anyone to know what it was until *I* knew what it was. So while Lizzie completes the questionnaire upstairs, I spend some time at a Web site reading a summary of last year's findings based on these surveys. Interesting data, but not the personal insight I am after. Then it occurs to me that the person who sent this questionnaire might be worth talking to. Our pediatrician, in practice for more than twenty years and herself the mother of three daughters, might be just the teen girl expert I'm looking for. A week later, she agrees to meet with me at the espresso place that has become my office away from home.

Catherine is a delicately pretty, soft-spoken woman, a doctor married to a doctor, with a girl who just graduated from college, a girl in college, and a third in the middle of high school. She looks ever so slightly worse for wear but a lot better than I'd look if I had three daughters. Maybe it was all those tough years in med school followed by those punishing twenty-four-hour shifts as an intern. Perhaps, next to that, mothering three daughters isn't so daunting. I ask her just one question—not even a question, really, but a prompt: Tell me about teen girls today—and for the next hour I listen and scribble notes.

Catherine's take is that a teen girl's life is all about stress. Although she talks about body image and sexuality, unhealthy eating habits, and cliquish friendships, the word she repeats again and again, the idea she circles back to every time, is stress. The stress she talks about first comes from what she sees as the loud, insistent—and mixed—messages about the female body. She begins with the expected "the female body is so sexualized in our culture and by our media" rap that I think to myself, I've heard this all before . . . Women's Studies 101 . . . but her ideas take a different turn. On the one hand, she says, the sexualized images promote "a

kind of freedom to be and do." But, competing with that cultural impera-
tive, there are also very powerful, equally insistent fear messages, from
elementary school warnings about "inappropriate touching" to sensation-
alized stories about kidnapping, rape, and sexual abuse to slasher movies
where the sexy girls are the first to go.

There is, Catherine says, "incredible tension" between what teen girls
think they have been given permission to do and what they are terrified
will happen to them if they do it. "Do you know," she says, lowering her
voice to a near whisper, "that there are girls so scared to be touched that
they won't even let me, a female doctor, perform a routine physical exam?"
The stress caused by this freedom-fear dynamic can be a kind of ever-
present background noise in a girl's life, which would be bad enough, or
it can grow into something bigger: extreme self-consciousness, low self-
esteem, poor body image, troubled eating habits. Add to this, says Catherine, who has seen several thousand teen girl bodies, the stress that
comes from the astonishingly wide variation in physical maturity. Some
twelve-year-olds are giggly and innocent and don't have their periods yet,
she says. Others look like grown women and have already given birth to
a baby. "Imagine dealing with that, every day, in a gym locker room."

Catherine is delighted by the doors that are now open to girls, the
whole girl-as-math-genius, girl-as-budding-scientist attitude of the last decade and a half. And she absolutely applauds the athletic opportunities
available to this second generation of post–Title IX girls. But she sees a
significant downside. "The bar is so high now," she says. "Academic achievement is one thing, but feeling that if you don't get *above* a four-point average your life is ruined is another. And athletics are the same. It's not
enough to play for fun or exercise. There are elite teams from sixth grade
on." She shakes her head. "Stress," she says again, "and more stress."

I must admit, I've never thought of Lizzie's life as particularly stressful.
She is not one of those overscheduled, overamped kids you read about
who needs her own personal assistant to keep her life in order. She isn't
overcommitted. She has plenty of downtime, plenty of lying on the floor
in her room listening to a Britney Spears CD time. She lives in a comfortable, stable, safe household where nutritious meals are placed before her
and clean clothes are delivered to her room. Someone—that would be

me—changes her bed linen, provides fresh towels, cleans her bathroom, and buys all the supplies, health, beauty, school, and otherwise, she needs. She is awoken, usually gently, on weekday mornings and driven, door-to-door, to school. When she arrives home by school bus, someone is always waiting to greet her. Interesting and entertaining material is readily available. There is both quality and quantity time with family. Her responsibilities number two: doing her homework and setting the dinner table. Where's the stress? Doesn't she know how good she has it? (And isn't that, I realize as soon as I think it, a mother's age-old lament?)

Or maybe she doesn't have it so good. I'm confused—and astonished—when I read the results of a 2006 nationwide study conducted by Girls Inc. that finds three-quarters of girls in high school, 56 percent in middle school, and a jaw-dropping 46 percent of those in grades three to five say they "often feel stressed." Maybe they just don't know what "stressed" means. Maybe they interpret the word colloquially, casually, the way a girl might say "I'm so depressed," when she doesn't mean she has clinical depression and is in need of treatment but rather that she's just had a bad day. But then I read further. Three-quarters of middle school girls, girls Lizzie's age, say they are "worried" about both achievement and appearance. Can this be true? Is Lizzie one of those girls?

I decide to check in with an old friend of mine, the mother of a girl my oldest son once had a crush on, and—more to the point—a veteran family therapist specializing in teens. For the past sixteen years, Elizabeth has talked to hundreds of girls—pampered girls with eating disorders, wards of the state with histories of sexual abuse, and everyone in between. The first thing she says, as we drink coffees alfresco at my usual hangout, is that middle school is the absolute toughest time on both girls and their mothers. She looks me in the eye and offers a kind smile. I can tell that she means to console me. I can tell that she sees I am in need of consoling.

I ask her about stress, and she starts talking about heightened expectations. Like Catherine the pediatrician, Elizabeth the therapist makes special note of the relatively new message that "girls can do anything," which is an offshoot of the slightly older but still relatively new message that "women can have it all." As a professional woman and mother she appreciates and has benefited from that message, just like Catherine has, just like I have. She recognizes that her daughter too has benefited. But she worries about the psychological costs. Most girls, she says, are told they can do it all, think they *should* do it all, but at the same time feel they can't *possibly* do it all. "That's a recipe for inner turmoil, for pressure, for high stress," she says.

I know what she's talking about. It would be hard not to know. The media are full of these Girl Power stories right now, big illustrated stories in the *New York Times* and in-depth features in the magazines about the new "supergirl." She is, as a piece in *The Nation* puts it, "at the top of her class, kicks ass on the soccer field and the debate team, plays a mean violin and is the life of every party." She is the poster girl for female empowerment, the "embodiment of the 'go-girl' feminism." And guess what? According to these stories (and Catherine and Elizabeth), she is not happy; she's stressed. Or, as one high schooler quoted in *The Nation* story succinctly puts it, "It sucks." This girl says she feels pressure to be everything at once— pretty, smart, athletic, popular, involved in loads of extracurricular activities, a leader. In a book I'm now reading, *Perfect Girls, Starving Daughters*, the author makes the argument that our generation of women "had the luxury of aspiring to be 'good,'" but our daughters are under pressure to achieve "effortless perfection."

The next morning as Lizzie and I go through our hectic routine trying to get out the door on time for school, I broach the subject of stress, perfection, and the supergirl. She is busy spooning Froot Loops into her mouth.

"So, Lizzie, tell me, do you ever feel stressed?" She keeps her head down, keeps shoveling in the cereal. I think she's ignoring me, but apparently she's actually considering the question.

"Let me think about it," she says thoughtfully, cocking her head. Then, hearing how grown-up that sounds, she adds, in an imitation-adult voice, "I'll have to get back to you on that." I smile and don't press the point. We're late anyway.

When she comes home from school that afternoon, I ask the question again. She seems a little mystified by the concept. "Well," she says, after a long pause, "I get stressed out when I forget something, like some homework I'm supposed to do, or like if I have a test and I forget to study."

I tell her I mean something more than brief moments of anxiety caused by a particular incident. I tell her just a little about the national survey and the articles I've been reading, wary of unintentionally planting the idea in her head, that I think she *should* feel stressed. But her attention is wandering. She's staring out the window. I'm about to give up the interrogation—which is undoubtedly how she sees this attempt at eliciting a response—but I decide to ask one last question. "Do you ever feel like you have to be perfect?"

She tears herself away from the view out the kitchen window and looks at me oddly.

"I just am who I am," she says.

In her voice I hear both defiance and impatience, and I am left, confused, parsing this statement. If said in defiance, then hooray! What a girl! If said in impatience, then it's just a door slammed in my face, a way to say butt out. Which is it? I don't know.

I relate this interchange to Kara a few days later. Kara is a quick, edgy, thirtyish woman with a sharp, pretty face and dyed, tomato red hair that she wears in the chopped, hacked style of an indic rock star. She's actually a mental health counselor who works with kids at three on-site health centers, one at a middle school, the others at high schools. Before she took the job a few years ago, she worked with homeless kids, disruptive teens, and teens with alcohol and drug problems. Kara is also one of the founding members of the Emerald City Roller Girls, a group of several dozen women—from their twenties to their fifties, from tattooed poets to fifth grade teachers—who've come together to play retro, full-body contact roller derby dressed in fishnets, skimpy tank tops, and outrageous hand-designed, hand-sewn outfits.

We sit on the grass talking during one of her breaks from Junior Roller

Derby, a first-time experiment she and several of her teammates have created to work with teen girls. It's kind of about roller derby, which is making a big comeback in young feminist women's circles. But it's more about body image, self-esteem, self-acceptance, and bedrock girl power. Kara smiles when I relate Lizzie's "I am who I am" statement.

"Awesome," she says. Then she tells me about workshops she has led where she asks girls to come up with descriptions of "the perfect girl." At first, she says, the girls chime in with physical attributes: blond, thin, rounded butt, big breasts but not too big, toned but not too muscly. "They are so specific, so exact," Kara says. "It's painful to listen to." When she pushes them to talk about attitudes and behavior, they say "sexy but not slutty" and "popular with lots of friends" and "confident but not a show-off." They even list "good manners," which both Kara and I think is pretty funny. "And how many of these girls *are* all of these things? And how does it feel to think you know what is perfect and not be able to *be* perfect?"

Does Lizzie feel she is coming up short, I wonder.

"You know," Kara goes on, "it's really all about power and control, and if your daughter feels she's got power over who she is, if she's fine with who she is . . . well, then . . ." She smiles and nods, leaving the thought hanging.

I wonder if maybe Lizzie's stubbornness, her attitude, her resistance— all the traits that make her hard to live with—are, in fact, the foundations for self-confidence. I hope so. On the other hand, I remind myself that Lizzie's quip—"I just am who I am"—might just be code for don't bother me. I did hear an undertone of attitude in her voice. But, then, I hear an undertone of attitude in her voice most of the time.

Kara goes on to give me a teen's-eye view of power and control issues, bringing up ideas that were absolutely core to my own teen years, that burned in my teenage soul, but which I've managed somehow to completely forget as a mother. Children, she says, by way of background, are part of a whole system their parents have set up and control: the house, their room, what and when they eat, when they can play, when they must do their homework, how long they can talk on the phone, the whole rhythm of their days. As little kids, they don't think anything of this. It's just life. It's just how it is. But as they get older, as they become teens, they begin to see that everyone doesn't live like they do, that their particular life has been, for the most part, fashioned by their parents' decisions. Meanwhile, they are also busy developing a sense of themselves as separate and individual people. So, Kara says, they recognize—often with a jolt—how powerless they are over much of their life. As she says this, I remember with great clarity an almost visceral memory: an imprisoned feeling, the weight of the family bearing down on me, the claustrophobia.

But, Kara says, when they are away from their parents, whether at school or out with friends or online, they are, within certain bounds, free to be who they want to be. A girl can have friends her parents don't know about, do things her parents don't know about—or wouldn't approve of—use language her parents wouldn't allow at home. So, continues Kara, "in one part of her life, her life away from parents, she feels powerful—which only makes her home life seem even more stifling." Put this way, it's easy to see how, without much extra effort on anyone's part, conflict could escalate at home.

"Okay, now get this," she says, taking a deep breath. "At home, the teen feels she has no power over her life, right? Yet, when she acts out, mouths off, doesn't play by the rules, she's told her actions are 'disruptive' to family life, that she is 'ruining it for everyone.' *Ruining it for everyone.*" Kara repeats the phrase slowly, carefully enunciating each word. "Now that's exerting an *enormous* power. She has the power to 'ruin it for everyone' but not the power to decide when she goes to bed?"

We're both silent for a moment thinking how deeply confounding this must be. I am also thinking, How many times have I said to Lizzie, "You're ruining it for everyone"? Dozens? Hundreds? I've made a good dinner. She sits and glares at the plate, refusing to eat, and her attitude changes the mood around the table. "You're ruining dinner for everyone," I am sure I said . . . many times. Or, the evening is going smoothly, all of us together in the family room, until I ask Lizzie if she has unfinished homework, and then all hell breaks loose. My sons quickly retreat to their rooms; my husband decides he needs to check his half dozen favorite news sites in case World War III has broken out since he read the *Times* that morning. Lizzie and I are left glowering at each other, and I'm thinking (and probably saying out loud), Thanks a lot for ruining the evening. I take a silent vow not to say this again. Not that I won't think it.

Kara has to go back inside to tend to the two dozen Roller Derby girls in training. But I want to ask her one more question. Although she spends most of her time talking to teens (and most of that with teen girls), she also talks with parents (mostly mothers), both with and without their daughters. What do mothers tell her about their feelings, I want to know. What I really want to know, of course, is whether these other mothers feel the way I do.

Kara takes another deep breath. Then the words come out in a rush: "They say their teen daughter shows blatant disregard for their feelings, that she seems not to consider that the mother is a human being, that she is disrespectful—hurtful and disrespectful." Kara is thirty-three. I ask her if she's interested in having kids. She is deeply ambivalent.

For several days after my talk with Kara, I think about this idea of power and how much it is at the core of both Lizzie's experience as a daughter and my experience as a mother. Lizzie doesn't have the power to decide on her own bedtime, but she has the power to ruin an evening at home. And I? I have the power to make all kinds of major decisions about her life—where and how she lives, where she goes to school—but I don't have the power to make her be civil to me. When you layer over this our stubbornness—a trait Lizzie and I share, in spades—it is little wonder that we are both so often frustrated and angry.

Yes, it's all about power, Kinlen agrees. Kinlen is a mother of two daughters, a teen educator, a registered nutritionist, and a practicing shaman. "The major challenge," she tells me as we sip our coffees at an outside table a few days after my talk with Kara, "is recognizing that you don't have power over your daughter anymore." Before she even finishes the sentence, I hear my own internal monologue: Oh yes, but I *want* the power. And I know what's best. And I want to control her, make her see things my way, force her to make the right choices. I am, after all, The Mother. And then another voice chimes in (is there such a thing as an internal dialog?): And, um, how's that working out for you?

Point taken. I stop listening to the voices and turn my attention back to Kinlen.

"You have to acknowledge their power," she is saying. Kinlen is both down-to-earth—straightforward, plain spoken—and somehow ethereal. A slender, graceful woman with luminous skin and clear blue eyes, she manages to communicate both inner calm and intense energy, a kind of banked fire. "You can't keep being boss. It just doesn't work. The relationship won't work. Her life will go underground." I hear that. My parents' lack of acknowledgment of my own power was probably, in retrospect, one of the reasons my life as a teen—and on through the adult years—went subterranean. But acknowledging the truth of something and acting on it are two very different things.

"How do I stop trying to be the boss?" I ask Kinlen. (This is a question to which I am sure my husband wouldn't mind my finding an answer.)

"Ask questions," she says, "don't make declarations. Find out what she wants, how she feels." I nod, thinking about all the declarations I make, how I often express myself in demands. Would it make a difference, I wonder, if instead of saying, "Do your homework," I posed a question: "How much time do you think you need for homework tonight?" Is this playing with words or is something more important going on? "It's about recasting yourself in the position of the nurturing coach," she tells me. "You don't want to be a dictator, and you don't want to be a buddy. You want to be the mentor whose love is always known." That's a very lovely thought. I hope I have it in me to play that role. Now that it has a name—"loving mentor"—it can be a goal.

We're finished talking. I pack up my notebook, and we both stand up. Then she says something, almost off the cuff, which is so profound I make her repeat it twice, as I fish notebook and pen out of my bag and scribble it down.

"I think teenage girls are here to help us heal the wounds of our own past," she says softly, "to help us deal with our own stuff."

So some of this is about me—I get that. Kinlen's remark cuts to the heart of that, punctuates it for me. Okay. I can work on myself by myself. But what's the next step with Lizzie? Through my reading and interviewing, I am beginning to understand something about teen girls and teen girl issues and teen girl brains. But I need to make more headway understanding one particular teen girl, my girl. It feels as if every time we make a connection, inch a little closer, there's a blow up or a wild mood swing, something I said or didn't say, some little psychodrama we find ourselves playing out, something that propels us backward and away from each other again. I am thinking about this when I remember what Kara, the Roller Girl/teen counselor, said: Kids feel far freer to be themselves at school than at home.

School. That's where I need to go. Of course I've visited her school, gone to all the parent-teacher conferences, the open houses, to events large and small. But I haven't spent any real time there. I haven't observed or experienced the daily life my daughter lives when she's not at home. At school, in an environment I don't control, making her own way, being who she is when she's not under my gaze, maybe she will reveal herself to me in new ways. And maybe this will bring us closer.

The next time we're in the car together, out doing the usual bank, gas station, grocery store, latte circuit, I ask Lizzie what she'd think about my tagging along with her to school, and we have a spirited discussion about the idea. Our best conversations seem to take place in the car. Actually, it's where pretty much *all* of our civil conversations take place. I've often wondered why this happens, why we snap and glare at each other at home but seem to get along famously in the car. I've heard other mothers say the same thing about these en route conversations. My friend Elizabeth, the teen therapist, thinks it's because in a car there's less opportunity for eye contact, which means the kid doesn't feel (literally) confronted, which means she relaxes. Whatever the dynamic, I cherish our car time. I am often happy to chauffeur her around for this reason. In the car this afternoon, I tell her that, regardless of how many books I read or how many adult experts I talk to, she is The Expert on her own life. Not only that. She is—or I would like her to be—my guide as I explore her middle school world.

This is how real anthropologists do their work, I tell her. They carefully and thoughtfully establish a connection with a contact among the population to be studied. (She snorts at "population to be studied.") This guide helps clear a small path for the researcher, maybe introducing her around, or maybe just by association, by showing others this person can be trusted. I can see that Lizzie likes that I am acknowledging her expertise and appealing for her help. My work as a writer is mysterious to her. What she sees is that I sit in a room by myself, clack away on a keyboard, and drink gallons of tea. How is that a job? What does that have to do with a book about her? But going to school with her, watching, asking questions—that makes sense. And *deferring* to her? What could be better.

She likes the idea, she says. But she wants to make sure I don't intend to Velcro myself to her side. Or, as she so sweetly puts it: "I'm gonna pretend I don't know you." That's just fine with me, I tell her. I want to be as unnoticeable as possible. I realize I may be a temporary curiosity in the classroom, in the hallways, in the cafeteria. I have read all about how the observer, simply by her presence, changes what is being observed. But I am counting on the utter solipsism of teens coupled with the universal invisibility of any adult to whom a young person is not forced to attend. I'll be all right. More important right now, it seems Lizzie will be all right too.

SEVEN

Here I am, 8:35 on a drizzly Monday morning in early February, just several hundred twelve- to fourteen-year-olds and I jostling for elbow room, waiting in the main hall of Spencer Butte Middle School for the first bell to ring. It has never before occurred to me that the expression "so loud you can't hear yourself think" could be literal, but truly it is so loud that I not only can't hear myself think, I am, for the moment, devoid of all thought, the din scouring my brain, a sensation both liberating and downright terrifying, a sensation not unlike what it feels like to be a teen—or so I remember. But I do need to have my adult wits about me. I am here this morning at Lizzie's school to begin a new phase of my exploration of her life, to further my understanding of what it means to be a teen girl today, and to, I hope, learn how to better connect with her. I am here not as a parent, not as a classroom guest or a casual visitor, but as a cultural anthropologist without portfolio.

Picture Margaret Mead hunkered down outside a thatched hut in Samoa. Imagine Jane Goodall crouched behind an outcropping in Tanzania, or John Nance sitting cross-legged in a Tasaday cave in the Philippines. These are my role models as I embark on a period of "sustained fieldwork" with the "indigenous population." I like to think of what I am about to do in these terms. Otherwise, it looks suspiciously like hanging out. Well, okay. I am going to hang out at my daughter's school for as long as it takes to make sense of this world she (and tens of thousands of other girls her age) inhabits for more than seven hours a day, five days a week—roughly the equivalent of a full-time job.

This anthropological fieldwork is not taking me to exotic places (I wish). This locale is anything but glamorous. It is a plain Jane school—a textbook example of early 1960's "modern" institutional architecture—a low, squat, glass and brick edifice located in an unremarkable residential neighborhood two miles south of downtown. The neighborhood is by and large middle-middle class, streets lined with well-preserved 1950s split-levels and 1960s-era ranches. But there's a working-class apartment complex a few blocks from the school and a small, low-income housing project on the edge of the neighborhood, plus some kids who transfer in from other areas. About a quarter of the student body qualifies for free lunch. There's nothing privileged or snooty about the place, yet it manages to be an extraordinary school—high-energy and innovative, warm and caring, staffed by seemingly tireless teachers who obviously love working here and a patient and always smiling support staff. Although modest in many ways (tax base, facilities), the school often scores near the top of district and state rating scales. Few students fall through the cracks. The teachers attribute this to the parents. The parents attribute it to the teachers. They're both right, and it is probably this mutual respect that fuels Spencer Butte's success.

The building may look familiar—in fact, my own junior high–high school was built right around the same time in the same unlovely style—but the world inside it, the world of the twenty-first-century teen girl, can seem more foreign than familiar to those of us who were twentieth-century teens. So I do see myself this morning as a traveler to a faraway land. Like my safari-vested compatriots who insert themselves into strange and wondrous cultures, I am driven by the same instinct to understand the lives of others. And like them, I believe that the clearest understanding comes from observing the routine, ordinary, everyday things these strangers do.

And so here I am, in the main hall of the middle school on a Monday morning surrounded by several hundred members of the subculture I plan to investigate: stringy-haired boys in camo; bouncy girls in skimpy tank tops and what look like flannel pajama bottoms; gangly, dermato-

logically challenged youth in basketball shorts three sizes too big that
hang to the calf; girls with matte black dyed hair who look like vampires;
hippie/urchin girls in gauzy layers and imitation Frye boots; tall, bony
girls in pencil skirts and cosmetician-quality eye makeup. And my honey-
haired, gray-eyed, peachy-skinned, jean-clad daughter, lugging her saxo-
phone and her twenty-pound backpack, making her way through the
throng to find her best friend, Nattie, looking over her shoulder every ten
seconds to see what I'm up to. She doesn't want eye contact. She doesn't
want to acknowledge me—and certainly doesn't want me to acknowledge her—but I know that not only is she okay with my being here; she
is kind of excited.

The bell rings, and we are off.

Lizzie's first class, a double period, is literature and language arts (or,
in layperson lingo, Reading and Writing). The teacher is Olivia, in her late
twenties, a lively, cheerful, ebullient woman who is already a seven-year
classroom veteran. She has arranged the room casually, with desks facing
each other in groupings of four. It's amazing how friendly and inviting a
standard classroom looks when the desks are not in rows all facing forward. It's also amazing—or maybe not—how much energy it is taking this
teacher to get the attention of these twenty-six kids given that they are
not all forced to face forward. I choose a seat in the very back of the
room, a chair against the back wall. Not one of the kids has so much as
glanced in my direction. I'm relieved, but not surprised. I was right to
count on the self-involvement of kids this age. My presence won't be an
issue.

Olivia begins the class the way teachers have jump-started Monday
morning classes since time immemorial: asking the kids what they did
during the weekend. Some answers are predictable and timelessly innocent: a birthday party, a trip to the humane society to get a puppy, a
grandmother's visit. Others are edgier. Our house got broken into, my
sister got out of rehab, my mother ran over a squirrel and couldn't stop
crying. I'm astonished at how easily some of these kids share this personal stuff, and I wonder—but don't really want to know—if Lizzie has
shared intimate details about our family in this forum. She doesn't today.
The kids seem to accept both the "grandma brought cookies" and "sister

has needle tracks" stories with equanimity. Or maybe they're not paying attention.

Next on the agenda is an overview of the homework due this week, greeted by theatrical sighs, audible groans, and much staring out the window. I look at the list Olivia has projected from her laptop and wonder if Lizzie is on top of this. There are two projects she should have already begun, but she's never mentioned them—nor, at least at home, worked on them. I start to write myself a note to ask her, then force myself to stop. Being here is not about checking up on my daughter. I have to remember that, or at least keep reminding myself. I am here to observe the tribe. Still, my gaze returns to her every few minutes: Is she taking notes? Is she paying attention? Does she seem engaged? The answer, at least today, at least in this class, is no, no, and no.

Now Olivia turns away to write on the board. "These are our topics for the week," she says as she prints:

Gender stereotypes
Ecological disaster
Cultural imperialism
Socially responsible science

Wow. What did *I* study in seventh grade? I remember memorizing the Indian tribes of Long Island. I remember a tortuous (for me to write and surely for my teacher to read) essay on why Hester Prynne did or did not deserve what she got. But cultural imperialism? Gender stereotypes? It makes me want to go back to school again. Okay, an exaggeration. Nothing could make me want to go back to do seventh grade again. But it does make me think kindly about what might be happening in today's classrooms—the good ones, that is, the ones overseen by thoughtful and enthusiastic teachers like this woman. I glance over at Lizzie. She is busy braiding a hank of hair.

The class is reading *As You Like It* in preparation for the much-anticipated annual seventh grade trip to the Ashland Shakespeare Festival. The much-anticipated part has more to do with a full day away from school, a reputedly raucous bus ride, and a restaurant lunch that in no way resembles cafeteria food than it has to do with Elizabethan drama, I am betting, but Olivia is forging ahead anyway. She's using a particular scene from the play—the heroine, Rosalind, is pretending to be a man when she encounters Orlando, the man she loves—to provoke a discussion on gender stereotypes. She asks the class to come up with words, attributes, behavior, whatever, that they would consider typically girl or typically guy. This is easy. Too easy.

Strong. Smart. Sports. Math. These guy stereotypes, interestingly, come mostly from the girls. *Ouch*. Obsessed with boys. Obsessed with clothes. Dainty. Scared of bugs. The girl stereotypes also come mostly from girls. I know they've been asked about stereotypes, but these quick answers, answers that could have been given thirty, forty, or a hundred years ago, are difficult to hear. It's not just the attributes themselves, but the fact that all the boy stereotypes are positive, and none of the girl attributes are. How long do girls and women have to keep proving their strength and intelligence? I thought we won that war, or at least some tide-turning battles. I can't tell what Olivia thinks about all this because her back is to the classroom as she writes the words on the board. I can tell what Lizzie thinks, though. I watch her as her classmates raise their hands to contribute to the discussion (trying not to stress that she is not raising her hand). She winces when "dainty" is offered by a (dainty) girl sitting just in front of her. I know how to read that wince: Both Lizzie and I have little patience with the dainty thing, with girls (or women, for that matter) who go *eeek* when they see an earthworm or don't like to sweat or couldn't change a flat tire if they had to. My daughter and I are decidedly undainty, and proud of it.

Now the kids listen to an audio recording of the scene with Rosalind as they follow along in the text. The language is difficult. The going is slow. The morning drizzle has stopped, and the sun has come out. Light streams through the big windows, and it's hard not to want to be outside.

"I don't get it," says a girl with bright green hair. Her tone is more exasperation than confusion, testy rather than questioning. Olivia has paused the recording to translate Shakespearean into Teen. "I mean, like, why doesn't she just tell him who she is?"

"Good question," says Olivia, ignoring the obvious attitude in the girl's tone. "What do the rest of you think?"

"Aw, she's, um, playing hard to get?" offers a boy sitting a few desks away from Lizzie. His knit cap is pulled down so far that his eyelashes touch the rim when he blinks. Doesn't that bother him?

"She thinks she'll be treated better as a boy than a girl?" This from the dainty girl.

I look over at Lizzie. She is doodling on the back of her notebook with her right hand and twirling a strand of hair with her left. No chance she's paying attention, I think. Then I see her raise her hair-twirling hand.

"She's just showing a part of herself that she couldn't show as a girl," Lizzie says matter-of-factly (and, I hasten to add, brilliantly). I hunch over my reporter's notebook, beaming, as I scribble down her remark.

The next class is history, presided over by the school's wrestling coach, a compact, muscular, prematurely balding guy with a big, booming voice. He is wearing a T-shirt and cargo pants and looks like he's ready to do yard work. Unlike Olivia's domain, this one is set up like all the classrooms of my youth: individual desks set apart from each other, little islands floating in a linoleum sea, lined up in careful rows facing forward. No question who the boss is here. The bell rings, and within seconds an assignment is given: The kids are to draw seven Mayan glyphs. The room is so quiet I can hear the distant drone of a neighborhood lawn mower.

It's jarring, this change from the first classroom of the day to this one. As a kid, I didn't give a thought to, much less appreciate, the fact that each classroom was a carefully managed, individually manipulated environment, a reflection of the teacher who inhabited it. But I see it clearly now. School is not of a piece. I am not talking about distinct academic subjects. That's obvious. I am talking about mood and ambience, expectations and behavior. School is not experienced as a building but rather as a series of discrete, self-contained spaces, all different from one another, all controlled by adults who make the rules, which are also different from one another. So a kid's job is not just to learn material, take tests, do homework, and generally stay out of trouble, but also to figure out how to act in each of these separate environments. What's permissible, what gets rewarded, what gets punished. How loudly can you talk? Can you eat that energy bar at your desk? Can you make a joke when answering a question? Is challenging what the teacher has said seen as laudable intellectual curiosity or disruptive behavior? Is collaborative work respected or called cheating? And what about gum?

These abrupt classroom-to-classroom changes in mood, expectation, and rules are one of the many sources of stress for middle schoolers. That's what the research suggests, and I am, just two hours into my first day of observation, a believer. Of course, learning how to negotiate these different classroom environments is an important part of a kid's education—maybe more important than mastering subject matter. And I can see how these changes from one teacher's world to another could be stimulating. But I can also see how, for Lizzie, they might serve to reinforce her mercurial behavior, or make her abrupt mood changes at home seem normal or expected—to her. After all, she might have to change her affect at school every time the bell rings.

After fifteen minutes of glyph drawing—"I'll give you time to finish up later," Mr. C. says, his big voice breaking the silence—the class moves on to an exploration of the Aztecs. He begins the lecture standing in front of the room, legs planted hip-width apart, hands on his waist, chin jutting forward—the Yul Brynner *The King and I* look—and says, apparently by way of introduction: "Hey, the Aztecs got *busy* with that sacrificing thing. Oh, dude, you won't even *believe* the Aztecs." I am alarmed by what might euphemistically be called his informality. But the kids eat it up. Mr. C. roams the classroom, walking with a rolling, wrestler's gait, talking blood and guts. Lizzie is tracking him with her eyes, laughing, occasionally scribbling something in her notebook. The kids want gory stories, and he delivers. They want gruesome details, and he delivers. This is perhaps not the way I'd teach about the civilization that achieved political and military dominance over large parts of Mesoamerica in the fourteenth, fifteenth, and sixteenth centuries, but clearly he knows his audience. And his audience is riveted by tales of human sacrifice.

Lizzie loves this teacher not because she loves history—Why should I care about old dead people? she snapped at me just the other night when I asked her how this class was going—but because she is one of three girls on the school's wrestling team, and Mr. C., the coach, pays a lot of attention to her. He admires her energy and encourages her participation. He enjoys her the way certain adults can enjoy other people's children when those children, in the presence of these other adults, become charming, engaging, and loquacious beings. That's Lizzie when she's around Mr. C.

With ten minutes remaining in the class, Mr. C. instructs the kids to go back to their glyphs. He walks up and down the aisles making sure everyone is on task, then motions me from my perch at the back of the room. He says he wants to have a word with me outside in the hallway. I knew I might have a hard time towing the line, maintaining my anthropological stance and ignoring my mother-of-a-student persona, but I didn't realize a teacher might have a problem with this too. Mr. C. wants to talk to me as a parent. I can't say no. I follow him into the hallway.

Lizzie is a great kid, he tells me, and she's smart. But she's not doing well in the class. He hates to say this, I can tell. Her less-than-adequate performance in the class is, of course, not news to me, but I didn't realize how bad it had gotten. We talk about how she can climb out of the C-hole she's dug herself into. Mr. C. is very gracious. He tells me about two or three different extra credit projects she can do. "She's a good kid," he says, again, as if to comfort me. I don't want to be comforted. I am now a Mom in Full, and in shock over the C-. No child of mine is getting a C-! A good strategy at this point would be to: 1. calm down, 2. remember that I am here to observe the middle school subculture and not act as a Helicopter Mom, and 3. remember what Kinlen said about being a loving mentor rather than a Bossy Mom.

I do none of these.

I troop back into the classroom and sit, fuming, until the bell rings. Then I walk straight over to Lizzie. She knows something is up, of course, because she saw Mr. C. call me outside to talk. I am sure she noted how long we spent in the hallway. She may even have seen the stony look on my face when I returned. "So," I say angrily, "you're headed for a C- in this class." Did I imagine this would be a conversation opener? She nails me with her best icy, squinty stare. She's good. I'll have to give her that. "A C-?" I repeat. My voice is maybe a little loud. "That is completely unacceptable." Her face is stony. With enormous effort, I reel myself in. "Listen," I say, "Mr. C. told me about a few extra credit projects. If you do two of them, you'll raise your grade to a B." She's still boring a hole through me. "I'll help you," I say, adding, a little weakly," it'll be fun."

"I'll *never* do anything if *you're* involved," she shoots back. Then she stalks down the hallway putting as much room as she can between the two of us. I'm stung by her words. But I also think it kind of serves me right. I did not handle this well. I got angry, and my lizard brain took over. I got angry, and I forgot why I was here, what I am trying to do. I follow her down the hall to gym class wondering how to make amends while not giving in on the C- thing. She is far ahead of me—maybe fifty noisy, jostling kids are between us—when she circles back and falls in step with me. She offers a smile, and I smile back. We both know we crossed the line, and we're both, by mutual and tacit agreement, crossing back.

"Gym, then Band, then lunch," she says gleefully. "The best part of my day."

But, as it turns out, gym is not the best part of this particular day. That's because her gym shorts are locked in someone else's locker, and that someone else is home sick. Why they are locked in someone else's locker is because Lizzie (apparently almost a month ago) lost the combination to her own lock and has been using various other girls' lockers ever since. This problem could have been easily remedied. We have spare combination locks at home in the drawer. I decide not to point that out, and pat myself on the back for the wise decision. Then I stand off to the side of the locker room and watch her run around trying to borrow a pair of shorts. And sneakers. And socks. It's like a scene out of *Goldilocks and the Three Bears*: These shorts are too big; these shorts are too tight; these shorts are *just* right. She is expending more energy finding appropriate clothing than I imagine she will playing games in gym class. And the whole thing is clearly stressful for her.

While she dashes around the locker room, I divert my attention to the other girls, noting that some grab their gym clothes and rush to change in the privacy of bathroom stalls and others parade around the open locker room in thongs. The two behaviors don't seem to correlate with body type—the girls parading around are no more or less shapely than the girls who have sequestered themselves in the stalls. What is it that makes a girl comfortable with her body? Many a teen self-help book has been devoted to that subject, I know. But the answer is elusive—both cultural and deeply idiosyncratic, as simple as "love the skin you're in" and as complex as the tangled relationship every woman who sighs and frowns at herself in the mirror has with the image she sees (or thinks she sees). Lizzie is, as I knew she would be, one of the paraders. Finally, she has put together semi-acceptable PE attire and sprints into the gym less than ten seconds before Bud, the teacher, begins the roll call.

I'm exhausted. And after three hours and fifteen minutes (but who's counting?) in this building, I am also claustrophobic. It's not a scary physical sensation, like being stuck in an elevator, but rather a mental dis-ease, a psychic discomfort. I have an urgent need to get out of these sealed-off, grown-up-controlled mini-environments and breathe the air of a free woman. Lizzie is sitting on the gym floor listening to Bud explain the rules for some extraordinarily complex game from Switzerland. I catch her eye and motion that I'll see her next period, in Band. Then I flee the building, get into my car, and make a beeline for the nearest drive-through coffee kiosk.

Unlike the coffee at my usual hangout, the drink I order is bitter and watery, and I drink it sitting in the car. Still, I can't remember when I've enjoyed a latte more. I sip it slowly, checking my watch to make sure I use up most of fourth period. Then I get an iced decaf version for Lizzie and run into a nearby grocery to buy four California roll sushi (her favorite) and a peach. After my brief immersion in her world this morning, I can't imagine—don't want to imagine—her standing in line in the cafeteria (yet another adult-controlled venue with more rules than a county jail—and a cuisine to match) waiting for a gray hamburger topped by one of those rock-hard tomatoes they strip-mine in Texas, to borrow a line from Garrison Keillor. She deserves real food! Her favorite food.

I have tried, off and on, to send her to school with a homemade lunch, which is what I did for both the boys. But toward the end of sixth grade, when I came to school to help her bring home art projects and science posters, I discovered fourteen lunch bags stuffed in her locker, the un-eaten sandwiches blue with mold, the bananas black and mushy, the apples brown and shriveled. Her locker smelled like a garbage truck. Since then, I have been stingy with the lunches from home, including only items I know she can't resist, like portions of leftover pad Thai or the saved half of a bean and cheese burrito from Baja Fresh.

By the time I make it back to school with my offerings, PE is over and Lizzie has changed back into her clothes and is in the band room assembling her instrument, a tenor sax. Around her, sixty other kids are either doing the same with their instruments or are already tuning and playing scales. Next to her is Damon, a short, cute, curly-haired eighth-grader. He has the sweet, soft face of a boy yet to turn the corner into manhood. If you could see his face, that is. Most of it is covered by his shoulder-length hair, which hangs like two curtains positioned an inch and a half on either side of his nose. But I have been privileged to catch occasional glimpses because this boy is Lizzie's latest crush, or what passes for a boyfriend in middle school. This means, as far as I can tell, that they hang out in front of either one of their lockers between classes, that they sometimes walk, shoulder to shoulder (holding hands being one of the many institutional no-nos) down the hallways, that his friends tease her and her friends tease him, and that, occasionally, Tom or I or Damon's father drive them to see a movie. It seems—and I hope it is—entirely innocent.

I hand Lizzie the coffee drink, and she gazes up at me with a look of pure love. "You're awesome, Mom," she says. This is definitely the best $3.25 I've spent in a long time. Not to mention worth crossing the line—yet again—between observer and mom.

I sit at the side of the room for the next fifty minutes and watch a master at work. The band teacher, Mr. Black, manages magic trick after magic trick, the first of which, the most impressive of which, is getting sixty-one kids to sit, instruments at the ready, focused on the baton he holds in his hand. He does it entirely, as far as I can tell, by standing stock-still and staring. He has very large, very blue eyes. He waits, and not all that long, and quiet descends. His other tricks rely on preternatural—actually kind of scary—peripheral vision. A trumpet player way off to the left, positioned almost behind the teacher's left ear, bends down to tie his shoe, and Mr. Black somehow sees the movement. He whips around and stares until the kid, sensing something, looks up from his shoe. Mr. Black holds his gaze a beat longer than necessary—*zap*—then turns back to his musicians. I see him nail three separate kids this way, one who is chewing gum, one who is fiddling with a music stand, and one—this is Damon—who is momentarily distracted by someone walking by the classroom door. In none of these instances is Mr. Black looking anywhere near the miscreant when the misconduct occurs. I watch as he fires Jolly Ranchers into the crowd like little missiles, each one hitting its target (a musician with whom Mr. Black is pleased), even though Mr. Black appears not to be looking at any of the kids.

Lizzie is one of the three kids today on the receiving end of the Jolly Ranchers. She pleases Mr. Black—she loves to play *and* she pays attention—which is one of the reasons Lizzie thinks Mr. Black is cool. Some of the other band kids think he's scary—that big, blue-eyed stare is unnerving—and Mr. Black is fine with that. The stare is his secret weapon. It's what keeps chaos at bay. Mr. Black is one of those teachers kids will remember—and tell stories about—for decades.

Lizzie is, right now, the happiest and most engaged I've seen her all day. She's got her Jolly Rancher. She's got her iced latte. She's got her boyfriend. She's got a new reed in her sax. And all is right with the world.

At least until the bell rings, that is, and it's time to rush to the cafeteria for lunch. I hang back and watch her make her way into the big dreary room with its long metal tables set in even rows. She scans the tables looking for her friend Nattie. But Nattie is already sitting with someone, their heads close together. Lizzie starts to walk over but hesitates. She can never be quite sure about Nattie. Sometimes it's like they are sisters. Other times, without warning, Nattie ignores her and attaches herself to someone else. Today is one of those other days, and Lizzie has too much pride (and, I think, too much fear) to walk over and sit next to Nattie and whoever Nattie's best friend du jour is and insert herself, uninvited. Lunch can be the cruelest time of day in middle school, the cafeteria being the most public showcase of cliques, a place where to eat alone marks you as a pariah, to eat with a friend cements the bond, and to eat with a group publicizes your affiliations and determines your image.

Lizzie finds herself alone, and it is a testament to how unbearable this is that she looks over her shoulder, makes eye contact with me, and beckons me to sit next to her at the end of one of the long tables. Across from us is a girl who could have been me back in the day. Her head is buried in a book. She remembers every once in a while to take a bite of the healthy-looking (brown bread, alfalfa sprouts) sandwich she brought from home. She is, as I was, oblivious to her loner status. She isn't alone at all. She is in the company of all those characters on the page.

As Lizzie and I sit side by side, I take the opportunity to quiz her about the lunchtime scene, both because I am truly interested—I am here to do research—and because it gives her the sense that we're sitting together not because she doesn't have another choice but because she's helping me with my work. We scan the room, and I ask her to describe what she sees. Her observations are quick and pointed.

"The preppies are over there by the 'Snack Zone,'" she says, motioning with her head to a counter on the far side of the room. "The populars are by the window, and those are the goths by the door." The preppies and populars look pretty much the same to me—mostly girls, carefully put together girls, who look like they spend more time getting ready for school than I would spend primping for an engagement at the White House. The goths—black, black, and more black—are easy to distinguish. Lizzie swivels her head to take in the rest of the room. "See those two tables in the middle? Those are the jocks." The room suddenly makes a new kind of sense to me. When I walked in a minute ago, trailing Lizzie by a respectful distance, I saw only a big room filled with noisy kids. Now I see distinct real estate. I see neighborhoods. I want to talk more about this, but Lizzie has finished gobbling her sushi and is ready to go outside. The kids are allowed to leave the building during lunch, provided they stay on the front walks or the lawn, like convicts allowed out in the exercise yard. Lizzie spies Nattie who is no longer in the company of her lunch mate. She and Lizzie go off toward the flagpole, whispering (Lizzie later tells me) about a boy who told Nattie, in confidence, that he likes Lizzie but doesn't want Lizzie to know. So much for telling your secrets to middle school girls.

A few minutes later, the bell rings, signaling the end of lunch period. The reaction would disappoint Pavlov. There are no quick movements, no upturned heads, no dashes to the doors to get inside and get to the next class. The boys who are tearing up clumps of grass from the lawn and throwing them at each other continue to do so. The girls who are painting their nails keep painting. The frizzy-haired bookworm reading in a patch of sunlight keeps reading. I count two minutes. Two and a half. At three minutes—the kids have five minutes between bells to get to the next class—the vice principal, a balding, burly, middle-aged man who inspires fear the way a good vice principal ought to—walks into the front courtyard. "That was the bell, people," he says, his voice booming. *Now* the reaction is Pavlovian.

What remains of Lizzie's day is the tough stuff: science and math. As many times as I sit through these classes during the three months, off and on, that I attend seventh grade with my daughter, I never cease to dread them—just as I did when I was her age. I feel that same suffocation when I enter the science classroom, that same tingling anxiety when I sit in her math class. Don't call on me. Don't make me go to the board and solve that equation. Don't hand back that quiz with all the red marks. I am happy that Lizzie does not fear these classes as I did. But I am *not* happy about one reason she doesn't: She just doesn't take school as seriously as I did, doesn't care as much as I did about being an A student. I feared bringing home a B, or God forbid, a C on a test. I *had* to do well. It was part of my (doomed) "perform for love" strategy. Lizzie, happily, healthily, doesn't play this game, which is great psychologically but has its academic downside. Her attitude toward these heavy-hitter classes is more like boredom—much to her science-writer father's chagrin—leavened by burden, the burden being that most science classes require actual participation, and there is math homework every night.

In science class today, the teacher shows a video that features spectacular footage of demolitions, the dramatic dynamiting of big, big buildings. Not surprisingly, the show is a hit. Lizzie is sitting at a table with three eighth-grade boys who either flunked this class last year or are on the slow track through the science curriculum. They stare at the TV monitor transfixed, whistling and exchanging high fives when a building crumbles. Lizzie is almost as interested in their antics as she is in the on-screen explosions.

When the video ends, the teacher segues into a mini-lecture on Alfred Nobel, the inventor of dynamite, and how scientific discoveries are not neutral.

"Take dynamite," he says, about to launch into his talk.

"Oh man, *I'll* take dynamite," one of the boys at Lizzie's table says, interrupting. "Just give it to me, man."

Lizzie laughs. The other kids laugh. The teacher does not laugh. He points at the kid, then points at the door. I have the distinct feeling this has happened before. The boy gets up and walks out of the classroom. The teacher follows. Lizzie looks over at me—I'm perched on a tall stool by the window—and rolls her eyes. After class, I cross the line to mother-hood again. I ask the science teacher to move my daughter to another table.

In math, the final period of the day, she has the formidable Mr. Z. I've been hearing about him since the school year began. He is the guy who makes you give up one of your hard-earned extra credit slips in exchange for being permitted to go to the bathroom during class time. He is the guy who charges the kids ten cents a pencil if they forget theirs. The parents have been in a state of revolt. I expect an ogre when I walk into the classroom. What I see is a short guy in Bermudas and flip-flops who just about any bartender would card. I'm inured to the beyond-casual, climate-inappropriate dress of the students—tank tops and minis in December, basketball shorts when there's snow on the ground—but it is startling to see teachers in such dishabille. Both Mr. C., the history teacher/wrestling coach, and Mr. Z. look as if they were on the way to a frat party, not a job. My hackles are raised until I consider the possibility that they dress this way not out of disinterest, sloth, or lack of professionalism, but rather on purpose. When I ask Lizzie about Mr. Z.'s attire, careful to hide my surprise (and disapproval), she smiles broadly. "Yeah, that's so cool," she says. Later she tells me that even though he's the strictest teacher she has, she's not afraid of him. Some of that, I bet, is the way he dresses, his constructed—or deconstructed—image.

Beach attire notwithstanding, Mr. Z. is a traditionalist. He stands in front of the classroom alongside a vintage overhead projector, scribbling equations on transparencies, sketching graphs, plotting x- and y-axes. I stare at the screen. These are the same equations I stared at uncompre-hendingly when I was in seventh grade. They baffle me still. Lizzie, how-ever, looks as if she gets it. She doesn't look particularly interested, but neither does she look, as I did, clueless. She dutifully takes notes, and twenty minutes later when Mr. Z. says the class can start on homework, she bends her head low over her worksheet and gets to it. I watch her. The minutes tick by. Her head gets lower and lower until it rests in the crook of her arm. It's been a long day.

When the final bell rings, I feel a sense of relief. Freedom! I can leave the building! I'm weary, but, except for a half hour during math, I was never bored. Shakespeare and gender stereotypes, the Mayans and the Aztecs, dynamite, Alfred Nobel—I am impressed by the material presented by these hardworking teachers. I am impressed by (and want to continue to learn more about) the challenges, both mental and emotional, that face Lizzie and her cohorts every day. And I am *really* impressed by my daughter.

"I can't believe how big your day is," I tell her as we drive home. "What a challenge. You're amazing!" I tell her. She drinks it in, smiling a tired smile.

"So," I say, not missing a beat, an instant morph from Mead to mom, "let's talk about that extra credit work for Mr. C. You've got to get on that right away if you want to raise your grade." She sighs. Her smile fades.

"Can you get back to the part where you just say how great I am?" she says.

EIGHT

"Why can't we be a *normal* family?" This is Lizzie's conversation opener at dinner one night. It's been three weeks since I started shadowing her at school, and one thing that has noticeably improved is our dinner table talk. Before I immersed myself in her middle school world, I'd pepper her with those generic (and, in her view, annoying) questions parents have always peppered their kids with at dinner, the ones that elicit monosyllabic responses: Anything interesting happen in school today? ("No.") What did you learn today? ("Nothing.") Now I know—or rather, I have relearned (because, of course, I knew this when I was Lizzie's age)—that school for her and millions of other teen girls is first and foremost social and only incidentally academic. What she cares about, what she thinks about and remembers, are friends and conversations, and the minidramas that take place in that sacred space between classes.

Now, based on what I've witnessed during the school day, my conversational prompts have completely changed. "So, Nattie's eye makeup was pretty intense, huh?" I said a few nights ago at dinner, which got us into a deep discussion about liquid versus pencil eyeliner and what a great store Sally's Beauty Supply is. Several nights before that, I mentioned that I had seen a few kids guzzling cans of Red Bull in the cafeteria during lunch, and that led to a spirited conversation about who drank what supercaffeinated beverage and whether the school was going to move in and ban such drinks. Okay, so these are not discussions about the beauty of a Shakespearean sonnet or the decline and fall of the Roman Empire, but they are points of connection, and I am enjoying the table talk these days.

So Lizzie's "normal family" crack takes me by surprise. Where is *that* coming from? We're all just about to tuck into our favorite meal of chicken Parmesan. I put my fork down. Tom and I look at each other across the table, wondering what Lizzie is talking about. I mean, we aren't exactly "normal"—two writers who work at home. We have no credit card debt. We don't get TV reception. How weird is that? But that's not what she means. We're not normal, she says, because we're not divorced. "All of my friends are from divorced families," she says.

Maybe she's bringing this up tonight because of the most recent Monday-morning debriefing in Olivia's class during which all five kids who shared their weekend experiences made references to split households. "I stayed over at my dad's Saturday night," one kid said. "I went to the movies with my mom and her boyfriend," said another. And so on.

I go through a list of Lizzie's friends in my head: Nattie, Allie, Evan, Micah, Damon—yep, all children of divorce. In Lizzie's seventh grade class, more than half of the twenty-six kids do not live with both biological parents in a single household. By that standard (these local figures are just about the same as the national stats), our family *is* aberrant. What a seismic shift over the last generation. I vividly remember the three—and only three—kids from divorced families I ever encountered growing up: my cousins, of course, whose mother, my aunt, caused a family scandal by jettisoning her first husband to marry her children's pediatrician; my friend Claudia, whose wild-haired, bangle-braceleted, single mother taught piano lessons; and the quiet, sad-eyed boy across the street whose father just disappeared one day. "Normal" was my family (if only statistically): one marriage, two parents, two kids.

Whatever the current—or preteen—definition of "normal" is, Lizzie has rarely been attracted to such kids. I am not referring to the marital status of the parents—although that might be a small part of it—I'm talking about the fact that she invariably befriends kids with "issues." Significant issues. Of course, I know kids have "issues." I've read the stories, from news of teenage binge drinkers and alerts about ADHD epidemics to the insistently scary stats on eating disorders and depression. But those things happen to *other people's* children. They certainly don't happen to my children, and they don't happen to my children's friends. In the serene mother-of-sons world to which I had become accustomed before Lizzie's arrival at the portals of teendom, "issues" were not an issue. An issue to a twelve-year-old boy is a misplaced Xbox control. Found. Solved.

Two years ago, the best friend Lizzie made at summer camp was a little girl with Asperger's and OCD who was fixated on *The Simpsons*. She came over to the house once, and we all tried hard to make it work. But after an hour, her discomfort was extreme, and even Lizzie could see that what might have worked out in the woods with structured activities and two trained counselors was not going to work for us. Then, last summer, her strongest attachment was to a thin, pale girl, three years older, who threatened suicide and cried herself to sleep every night because, among other things, her mothers were in the middle of an ugly custody battle over her. It's like Lizzie purposefully goes after the wounded kids.

Now there's Nattie, her best friend since last year. Nattie is a year older, although in the same grade. "I just didn't want to go to school one year," she once told me. Nattie's mother, who is not yet thirty, had her when she was sixteen. Then she had two more kids. Now she's trying to finish school while working full time, and it's Nattie who provides the stability at home, caring for her younger sister and brother, worrying over them, worrying about money, about whether her semi-employed father, who lives a few blocks away, has food in his refrigerator. Lizzie tells me one morning that she dreamed that Nattie was about to fall off a cliff, and Lizzie saved her.

That's a powerful dream, I think to myself, and an *em*powering one for Lizzie. It's interesting that Lizzie dreams of herself as the savior, the one in control, when it's clear that in nondreaming life Nattie calls the shots. I have been watching their interactions carefully these past weeks. Some days they find each other in the main hall before the bell rings, exchange hugs, troop off to the band room to stash their instruments (Nattie plays trumpet) and are inseparable all day. In Olivia's class they form a two-person work group and bend their heads over that morning's project, talking, writing, drawing, laughing. They walk side by side down the hallway. They sit together at lunch.

But there are also days when, if I didn't know these two were best friends, nothing I observed would hint at that. Nattie chooses another girl to work with in class. She spends between-class and locker-hang-out time with others, sits with another group at lunch. Lizzie waits it out. Or she hangs out with a group of boys. She knows that Nattie will eventually invite closeness again, probably the next day, maybe even that afternoon. And she is willing to put up with the seesaw of that relationship. After all, Nattie's personal life is *so very interesting*, and Nattie's style, with exotic piercings and a new hairstyle and color almost weekly, pushes the envelope in a way I think Lizzie admires. Nattie seems mature, confident, in control. Yet part of Lizzie—the subconscious, dream Lizzie—knows Nattie isn't in control at all, that she needs help.

Then there's her other girlfriend, Allie. Allie lives with her divorced mother in an apartment complex two long bus rides away from school. Her mother works the dawn shift at a convenience store, and Allie wakes up to and usually comes home to an empty apartment. It's easy to see—at least it's easy for me to see—how she pretends to be so much more grown-up than she is. She entertains Lizzie with all-too-colorful tales about who the police came and took away the night before and who got a black eye from a boyfriend, about the fifteen-year-old next door who just had a baby and the woman who didn't pay the rent so the manager put all her furniture out front and changed the locks on her door. Lizzie listens, entranced. This is so not her world, not our world. These two girls, her closest friends, are among the neediest—economically and emotionally—kids at school. They are among the small percentage of kids not from the surrounding neighborhood who are permitted to transfer in. It's not that easy to find kids like this at Lizzie's school. Yet she does.

I am worried about her choice of friends. Isn't she too young to be taking on the burdens of other kids? She's not yet figured out who she is, what she wants, where she fits. To be faced with these very adult issues seems not just premature but potentially scarring. Does she really have to know how stupid and cruel adults can be to each other at this point in her life? Does she have to know how scary life can be as an adult, how much risk is involved, how stability and comfort are luxuries, not givens? These may all be important life lessons, but at twelve? I've worked hard, Tom has worked hard—and together we've made good choices—so that our kids don't have to worry if there's food in the refrigerator. We've arranged our lives, made sacrifices, figured it out so that our kids don't have to come home to an empty house. We've worked and planned and saved so that we can live somewhere where the neighbors don't beat up on each other, where the police don't make routine house calls. To see Lizzie begin to learn about a world we have tried so hard to shield her from, to see her seek out and befriend the kids—and *only* the kids—who live in that world is confusing and upsetting.

I talk about this to Joyce, a therapist I know. She's seen a lot of teen girls in her decades-long private practice. "It could be," she says, after hearing the details of Lizzie's various friendships, "that your daughter is a born 'rescuer.' Lots of girls—and women—are." I nod, thinking of Lizzie's very literal dream of saving Nattie from falling off a cliff. It's enlightening to consider that, although my daughter may not be sensitive to *my* feelings, she might be finely attuned to the feelings of others. That's a good thing. "Maybe she just feels the need to nurture and help," Joyce says. That's another good thing.

I see evidence of this at school. Lizzie is—on those days Nattie and she are close—very involved in helping her friend work out boyfriend issues. Lizzie has a current crush, Damon; Nattie has admirers, boys too shy to approach her. Lizzie works the angles for Nattie, corralling one boy after lunch and getting him to talk to his friend (a shy Nattie admirer). I hear her assuring the boy that Nattie really likes the shy boy and would be amenable to his approach.

What I see more of at school, though, is Lizzie as listener. I don't hear a lot of what Nattie or Allie tell Lizzie in the hallways when they walk together or linger in front of their lockers—I cannot get close enough to eavesdrop over the din—but I see that Lizzie is listening and nodding, that sometimes she laughs, but other times she looks concerned, that when she talks she often seems earnest, that she gives them hugs.

I am working myself up into a truly sanguineous state about my preternaturally empathetic daughter when Joyce delivers the bad news. Girls who are rescuers often go for "bad boys," thinking—incorrectly—that they can reform them. Women who are rescuers are so busy trying to save others that they neglect themselves. Rescuers can be one-half of an unhealthy codependent relationship. Enough already. Joyce must be reading my face (I have a very readable face). She reaches out to pat me on the arm. "Or," she says kindly, "you just have a lovely, sensitive young woman in your house."

It would be nice if she left it at that, but she doesn't. Joyce has two other theories about Lizzie's choice of friends. She asks if Lizzie has siblings, and when I tell her she has two older brothers, she zeroes in on that. Are the brothers high achievers, she asks with no preliminaries. In fact, they are. I tell her that my first son is a National Merit scholar and an Eagle Scout, a top scholarship recipient, and my second son is a talented musician, an AP student, and, oh yeah, prom king. Joyce looks at me and shakes her head. "That's a pretty steep hill to climb to be like her brothers," she says. "Maybe your daughter just decided to opt out." I look at her quizzically. "What I'm saying is that she saw how high the bar was, and she decided she could not—or would not attempt to—compete. So, what could she do to feel as accomplished as her brothers? She could choose friends over whom she had an advantage."

She's not doing this consciously, Joyce says, trying to reassure me. I am not reassured. I hate the idea that one person's success (or in this case, two brothers' successes) can sideline a third person. Why not look at the boys as role models? Why not see how, although both are highly accomplished, they are very different from one another, surely a lesson that there is room at the top, that brother number two didn't opt out because brother number one was an achiever, that there are many ways to excel. I know this is a message in our household, a powerful but unspoken one. Maybe I should speak it? Maybe I should find those "teaching moments" in our life together to impress this on my daughter. Then I force myself to remember what Kinlen, the nutritionist/shaman, told me about the power I no longer have, the power I must recognize in my daughter, how I must train myself to ask questions rather than make pronouncements.

I like Joyce's third theory the least: Lizzie has a self-esteem issue. She doesn't think she's as good as the kids who are doing well. She feels she's not worthy to be their friends, not up to par, so she chooses the kids who are hurting, the kids with issues. I don't want to dismiss this out of hand, but I'm pretty sure, after living with this girl for a dozen years, that she has a healthy ego. It's true, though, that Lizzie is not a straight-A student. I don't think this bothers her. I *wish* it bothered her more. But I think she is confident, as she should be, in her own intelligence. I think she knows (and I have certainly told her) that she *could* be a straight-A student if she spent even half the time on math that she does on Tomb Raider. She gets kudos at home and at school for nonacademic achievements: her growing prowess on the tenor sax, her emerging athletic ability.

In PE class, I can see that she absolutely shines. She has a natural athleticism that makes her good at almost every activity and, unlike many of the kids in that class, she pays attention. She listens while Bud explains things. She lines up when she should. She throws herself into every activity. She volunteers to get equipment, set up, to run a quick errand to the office. And in Band, she is one of Mr. Black's favorites not just because she is learning to coax a lovely, smooth sound out of her sax but because, as in PE, she is attentive. Although she sits next to Damon and could easily be distracted, most days she isn't. Most days it's clear she is genuinely interested in the music, in the way the various sections have their own parts, in how a piece the band is practicing is slowly coming together. Most days she comes home with a Jolly Rancher or two in the pocket of her jeans, evidence of Mr. Black's approval. She knows she's good. She's told she's good. I don't see low self-esteem playing into the mix.

The truth is, I don't know why she chooses the less-fortunate, issue-burdened friends she does. She may not know herself. What I do know is that while having friends is always important, at this age, it can be *everything*. That's what more than a few middle school teachers have told me. The biggest, most important challenge facing girls in middle school, they say, is learning how to negotiate friendships, learning what makes a friend and how to be one. Maybe it's because the stakes are so high, or because the girls' brains are now wired for drama, or both, but girl-girl friendships at this age are reputed to be among the ugliest and nastiest on earth. One of the therapists I talk with goes on for a solid fifteen minutes about how malicious and cruel girls can be toward each other. Beyond the cinematic "mean girls" who cluster in exclusive cliques and make life miserable for outsiders, there is, the therapist tells me, cruelty so over the top that it qualifies as "verbal torture." There's bullying and backstabbing. Girls will start ugly rumors about other girls to inflict pain, to cut them down to size should they be doing well at school or have a particularly hunky boyfriend.

A middle school counselor calls girl-girl relationships "merciless." Girls store up information to use against each other, she says. They zero in on one another's vulnerability and work it, pick at it, poke at it, make it bleed. She doesn't think for a moment that girls are inherently vicious. She thinks all this cruelty stems from a new and overwhelming sense of powerlessness. The girls feel powerless over the changes in their bodies. They feel powerless in their relationships with their parents. They feel vulnerable and flawed, and the nastiness they inflict on other girls has, she says, much to do with making sure everyone else feels just as imperfect as they feel, making sure other girls are down at least one more peg than they are.

I don't see this with Lizzie and Nattie. The cruelty, if it could be said to be that, is in Nattie's periodic cold-shouldering of Lizzie, not in any verbal sparring. I do make an effort to eavesdrop on other girl-girl conversations in the hallway. I am less concerned with being obvious with these girls I don't know than I am when I hover around Lizzie. I occasionally hear girls critiquing the clothes, hair, makeup, and boyfriends of other girls. They are harsh—and sometimes clever, even funny—in their remarks, but not downright cruel. Whatever nastiness there is, assuming it exists as all the experts say it does, remains hidden from my purview. I think it must happen in notes passed in classrooms, in text messages and at MySpace, at sleepovers.

I ask Lizzie about this, if she's experienced the kind of cruelty I've been hearing and reading about. At first she says no. "My friends are all cool," she tells me. Then, a few days later, she wordlessly hands me a little spiral notebook I gave her maybe a year ago. It has a pen and ink drawing of a lioness on the cover. Sometimes, when we are not locked in battle and I can appreciate her ferocity, I call her "Lizzie the Lionheart." She has used the notebook, or at least the first seven pages of it, as a diary.

"I can read this?" I ask incredulously. I remember going to great pains to hide my childhood diary in a drawer in my nightstand under a stack of *Seventeen* magazines, and then later, wedged between the mattress and box springs of my bed. I can't believe Lizzie is just handing this to me.

"Yeah, sure," she says. "Like, it's no big deal. It was from a *long* time ago."

"Wow," I say, just about speechless. "This is just amazing of you."

"Yeah, I know," she says, grinning. "Anyway, it's for the book, right?"

"Right."

After she hands me the notebook, she disappears upstairs. I don't waste a moment. Quickly, I open to the first page. "Best friends: Nattie and Allie," she has printed at the top. The date is, in Lizzie time, "a long time ago": late October, almost five months ago. I start reading.

"My cat is my life," the first entry begins. "He is always there for me." This is, apparently, in contrast to the *humans* in her life, the kids at school. About them, she writes: "People at school say nice things to me, but other times they are mean. What should I do? This happens every school day. What did I do to them to be so angry and mean to me? Someday I really hope they will stop."

On another page she writes: "Whoever is mean to me I am mean right back. I don't like being mean to people, but everyone has a temper and mine is very big at times."

I find Lizzie in her bedroom sitting on the floor going through a stack of CDs. I give her a huge hug and thank her, again, for sharing her diary. I want to follow up on something, I say. Is that okay? Sure, she says. And so I ask for details. I want to know exactly what mean things were said and by whom. I won't use names, I reassure her. But I need specifics. She says this happened so long ago that she doesn't remember. I press the issue. She sighs, and I know in that moment she regrets giving me the diary. Oh, great. Yet another big talk with my mom, she is thinking. Can't she just disappear and let me listen to my music? I back off. We're in this for the long haul, after all. There's always tomorrow. I'm learning.

The following morning, we are in the car on the way to school—our prime conversation time—when I ask again for details. Now she says she remembers a number of times when supposed "good friends"—she mentions Nattie and Evan, a boy she's known since preschool—all of a sudden, for no reason, shunned her. "Like I'd be walking down the hall, and I'd see Evan, and he'd look the other way. Or when we had to get in groups in class, and I'd walk over to Nattie, she'd turn her back and walk over to start a group with someone else." I've actually seen this happen once since I've been observing.

"No explanation?" I ask gently. "No one said anything?"

"Nothing," Lizzie says. "That's, like, what made it so bad."

Then, as I'm pulling into the parking lot, she remembers a note Nattie wrote to her around the time of those entries last fall. "I don't want to be friends with you right now," the note said. It came out of the blue, Lizzie says, just like the snubs in the classroom and hallway.

"So what was going on?" I ask. It's the first time I've heard this story—and I feel sad that Lizzie had to go through this without my support at the time. She says she doesn't remember. I'm surprised. Wouldn't this have been a traumatic event? But I remind myself that five months can be an eon in the life of a twelve-year-old. This note is ancient history. She and Nattie are best friends again.

A few hours later, Lizzie calls me from school. It's lunch period, and I can hear pandemonium on the other end of the line. I can also hear Nattie's voice. Lizzie is asking her about the note. She is, in fact, interviewing her for my benefit. It turns out, according to Nattie—who does remember the details and, once she remembers, sparks Lizzie's memory—that Nattie wrote the Dear John note because she thought Lizzie was being "mean and bossy." I hear the story unfold from both sides. It involves one of those complex choreographies of friendship unique to this age, with Nattie (according to Lizzie) horning in on Lizzie's longtime comradeship with Evan and two of his pals and Lizzie (according to Nattie) becoming short-tempered and snippy, and Nattie (according to Lizzie) acting snooty and stuck-up. There's also an unsurprising subplot involving Evan, who Lizzie has had a secret crush on for years, paying just a bit too much attention to the very attractive Nattie. I know that on the psychoemotional Geiger counter that measures teen cruelty, this barely makes a clicking sound. There are kids who are so verbally brutalized, taunted, and humiliated by other kids that they fall into deep depression or even take their own lives. But I also know—both from my own past and the teen brain research—that even small emotional glitches can feel like out-of-control rollercoaster rides at this age.

On the final page of Lizzie's diary, I read: "Everyone thinks being liked by a guy at school is a big deal. Girls say they know when a guy likes a girl but they really don't. Every day we get new feelings for a person. One day you will have a boyfriend and the next day you will break up. Life is hard this way and that's why I think I'm going to grow old and lonely and die old and lonely."

I want to cry when I read this. I do cry. But I am also—and I know this sounds strange—reassured by her words. This is just what I felt at her age, almost exactly what I wrote in my own diary. This is teen angst I understand, and it makes me feel emotionally connected to this girl from whom I sometimes feel so distant. The fact that she wrote about it comforts me. It shows that she already understands the therapeutic power of chronicling one's own insecurities. It shows that she's working through some of the tough coming-of-age stuff we all have to face.

This age in particular, with its laser focus on friendships and its budding awareness of romance, brings with it such fears of ostracism and abandonment, of unbearable everlasting solitude. Friendless. Boyfriendless. What could be worse? More terrifying? And even more important to a teen girl, more *embarrassing*? Happily, this age also brings with it wildly wandering attention and swiftly changing moods. Yesterday's deep funk over a real or imagined slight, an overheard nasty remark, an exclusion from a tête-a-tête in the girls' locker room is replaced by the euphoria of a surprise phone call or someone in the hallway saying that your hair looks good. Or maybe you look in the mirror that morning, and a pimple is gone.

Volatility is the name of the game, and Lizzie plays it well. It occurs to me that this hints at what may be the best explanation for her attraction to girls with issues: a craving for theatrics, a need to vicariously experience the kind of domestic upheaval, excitement, and commotion she does not often get living in our staid and stable home. And maybe, in reverse, this also explains why she has so few girlfriends. Nattie and Allie are it. Their drama is exciting, but it is quite enough.

All the other kids in her life are boys. In the cafeteria, when not with Nattie, she sits with Evan and two other boys. After school, I see her hanging out with the same threesome. They joke and laugh and seem entirely at ease with each other. They talk about video games, computer games, music, movies. I hear nothing personal, nothing intimate. On weekends her playdates aren't with Nattie (who is often busy caring for her two younger siblings) but rather with Evan and company. I take her to Evan's house, or sometimes he comes here, and they play video games for hours, barely talking. It's such a stark departure from her interaction with girls that I presume their silence must be a respite for Lizzie.

It turns out that boy-centric girls are not uncommon, especially among girls who grow up, as Lizzie has, with brothers. Kara, the school counselor, tells me that some girls just opt out of the world of girl-girl friendships and instead gravitate to guy friends. She tells me what I already know: Guys don't do drama. They don't process emotions in front of you. They are not interested in dissecting relationships and puzzling over the subtext of conversations and discerning the real meaning behind a certain look given by a certain someone. They are not so unpredictable. I listen to Kara list these male attributes, and one part of me silently screams sexist! sexist! and another part of me says yep, uh huh, that's just how my sons are. And that's pretty much the nature of my adult interactions with most men.

The problem with boy-centric girls, Kara says, is that they are learning early on what so many women need to *un*learn later: to define their lives by the men (or boys) around them, to see themselves only in relation to the guys, to lose themselves in male culture. There's another problem too: At a certain age—that is, *this* very age—boys become less interested in having girls as friends and more interested in having girlfriends. This means, according to Kara, that boy-centric girls either are left out in the cold or start, perhaps too early, to have boyfriends.

I can see that both are beginning to happen with Lizzie. Evan's two buddies seem to be moving away from the girls-as-just-friends period, just as Kara predicted. I've noticed maybe a half dozen times since I've been shadowing Lizzie that the two boys separate themselves from the group outside after lunch, leaving Lizzie and Evan alone. And several times when Lizzie has called Evan to invite him over, he declines, saying that either or both of the other boys are coming over. Lizzie is usually not invited to join.

And Kara is right about the precocious romance also. At the tender age of twelve and three-quarters, Lizzie has already had three boyfriends. Most of the relationship drama around our household is not about mean girls but about hot guys. Tom finds this astonishing, and more than that, scary, as I think many fathers do. *His* little girl with a boy. It is almost too much to rationally contemplate. I am both less astonished and less frightened, having had my first all-consuming crush at age twelve. For Lizzie, it began this past fall at the start of seventh grade. He was a cute, curly-haired, generously proportioned boy on the wrestling team who came from—you guessed it—a divorced family. The particular quirk here was that his mother and father were living together again after five years apart, which was making for what might euphemistically be considered a "dynamic" domestic scene. The boy, Micah, was very sweet to Lizzie: attentive at school, calling her at home, inviting her to come along with his family to movies and football games. During Christmas break he had his mother drive him out to our house to hand deliver three presents—gloves and a scarf his mother bought and a little locket he picked out himself. There was a precious, aw-shucks moment out on the porch. This boy was sweet to Lizzie right up until the moment he dumped her. *Unceremonious* is the word that comes to mind. Unceremoniously dumped her. There was another week and a half until the end of winter break, but after being given the presents, Lizzie heard not a word from Micah. Early on New Year's Eve, she got a call. He had another girlfriend, he said, and had been "dating" her for the past week. And that was that.

When Lizzie told me—which she did seconds after getting off the phone with him—I was furious. How dare this kid dump my daughter? Who does he think he is? And I hurt inside for Lizzie. I remember the physical, palpable ache in heart*ache* after my own first dumping, and I wanted to be there for Lizzie, to honor the significance of the occasion and to salve her wounds. I remember, at her age, feeling as if adults did not take me seriously, had no clue about the depth of my inner life, how much I actually understood and felt. I would not make that mistake with Lizzie. But neither would I make this two-month, occasional-peck-on-the-cheek relationship into something it wasn't.

I wasn't sure how to handle it until, at breakfast the next morning, after the tawdry tale of Micah's call was related to one and all, one of my sons commented: "What a dick that guy is." And I said, could we please not say stuff like that at the table. And everyone laughed because we've—I've—said much worse. Let's just say he is a *phallus*, I said, with exaggerated prissiness. And that's how Micah—who was an ardent fan of the sports teams of Oregon State University, located in the town of Corvallis—became known in our household as the Phallus From Corvallis. No one laughed harder about this than Lizzie.

Then, within a few weeks, we started hearing about Jay, a quiet kid in Lizzie's math class whom she had befriended. There were occasional e-mails, then daily e-mails, then entire evenings, after homework, spent on the phone. There were a few Saturday afternoon video game "dates" at his house or ours. It all happened (and ended) so fast that, although this was just three months ago, I hardly remember it. More to the point, Lizzie hardly remembers it.

Now, this being spring, we are deep into Damon territory. Damon is the eighth-grader who often sits next to Lizzie in Band. He has wavy, shoulder-length hair which is almost the exact same in-between color as Lizzie's—a honey blond veering to light brown—and a soft, appealing, slightly impish face. At school they meet up at Lizzie's locker between classes. They walk the halls together. They are, I can see from the looks the other kids give them, acknowledged as a "couple." One time, trailing behind them as they left Band together, I saw Evan study them surreptitiously. I tried to read his look. Did he fear losing Lizzie's friendship? (No, that couldn't be right. Lizzie still hung out with him, still asked him over for video game fests.) Did he wish he had made a move and that he was walking by her side instead of Damon? (Probably not. Although Lizzie admitted to having a perennial crush on Evan, there had been no hint of reciprocity—and many opportunities for same.) Maybe it was simpler than that: sheer curiosity. Evan still thought of girls as friends, not potential girlfriends. Maybe he was studying Lizzie and Damon for hints to his own future.

At school, I overhear Lizzie and Damon make plans. At home, there are phone calls and e-mails, invitations to spend (parent-supervised) afternoons at his house, return invitations with afternoons spent here. I know this relationship is something a little more than the other two because when Damon comes here they don't just play video games. Lizzie takes him for walks in our woods. When I pick them up from seeing a movie at the mall, she shows me a strip of photos they took at one of those little booths. In one picture, their cheeks are touching. In another, they are grinning with their arms flung around each other's necks. In a third, he is looking at her, not the camera, and he looks smitten. How could I not like a boy who is smitten with my daughter?

The answer comes two weeks later. I am at school at five to pick up Lizzie from track practice. She is waiting for me, sitting next to Damon on the cement walkway in front of the building. Her face is nicely flushed, rosy, glowing, which I attribute to two hours of track practice. Apparently, there is another reason for her high color.

"We made out!" she tells me the second we get into the car. I am more floored *that* she is telling me than *what* she is telling me, although the sentiments run neck and neck in intensity. I would have withstood a red-hot branding iron to the soles of my feet, waterboarding, whatever, before I would have told my mother something like this, before I would have told her *anything* about boys or any details about what I considered, even at eleven or twelve, my "private life." I look over at Lizzie, her bright eyes, her pink cheeks, and I am struck again at how different in some important ways—some good, healthy ways—she is from the daughter I was. Which means, which must mean, that *I* am different in some important ways from my mother. I think this all in a flash, and then it's gone, obliterated by the issue of the moment.

"Making out?!" I try not to yell. "What do you mean 'making out'?"

She looks at me with a mix of pity and exasperation.

"Like kissing. A lot of kissing."

"Anything else?"

She hesitates. I sense her hesitation. She senses my sensing her hesitation. Now she has to go on.

"Well, when we were kissing, his arm, like, accidentally, um, touched my, you know, breast."

Oh yeah, I am quite familiar with such "accidents."

"Listen," I say, slowing the car to a stop, "you should not let him feel you up. You should *really* not let him feel you up." I can tell that, despite the urgency of my voice—not to mention the volume—this is not making an impression. I need to give her a reason. She and her twenty-first-century teen cohort live in a world surrounded by, inundated by, sexual messages, images, and symbols. Feeling up is tame next to what she sees on the Internet, what she hears in lyrics. I think back to my own teen-era mistakes. "Boys this age are really immature," I say. "If you let him feel you up, he'll tell all his friends, and they will tell all their friends, and then everyone at school will be talking about you." *That* gets her attention.

"Okay, okay," she says. "I get it." I can see that she gets it. I start driving again, and we're both quiet for a long moment. "So," she says sweetly, as we near the house, "like, how do you feel about dry humping?"

As the sweat trickles down my back, I wonder if it is possible for a woman my age in perfect health to have a heart attack. Maybe what I'm feeling in my chest is merely transient arrhythmia.

"I'm *kidding*," she says. "I'm just kidding. It's, like, a *joke*."

A joke? I want to know how my twelve-year-old daughter even knows the *term* "dry humping." I want to run home and Google "convent" and dispatch her to one posthaste. Instead, I try to appreciate the fact that she tells me what she tells me, that she feels she can make jokes like this, that despite the stormy seas we travel, we do have these moments of connection. I keep my mouth shut.

NINE

My final foray into the world of seventh grade takes place on a mild, sunny day in late April. Today I am not roaming the hallways or eavesdropping by the lockers or scribbling notes from a perch at the back of a classroom, where I've learned all I am going to learn from that routine. I continue to be impressed by the energy—the creativity, determination, patience, and humor—of the teachers. I continue to be impressed by how the kids, Lizzie included, manage to successfully negotiate the herky-jerky rhythms of the day, how, in the midst of teen turmoil and teen angst and incompletely wired brains, they manage to figure out what teachers want and give it to them. What has caught my attention a lot in recent visits to school has been the way the kids manage to sandwich in full, complicated lives during the five-minute breaks between classes. Entire soap operas are played out in those five-minute breaks: friends fight and reconcile, tears are shed, boyfriends are shed; alliances are made, cliques defined, secrets shared, confidences broken. Somewhere in there, books get taken out of lockers, and homework is retrieved. But that's really not what school is about for these kids, for my kid.

I've paid attention to Lizzie's friendships and listened in on friend-to-friend conversations. What I'm after now is a broader sense of how Lizzie and her peers interact—not observed from afar as I check out crowds of kids rushing down the halls or take note of clusters of kids gathering in the corners of the cafeteria, but up close where I can study their interactions and hear what they say to each other. Not in those stolen minutes between classes, but when they have time to laze around with each other, time to talk. I want to know what kids talk about when they're not at school and when they're not just hanging with close friends.

And so I've signed up to help chaperone a day-long, out-of-school activity that involves ten seventh-graders. The outing is part of a school-wide project called "A Day of Caring." The kids have all done preliminary research on issues affecting the community—everything from homeless-ness and teen pregnancy to animal overpopulation—and are now set to perform a day of grunt work at local nonprofits that deal with these is-sues. Lizzie has chosen animal control (or lack thereof) as her issue, and she—along with nine other kids—will be volunteering at the county's animal control agency (aka the pound).

I've got four kids in the car this morning: Lizzie; her apartment-life tale-teller friend, Allie; a girl I don't know with a meticulously torn T-shirt and red streaky hair; and a small, skinny, slightly wild-eyed boy. We are driving out West 11th, more a five-plus-mile strip mall than a street. We pass TacoTime, Taco Bell, Burger King, Carl's Jr., Round Table, McDon-ald's. When we pass by Wendy's, the skinny boy, who is sandwiched between two girls in the backseat of my Prius, pipes up.

"I could go for a triple bacon cheese patty melt," he says.

"I hear that!" says Allie. The boy extends his hand for a high five, then grabs the twenty-ounce Nalgene bottle wedged between his thighs and chugs it.

"What is that? Like, vodka?" This is Allie again.

"I wish," says the boy. "Naw, it's just coffee." A twenty-ounce Nalgene bottle of coffee? He can't be serious. I call him on it, and he passes the bottle up to the driver's seat. Yes, it is coffee.

"Here's the rest of my lunch," the kid says, pulling a half-pound bar of Nestlé milk chocolate from his backpack and holding it above his head for all to see. The girl with the streaky hair reaches into her backpack and pulls out a stomach-size bag of Skittles, which she passes around. The kids take generous handfuls and stuff them. It is 8:40 in the morning.

"My mom is always trying to lose weight, so all we have is all this low-fat crap in the house," says the streaky-haired girl, her mouth full of Skittles. Lizzie, who is up front in the passenger seat, shoots me a side-long look and takes another handful from the bag.

"That's why we all go for the junk food," Lizzie says, her remarks obviously directed to me and not the kids in the car. "It's all the stuff we can't have at home."

"Junk food?!" The skinny boy pretends outrage. "Hey, this is the food of the gods."

When we arrive at the animal control agency, the kids discover that they won't be helping out with the animals themselves, which is a big disappointment. Lizzie signed up for this agency because she is nuts about cats and dogs. She thought they'd be grooming, feeding, walking the animals. She was even prepared for cleaning cages. But pound animals are sometimes pound animals for a reason, and there are "liability issues," according to the guy who greets us at the door. Instead, we—ten kids and three mothers—will be doing landscaping work. The area in front of the building is a weedy expanse of erstwhile lawn with a few outcroppings of shriveled petunias. We are given trowels, rakes, hoes, shovels, and wheelbarrows, and are set free. The two other mothers go off to a far corner of the property with four girls in tow. I stake out a small plot to work on, close enough to easily eavesdrop on the six remaining kids but far enough away to be out of direct line of sight.

The talk turns, almost immediately, to sex. They are, with no preamble I've heard, discussing the meaning of "sixty-nine."

"You don't know what it means?" This is Lizzie, *my* Lizzie, talking. We've had all kinds of sex talks. But not this one. Lizzie is apparently incredulous that her sometimes-friend Starr does not know what sixty-nine means. The other kids look at Starr like she's told them she doesn't own a cell phone or some equally ludicrous statement. Of all the kids digging in the dirt this morning, she looks like the one who would know. At five feet nine, with a generous, precociously womanly body and a face made theatric by the overenthusiastic application of cosmetic products, she could pass for twenty.

"Tell me, tell me," she pleads. Lizzie looks over at me. I look down quickly, avoiding eye contact. I'd like her to think I'm not listening.

"Even *my mother* knows what it means, don't ya, Mom?" she says. I keep my eyes focused on the weeds. Rob, the coffee-swilling chocoholic, laughs. Then he grabs a stick and draws an illustrative picture in the dirt. Starr studies it, her face flushing. The others crowd around to take a look.

Now the conversation turns to masturbation, which Rob, font of all important information, tells everyone is "healthy."

"Well," says Allie, "maybe for *guys*." And I think, So much for the four-decade-old sexual revolution, so much for second-, third-, and fourth-wave feminism.

"And porn," says Rob. "Porn is good too." This is what seventh-graders talk about? I wanted to know, and now that I do, I am considerably less than thrilled. My mother instinct kicks in, and all I want to do is grab Lizzie, walk her away from her "peers," and give her an earful about the harm porn does to healthy sexuality, how it is mostly antifemale and how Rob is a complete jerk. But I resist the urge. Lizzie is allowing me this access to her life, giving me permission to be here. I need to respect that by maintaining my interested-observer stance. We can talk later.

"So, do you think X"—Rob mentions the name of a boy they all know—"is gay? I *know* he is. I mean he doesn't masturbate and he doesn't watch porn, so he must be, right?" Silence. Lizzie and Starr exchange looks. Allie stares off into the distance. The spiky-haired girl stares at Rob. It's clear that he's gone over some line with that last remark. But I don't think it's the "gay" comment. In school I've often heard kids use the word "gay" with an offhand casualness that belies what is clearly intended as an insult. ("That is *so gay*," someone—a boy, that is—will say about, well, about anything he notices about another boy—a pair of socks, a book, the way the kid laughs.) Kids are accustomed to bandying around the word "gay." I think Rob has lost his audience because of the cumulative effect: masturbation *plus* porn *plus* homosexuality. It's just too much. The uncomfortable silence is followed by long minutes of actual weeding.

Then it's time for lunch break. Rob sits under a tree and attacks his half-pound block of chocolate. The streaky-haired girl still has her Skittles, which she now supplements with a bag of Red Ropes. Lizzie hands off the lunch I prepared for her (which contains, embarrassment of embarrassments, a piece of fresh fruit) to another girl—she thinks I don't see this, but of course I do—and cozies up to Starr, who has brought along a mega-sized bag of barbecued potato chips. Everyone gets soda from a vending machine inside, then settles back in a patch of shade. The conversation turns to drinking. Alcohol, that is.

Two of the kids—Rob, of course, being one of them—say they've had drinks, and the others want to know: What did it taste like? Did you get wasted? Rob says, proudly, that his parents caught him and grounded him for a month.

All of this is quite enlightening to the researcher delving into the dark heart of teendom. But it is pretty hard to take for the mother whose daughter, surrounded by kids who eat Skittles for breakfast and brag about getting drunk, is professing to know what sixty-nine means. (Turns out, I discover later, that before Rob's stick-in-the-dirt graphic, she thought it was just general code for "sex"—small consolation.) Except for Allie, these are not her close friends, a fact for which I am thankful. But as the day goes on, and I listen to more edgy talk, I think: This is her world. And I worry—like every other parent on the planet—about peer pressure. Lizzie does not drink, smoke, do drugs, or have sex. Of that, I am sure. But if she hangs out with kids who do, or who talk about it, and with the issue-burdened kids she seems to invariably befriend, what will happen to her? Will my as-yet innocent daughter go bad? How much will the values she learns at home matter in the face of peer pressure?

The research—and yes, I hasten home to do the research—says I should calm down about this. "Peer pressure" is not really what we think it is. What we think is that other kids will corrupt our kid, that our innocent, unassuming child will go over to the dark side because friends or acquaintances coerce or compel her to adopt bad behaviors. When I express it to myself in these simplistic terms, the silly, overblown stereotypes pop right up, the very ones I scoffed at when I was a kid—the *Reefer Madness*–type scenarios with sketchy kids pushing joints on you out in the schoolyard, the educational videos we were forced to watch with some adult's vision of a teen party (unlike any we had ever attended) with liquor flowing and snarky kids urging you to "just have one drink . . . what are you, a wuss?"

I am not saying that some little lambs aren't led to the slaughter. But it is a "myth," say child psychologists and others, that a good kid turns bad because of peer pressure. Kids, the research says, are by and large attracted to their own kind. Rather than being pushed into various behaviors or attitudes, teens purposely select friends who are similar to themselves in sometimes not obvious ways.

So let's say a girl with a healthy attitude toward food (if there exists such a teen girl) hangs out with a girl who is bulimic, and the mother of the unaffected girl fears the worst. But her daughter is not a victim-in-waiting. She is not primed to be pulled into the world of disordered eating. She has, the research would indicate, selected her bulimic girlfriend for a deeper, less obvious reason: Maybe they are both perfectionists who do not feel in control of their own lives, and she feels an emotional connection to the girl. Will the bulimic girl pressure the other one to start throwing up in the bathroom stall after lunch period? Unlikely. More likely, the healthy girl will take something else away from the friendship. Maybe she will see how the other girl is handling the emotional and psychological baggage she carries, and that will help her decide whether that particular "solution" is working or not working.

The research also suggests that, rather than being dragged into something they are totally unprepared for (the swig of alcohol in the back of the school bus), kids are attracted to kids who are doing the things they would secretly like to do (which could be getting As in school as well as getting high). Some kids who are fascinated with certain behavior in other kids are just waiting for an opportunity to try it out themselves. (Read: Your darling is not the Snow White you thought.) But others just want to watch. They are after a voyeuristic thrill, not a participatory one. Seen in this light, hanging out with evildoers can be a good thing: The kid doesn't actually have to get plowed. It's enough to see others do it. Whatever the case, the message from those who study such things is that, in general, bad kids don't turn good kids bad.

I am relieved. And I am thankful that I restrained myself when I listened to Rob spin tales about getting drunk at a party of high schoolers and then detected interest and curiosity on the faces of the other kids, Lizzie included. I did not blow my cover as the fly on the wall. I thought then, just wait until I get Lizzie home . . . we will have quite a talk about all this—"quite a talk," I fully acknowledge, being parent code for fire-and-brimstone lecture. But as luck would have it, it was my night to make dinner, and after the Day of Caring activities ended, there was shopping and prep and cooking to do. And then Lizzie had homework to do, during which time I slipped off to look at the research on peer groups.

So by the time I emerge, just before Lizzie's bedtime, I no longer want to deliver the lecture. I want, instead, to think more deeply—more intelligently—about Lizzie's friends.

My reading about peer pressure is leading me to another place. It makes me think about Lizzie's choice of Friends with Issues in a new way. Their issues—poverty, divorce, domestic instability—are not her issues. It may be that part of the attraction is, as I had been thinking, voyeuristic: the attraction of drama to a girl who considers her own home life boring. But if the research is right, it may be that Lizzie is choosing friends who, while they do not have obvious similarities to her, are kindred spirits emotionally. When I think of Nattie, I can think of her as the impoverished, beleaguered kid of a teen mother. Or I can look deeper for the connection Lizzie might feel to her. Nattie is a problem solver. She is upbeat and resilient. She has a calmness about her. Maybe it's her emotional stability and not her domestic instability that appeals to my daughter.

At any rate, I need to disabuse myself of the idea that hanging out with Nattie and seeing how her family works (or doesn't) is going to turn my child into someone who gets pregnant at sixteen. A teen, writes one child psychologist, has "pretty much learned most of the really important things she can get from you by the onset of adolescence." Things like values, morals, ethics.

And so, making use of this newfound wisdom, the next day when we are in the car together doing errands, I jump-start a conversation about how resourceful Nattie is and what a sweet kid Allie seems to be. Lizzie warms to the topic. She tells me how good Nattie is with her little brother, and how Nattie plans to get a job next year so she can earn spending money. She tells me how Allie is sleeping in the living room of the apartment because her mother has brought in a paying tenant for the bedroom that was hers, but how that's cool because now Allie gets to stay up as late as she wants watching TV. I show Lizzie, I hope, by my interest, by the admiration I express for Nattie's maturity and Allie's grit, that I understand what she might see in these girls, and that I see it too.

What a wise and understanding mother I am becoming, I think to myself . . . for about half a second. Okay, maybe the delusion lasts for a few hours—the few hours between our sweet and earnest conversation in the car in the afternoon and the next blowup (that night).

Lizzie is upstairs supposedly working on a report about the Day of Caring for Olivia's class. She is supposedly searching the Internet for information about animal overpopulation. But when I go upstairs to check on her progress (knocking on her closed door before entering), I see Oni on her computer screen. Oni is a purple-haired cyborg from a computer game.

"What does this have to do with your project?" I ask, pointing an accusing finger at Oni.

"I'm just *so* glad I let you come into my room," Lizzie shoots back. The best defense is a good offense. I am afraid she learned that one from me.

"Listen," I say, undeterred, "the paper is due tomorrow, and it's nine o'clock. Get to it." We both know she hasn't been doing her work. If she had been busily perusing the ASPCA Web site or PETA, or anything vaguely relevant to her topic, she would not have hidden it from my view when I walked into her room. She would not have exited the site or clicked the window closed so that all I saw was her Oni screensaver. What *was* she doing?

TEN

W hat *is* she doing?

I find I am asking myself this question a lot these days, and it is almost always in reference to the time Lizzie spends up in her room, in front of her computer, online. The world of school is real and visible. I've seen it, lived it. The world of her friends and peers is real and visible. I've been there too. But she spends long hours, whole evenings, entire weekends in another world I know little about: her online world.

I knew this had to be my next area of investigation the moment I saw the Oni wallpaper on her screen a few nights ago. Honestly, I knew it before that, months before that, but I had been actively repressing both curiosity and concern. I didn't have—don't have—a devil-may-care attitude about Lizzie's online life, but I have long accepted the fact that she is a member in very good standing of the Born Digital generation. Computers have always been a part of her life. Going online for her is like picking up the phone was for me. She is one of those kids who are, as a PBS special I saw a while ago put it, "growing up online." In the house, upstairs in a darkened room—spring sunshine be damned . . . there must be no glare on the screen!—Lizzie is immersed in what I think of as an alternate world, not the "real" world. But the Born Digitals apparently don't make that distinction. They don't regard "online" as a separate (virtual) place but rather as a fully integrated part of their existence. This is Lizzie's natural habitat.

She did not have to learn to live comfortably in this world as I did—or even as her older brothers did. Although, respectively, only six and eight years her senior, my sons had very different early childhoods than Lizzie had. They sat on the living room floor building pioneer cabins out of Lincoln Logs and pirate ships out of LEGOs and windmills out of K'NEX, all of which seems positively nineteenth-century to me now (except for the fact that everything was made of plastic). Playtime meant the family was together in one room. We talked, joked, listened to music. The boys rolled around on the carpet, chucked LEGO blocks at each other, invented weird and impossible structures. They built with their hands. They demolished—which they enjoyed even more—with full body blows.

Lizzie, at the same tender age, was upstairs in front of her computer building six-room, fully furnished, lushly landscaped homes with swimming pools and cabanas by clicking a mouse and dragging items across a screen. This game is called The Sims, and here's where I have to admit that I love playing it as much as she does. It's an inspired mix of the old-fashioned (playing with dolls), the contemporary (endless shopping, conspicuous consumption), and the timeless (the opportunity for omnipotence, the chance to create, boss around, and otherwise control the lives of on-screen characters). In kindergarten Lizzie was tracking Carmen Sandiego across the globe, playing digital Candy Land, and learning French from an interactive Madeline program. By third grade she had an e-mail account. By sixth grade, e-mail was already becoming passé. Now, like more than eight out of ten kids her age, Lizzie instant-messages or texts her friends instead, preferring truncated, acronym-rich, immediate-response convos to the leisurely, full-sentence world of e-mail. To Lizzie, e-mail—which is both the staple and the bane of my life—looks downright quaint, like handwritten USPS mail looks to most of us. "It's so totally old school, Mom," she told me when she was in sixth grade. She looked over my shoulder as I tackled my overflowing in-box, and she shook her head. "I mean, e-mail is for old people."

It's easy to be astonished by the differences between my technologically bereft childhood and Lizzie's, but it's practically heart-stopping to realize what has changed just within the narrow window of my children's childhoods. All these gadgets and applications (I am out of date before I even know what the date is); a jungle of blogs and microblogs; a universe of online predators and unregulated content, from scurrilous, scatological

Web pages to sites that detail ways to kill yourself (or others), to chat groups that glorify self-mutilation. And then there are the multitudinous opportunities for soul-baring (and sometimes body-baring) on MySpace, Facebook, YouTube.

The PBS special likens the online world to a frightening cyber Wild West where anything goes. I've read that teens who spend too much time online can withdraw from active life and increase their risk of depression and even suicide. I've read that cyber relationships are anything but harmless. Because they are easier to maintain than real friendships, because frailties and insecurities can be hidden and identities masked, online liaisons are enticing for many teens (adults too) and can supplant real relationships.

Is all this as nail-bitingly scary as the media would have us believe? I am trying to figure out just how worried I should be. Fear may be a good motivator, but it is an awfully thick (and usually distorting) lens through which to view the world, online or otherwise. If I go into this investigation fearful rather than, say, curious, I am setting myself up to see the worst. And so I do a bit of background research, and what I find is that wild-eyed panic and widespread gloom and doom have often accompanied the new habits of the young. In the 1920s, for example, the panic was over jazz music—listening to it and especially dancing to it. The fear? Interracial contact, interracial dating, moral turpitude. In the 1940s, I discover that comic books were the sworn enemy of upstanding youth. Horror and crime comics with graphic violence and gore—"lurid, unsavory, gruesome illustrations" were the exact words—and "sexy, wonton comics" apparently caused such an uproar that congressional hearings were held, and the comic book industry, just a step ahead of the government, instituted its own censorship code. The fear? Crime sprees, juvenile delinquency, sexual perversion. And then along came Elvis, followed by sixties rock 'n' roll, which would, declared the pundits of the day, surely be the death of all things good and moral. Sexual promiscuity and drug addiction would most certainly be the result of gyrating pelvises and reading deep meaning into "Lucy in the Sky with Diamonds."

When I allow myself to think this way—calmly, historically—rather than reacting to the latest scare story about, to name a recent headliner, cyber bullying and teen suicide, I see two things: 1. that whatever is new in the life of teens is often perceived by parents as threatening; and 2. that although the form may change, the technology may change, I believe that the issues at the heart of being a teen do not. I will not let these twenty-first-century bells and whistles obscure this. I will not let technology, by itself, be the issue.

After all, at Lizzie's age, I too was immersed in virtual worlds, spending most of my time alone in my room, shunning my parents, saying no to any family activity I could get away with saying no to—and making my parents pay for forcing me to participate in the other ones. These other realities, these virtual worlds, were far more interesting, more exciting, and more involving than my own boring suburban early teen reality. I fell into these worlds, lost myself in these worlds, imagined myself as part of these worlds.

That is, I read.

And, although I began with teacher-suggested, parent-approved books like *A Tree Grows in Brooklyn* and *Little Women*, I moved swiftly and secretly to the raciest stuff I could find on my parents' bookshelf: *Lady Chatterley's Lover, Lolita,* anything by Harold Robbins or Ian Fleming. I became a temporary citizen of these raunchy worlds as I read by official Girl Scout flashlight under the covers after lights-out. How different is this from Lizzie's forays into whatever online worlds she is attracted to? How different is her absorption from mine? Her need, like just about every other curious, independence-seeking teen, to be anywhere other than where she is?

And so, I resolve to focus on what unites Lizzie and me rather than what separates us. If I think of her Born Digital life as alien and incomprehensible, *she* will become alien and incomprehensible to me. If I allow myself to be stymied by or resistant to or just blinded by the new technology she is so entirely comfortable with, I'll drive a wedge between us. If I allow myself to feel resentful that Lizzie's virtual world is more interesting to her than the real world of which I am a part, then I come to this investigation with attitude rather than openness.

Call me Sandee. I have ocean eyes and a midnight black ponytail. I'm wearing Blue Chaos hip-huggers, a Sparkle Rocket baby-T, and a pair of red Strap Happy sandals. Right now, I'm sitting at a little table at "Buck-stars," a coffee shop, talking manga, music, and movies with a girl who says she's sixteen and calls herself Lerz.

I know better. She's twelve, and her name is Lizzie. She's my daughter, and she's not at a coffee shop. She's sitting upstairs in her room in front of her computer clicking on menu choices that animate Lerz, her online avatar. Lerz is not just four years older than Lizzie, she is also much hipper. Lizzie has braces and wears musty T-shirts and jeans that sag in the butt. Lerz, on the other hand, with her micromini, midriff-bearing tank top and platform heels, looks as if she could earn a good living on the street.

Downstairs, in front of my computer, I type words that fill the bubble over Sandee's head. Sandee is my avatar. She is sleeker, trimmer, trendier, and several decades younger than I am—although I must say, in my own defense, that I have better hair. With Lizzie's help, I've created this 3-D projection, customized her look, and learned the basics of how to have a conversation on www.imvu.com. IMVU, for the uninitiated, is a ditzy teenage but seriously sophisticated Web site, an anime-inspired "Second Life"–style combination of instant messaging tool, chat space, social net-work, and celebration of consumer capitalism. Right now, this is Lizzie's favorite thing to do.

Lerz and Sandee are, essentially, just text messaging, but with IMVU our characters converse while cyber-physically in the presence of each other. These avatars we create to represent—or *mis*represent—ourselves can react and interact on the screen. They can shake hands, high-five, nod, glare, smile, wink, laugh, flirt, or shrug shoulders as the conversation appears in bubbles over their heads. It's kind of like being a puppeteer, only edgier, more subversive. It's fun.

It's also simple—and I say this as a person who has trouble program-ming the alarm clock in a hotel room. All you do is create an on-screen alter ego and then use it to meet and chat with other people's on-screen alter egos in virtual environments created by IMVU users. There is no cost to do this. The software is free and easily downloadable, although for a wide array of price points one can participate in a thriving entrepreneur-ial IMVU community made up of users who trade in online credits for specially designed outfits for their avatars. Still, if you settle for the free stuff, you can start "playing" within minutes.

It's simple, but as I get into it over the course of a few intense evening sessions, as I chat with Lerz or go off on my own to meet others, I see that this pastime (it is far more than a "game") is so packed with meaning that it's ripe for a doctoral dissertation or two. For starters, although there are a staggering number of choices when creating your avatar (hair color, hairstyle, eye and skin color, clothes and accessories), all the female avatars essentially look alike. They are rail-thin, baseball-boobed, edgy-looking, anime-like figures with round faces and huge Keane eyes. You can dress them in many styles—punk, fancy, sport, geek, cheerleader, fairy—but all the outfits have basically the same look: slut (the geek accessorizes with glasses).

I notice that Lizzie changes the look of her avatar every day. When we meet at a little table at Buckstars, where all initial IMVU rendezvous begin, Lerz sometimes has straight black hair with bloodred streaks, sometimes ankle-length platinum hair, other times pumpkin-colored locks with hacked bangs and a spiky ponytail. These are just a few of the many things I will not permit my real daughter to do to her own lovely head of honey-blond hair. Lerz also wears clothes Lizzie would never wear—or be permitted to wear: a red and black micromini accessorized with thigh-high black boots, a black leather ninja outfit with visible thong and push-up bra. If Lizzie somehow managed to get her hands on such outfits, or anything vaguely approximating such outfits, I would chain her to her four-poster bed and risk a visit from the Children's Services Division before I'd let her out of the house. But when I see her tarted-up avatar, I just laugh.

There's no tactile experience in the online world—the satiny feel of a Barbie prom dress, the rubbery stretch of a Polly Pocket ensemble, the slickness of long viscose hair as you braid it—but the idea of dress-up is the same: It's about pretending, dreaming, trying on different identities without actually changing yourself. It's about freedom with little consequence, experiment without risk.

Once coiffed, dressed, and accessorized, Sandee can visit different environments, kind of like a doll moving from one room to another in a dollhouse, or like positioning Polly in any one of those seemingly endless add-ons in the Polly Pocket world (cars, swimming pools, performance stages, beauty salons). In IMVU, the environments are, of course, only virtual. But they are varied and imaginative—from a coffeehouse to a castle, a water park to a mountain peak, a disco to an enchanted forest, from (yes) heaven to hell. When not mentoring Sandee in the ways of IMVU, Lerz hangs out with "Devilkiller," who says he's sixteen, at a beach with swaying palm trees. She and "Babyzbreath" (boy, fifteen) go horseback riding in a western landscape. She and "Crazzyyyyyy" (boy, seventeen) float on a magic carpet and ride on a Ferris wheel. Of course, this being twenty-first-century cyberspace, some of the environments are significantly less than wholesome. Lerz has taken Sandee on a tour of such places as Kinky Mansion (complete with stripper pole), Sexy Teen Club, Dark Playground, Truth or Dare, Lez and Bi Palace.

In addition to Lerz's hectic social life, she has also become, courtesy of the global reach and popularity of IMVU, a citizen of the world, meeting and conversing (via text bubbles) with kids (via their avatars) from India, China, Iraq, Germany, Egypt, Australia, England, Mexico, and Canada. When Lizzie first tells me of her international interactions, I go directly to panic mode: Oh great, a United Nations of predators. But, when I sit next to Lizzie as Lerz meets and talks with these strangers, when I pay very close attention to the conversations, I exhale. For the most part, what she's doing is just a cyber version of being a pen pal, a hallowed tradition of my own childhood, a Girl Scout badge requirement, an ongoing assignment in junior high and high school language classes. She's chatting with kids from other lands, talking about many of the same things I wrote about to my French and Italian pen pals: friends, crushes, school, music, family, hobbies, assorted weird stuff that happened that day. (Okay, so I also, at age ten, wrote my Toulouse pen pal asking for a precise definition of "French kiss" and, maybe a year later, based on a mysterious bathroom stall scribble, ventured a query about French ticklers. So much for the innocence of another time.)

I allow myself to relax into the IMVU experience, joining Lizzie/Lerz as often as I can. I am once again playing my two roles: cultural anthropologist, immersing myself in this virtual world with Lerz as my guide, and parent, working all the angles, working to make new connections with my daughter while scanning the terrain like a mother lion. Tonight Lerz and Sandee are hanging out at Buckstars. They are chatting, high-fiving, laughing, sending each other links to YouTube videos. Sandee doesn't tell Lerz it's time to do homework or clean up her room. She doesn't shoot her a dirty look, which can be done with a mouse click, about that dish of ice cream that was sneaked upstairs. Sandee comes without baggage. Lerz comes without adolescent attitude. And so, we connect. What sometimes seems so difficult in real life is easy in cyberspace.

But after a week and a half as Sandee, I am tiring of this whole avatar/text bubble thing. When it's Lizzie and I, that's great. But Lerz doesn't want to spend all her online time with Sandee. And Sandee is, after the initial thrill of the "game," stupendously uninterested in making small talk with random teenage boys. And so I watch instead. I sit on the floor next to Lizzie as she types and clicks her way through multiple conversations with multiple strangers. Some conversations are over almost before they begin—as when Lerz encounters a girl avatar at Buckstars who is interested in flirting with boys, not talking with girls. The other avatar exits before Lerz can introduce herself. Other interchanges are like the chitchat between classes at school, inquiries about favorite bands or cool movies. But sometimes Lerz will have a conversation like this one I witness:

> LERZ: Hey.
> BOY AVATAR (jeans, red jacket, sunglasses, fifties' slicked back hair): Hey.
> LERZ: Whazzup?
> BOY: Do you have MSN?

Lizzie turns to me. "That's a way to IM," she explains. "He might want to do that instead of IMVU. It's much quicker."

> LERZ: Yes.
> BOY: Are you logged on?
> LERZ: Yeah.
> BOY: Do you have a webcam?
> LERZ: Yes.
> BOY: Can I see you?

Lizzie gives me a knowing look. I give her a concerned look in return. The most comforting aspect to IMVU, I think, is anonymity. This boy wants to see her?

LERZ: My brother is using the webcam.

She is lying. The webcam is sitting on top of her CPU. I hope she is lying because she wants to protect her privacy and not because I happen to be in the room.

BOY: What do you look like?
LERZ: What do you think I look like?

Wow. She is flirting, toying with him. Is that okay? I don't know. It takes a great deal of willpower to keep my mouth shut and see what unfolds.

BOY: You're hot.

Avatar Lerz winks.

BOY: Can't you go get the webcam?

Lerz does not reply.

BOY: Can't you go get the webcam?

No reply.

BOY: Are you home alone?

Lizzie clicks, and Lerz disappears from the screen. Then she turns to me. "This guy just wants cybersex," she says, with the same inflection and emotion she would use if she were saying, "This boy just wants a peanut butter and jelly sandwich." Apparently, she has been approached before in far more direct ways. This is the first I've heard of it. But not the last. Two days later, I witness this conversation:

> **LERZ**: Hey.
> **BOY**: Have sex with me.
> **LERZ**: LOL

She thinks he's joking. "LOL" is "laugh out loud."

> **BOY**: Cybersex.
> **LERZ**: If you were the last boy on the planet, the answer would be the same . . . no.
> **BOY**: I get sad.

"I bet this kid is from India or China or somewhere like that," Lizzie says to me. "You can tell by how they leave out words."

> **LERZ**: Where are you from?

The boy avatar disappears. This is not the conversation he is interested in having.

Lizzie turns to me. "Guys like this are losers," she says dismissively. "I mean, they should be romantic with their *real* girlfriends. They should be thinking about sex or having sex with someone they love or like—or at least *know*."

"Why do you talk to them at all?" I ask. "When you see what they want, why don't you just get out of there fast?" She thinks about that for a moment.

"They're jerks," she says. "And I want them to *know* they're jerks, so I'm treating them like jerks. I wish lots of girls on IMVU would do this so then these guys would realize that they're not going to get anywhere."

As I listen to her, the protective, Puritan parent part of me is, of course, aghast. I want to forbid her from ever going on IMVU again. I want to remove the computer from her room. I want to dress her in gingham and send her off to a quilting bee. The modern-day mother part of me, however, the part that recognizes and has been forced to accept the dangerous worlds, both real and virtual, facing teens like my daughter, that part of me is unexpectedly proud. My daughter doesn't need lectures from me about scurrilous online prowlers. In fact, she could sit me down for a lecture. She does not require tutorials in how to avoid Internet nastiness. She's figured it out already.

I am impressed, and I tell her so. She smiles indulgently. "No biggie," she says, but I can tell she's pleased. This is the kind of attitude and independence of thought I can (and do) applaud. Maybe it's even evidence that I'm doing something right. She hasn't learned to be a savvy cyber chatter from me—there are many things I can't teach her, and that's okay. But maybe in practicing her attitude on me, she has honed it for her dealings with Internet scum. Maybe in battling me, she is learning how to do battle in the world.

Then, all of a sudden, three weeks into my online life as raven-haired Sandee, Lizzie wants nothing more to do with IMVU. Although I started to take notice only a few weeks ago, Lizzie has been living the life of Lerz for many months. Now, after school one day, she unceremoniously wipes the software from her hard drive. Why this sudden change, I ask. It's not because of the losers looking for cybersex, she says. It's not because I will not let her use my credit card to buy more outfits for Lerz. It's not even because of Sandee's intrusion into Lerz's domain. It's because her "good friends" from IMVU have all migrated over to MSN where they IM each other quickly and efficiently. No avatars, no fanciful environments, no gewgaws. Just convo.

And so begins the MSN chat phase. Her IMVU-to-IM friends include a boy from Louisiana she had a crush on (unrequited) who is now "dating" a girl from California, an IMVU friend whom Lizzie introduced him to; a boy from Australia whom Lizzie finds fascinating because he is living his life a day ahead of her; a skater dude; a boy from Wisconsin with girl troubles who depends on Lizzie for advice; and a born-again Christian from Illinois who is trying to convert her. She also, just a week into the MSN chat era, has a new cyber passion that is both cutting into and augmenting her busy IM activities. She is now a MySpace enthusiast.

Once she finds out about MySpace from her IMVU-to-IM buddies, she devotes an entire weekend—I mean eight or nine hours a day for two days—to creating her page. If she spent this time on a science project or an English essay, she would be . . . well, she would be like Leah, my friend Sarah's brilliant, overachieving daughter. But this MySpace page is far more important than schoolwork. This page is her public persona, her unique presence in a world that numbers more than a hundred million inhabitants, most of them teens.

She begins her foray into MySpace by creating her personal profile, answering questions—some more truthfully than others—about who she is and what she likes. As you have to be fourteen to join MySpace, and as Lizzie is still only twelve, her year of birth will be her first fabrication. But she doesn't think of it this way. After all, Lerz on IMVU was sixteen, so Lizzie's proclaiming herself a mere fourteen is a step backward, two years closer to the truth.

Lizzie works hard on her page, selecting and rejecting several dozen wallpaper schemes before settling on a retro disco background, then searching for the better part of an afternoon for the right song to feature. She spends hours searching YouTube and music video sites for clips. She finds anime art, animated cartoon characters, glitter words, snazzy graphics. "I'm pimping out my page," she tells me happily. She nags her older brother into taking several dozen photos of her, posing with soulful eyes and pursed lips for the camera, her bangs artfully positioned to look carelessly flung across her face. She downloads ten of her favorites, supplementing these with two of the cat and two of her brothers. She adds a flickering angel-with-horns graphic, a light show, objects falling from the sky. Her page, to my eye, is all energy and confusion, lights and sounds, graphic explosions, no cohesive or coherent mood. A lot like her. By the end of her first week on MySpace, she has ninety friends and seventy-four posted comments and conversations.

Now her typical day looks like this: She sets her clock radio thirty minutes early so she has time to check in with her MySpace and MSN friends before school. Some of these friends are actual (not virtual) friends. She and Damon chat daily, and she maintains an active online relationship with Evan and his buddies. But most of them are cyber friends. When she gets home, she immediately and with no coaxing attends to her homework, then disappears upstairs and into MySpace, where she stays—with the exception of a twenty-minute hiatus for dinner—until her

9:30 bedtime. She doesn't talk on the phone. She doesn't play computer games, her erstwhile obsession. She doesn't watch movies. And of course, she doesn't interact with her family. I ask her, repeatedly—and much to her annoyance—what the attraction is to these superficial conversations with kids she's never met and will never spend face time with. She tells me she loves being able to "just talk" to people without all the baggage of real life, without knowing what they look like or what crowd they're in at school or whether your friends think they're cool or not. She says that at school she would never dream of starting up a conversation with someone she didn't know. But on MySpace, that's normal. That's what everyone does.

She knows—I have certainly told her—that I think she is spending way too much time in cyberspace. I'm confused about the nature of my own criticism, though, as I suspect I would be not all that displeased if she were spending the same amount of time lost in the virtual world of books. After all, if she were buried in some book upstairs she wouldn't be part of family life either, and I have no reasonable explanation for why I value immersion in one imaginative world over another—but I can't help it. At least I get an inkling of my own hypocrisy here, and it makes me pull back from the position I would really like to take: putting a strict limit on online time. My husband is also reticent to impose time limits. As long as she's doing well in school and doing her homework, as long as she's attending to the few chores we require of her, as long as she seems happy, why step in? he asks. He makes a good point too: We live in the country, not in a residential neighborhood. Lizzie can't walk out the door, down the street, and over to someone's house to play. Every social inter-action involves advance planning, multiple phone calls between families for scheduling, and car ferrying. Online she has an instant social life, a community of easily available friends—and more where they came from. The positive spin is that it hones her social skills. Plus she is becoming a lightning-quick typist.

But then comes the next chapter of her online life. Yes, there is a *next* chapter. It seems that the moment I get in anyway comfortable with, or just get a handle on, what's going on, the game changes. In this case, it literally *is* a game: Halo 3. Connoisseurs of futuristic 3-D combat games maintain that the story is so complex and the graphics so rich that Halo is in a class by itself. In Lizzie's life it is now taking the place of MySpace, which replaced MSN, which replaced IMVU, which obliterated e-mail. I am suddenly behind the curve again. I ask Lizzie for a tutorial. I'll learn to play the game, and maybe learn something about her as I do.

We sit on a couch, shoulder to shoulder, staring at the forty-six-inch rear projection TV my husband bought several years ago that is hooked up to both Xbox 360 and the Internet. Out in the cyber gaming community of Halo 3, Lizzie meets guys (always guys) from all over the country. They form teams and play against other teams, all the while either texting each other on-screen or talking through the headphones. Lizzie's favorite teammates are a college football player from Alabama and his friend, both of whom seem to have copious amounts of free time. For the tutorial, though, it is just Lizzie and I. I don't dare venture online without significant skills.

Lizzie fires up the machine, hands me a controller, and takes another for herself. The unpleasant-looking robot dude I see on the screen represents me, and I have to learn how to make it/me walk, drive a tank, fire weapons, toss grenades, and smash other unpleasant-looking robot dudes. It turns out that the variously colored and shaped buttons, triggers, bumpers, and thumbsticks on this molded plastic control gizmo regulate nineteen different functions—*nineteen*—the instructions for which I forget as soon as Lizzie tells me. Oops, my character sees a bad guy! Red button to punch the guy in the face, or left bumper to pick up a weapon, unless it's a grenade, in which case use the left trigger to pick it up, and then—quickly now—the right trigger to fire it. If, on the other hand, you wanted to zap the bad guy with an exploding magnet, then that's the blue button. And I haven't even mentioned the thumb pad.

"Got it?" Lizzie asks. She has been very patient with me.

The last time I felt this stressed out, the last time I practically *tasted* cortisol in the back of my throat, was when my plane was landing on a foamed runway at LaGuardia. That's how much fun I am not having.

"Lizzie, I just can't do this anymore," I say, putting down my controller. My hand is actually shaking. "This is really, really hard for me."

She gives me a consoling smile. "Yeah, it takes a while," she says. I know she is saying this to make me feel better, which is very sweet. And she knows that I know, which is also sweet.

And what passes between us in that moment—that flash of connection and warmth—feels important and meaningful. I don't understand her attraction to this game, and I don't think I will, and I don't think that matters. What matters is this moment, her patience with me, her sensitivity to my feelings, the place on my shoulder where I can still feel the imprint of hers.

"Let me watch you," I say. And then, for the next two hours I stare at the TV screen as Lizzie and her two Alabama buddies wreak nonstop cyber havoc. I am both deeply, genuinely, numbingly bored and totally in awe of Lizzie's skill. Her reactions approach warp speed. Her hand-eye coordination is extraordinary. Her fingers dance across the controller. She is quick, decisive, unflappable. And all the while, she is keeping up a steady patter of trash talk with her online compadres.

How does she do it? And how does she do it for hours and hours and hours, every day after school and all weekend? And who are these twenty-year-old slackers who play online with her? I quiz her repeatedly about her Alabama buddies. When one of them calls her a few days later, I quiz him personally before I hand over the phone. He seems okay in a game-crazed geeky way, but what about the others she plays with and talks to? Should I be vetting all of them? I am back to being worried again.

And then Lizzie saves the day.

It is nearing the end of spring term, just a few weeks from the end of seventh grade, and she has let one of her grades slip below a B. She knows—has known since we opened up the world of the Internet to her a year ago—that any grade less than B will scuttle her online privileges. That's been our one rule. With the aid of extra credit assignments, she has gotten the grade for Mr. C.'s history class up to par. But she has known for months that she was headed for a C in math. She's gotten written warnings from the math teacher and repeated verbal warnings from us. We ask if she needs help with homework. We plead with her to let us help her study for an upcoming test. We offer to get her a tutor. No, she says, I've got it covered. And so, when we see the grade update from her teacher and the news is bad, as we all knew it would be, our response is swift.

"That means no Internet until you raise the grade to a B," Tom tells her at dinner that night. "You are officially, as of this moment, off-line."

"We need to see a B on your semester grade report," I add. "That gives you three weeks to work on it."

"You mean three weeks without the Internet?" Lizzie says. "That's, like, *forever*." She's whining but she hasn't slammed down her fork and stormed out of the room. She is, in fact, oddly calm. True, she was expecting this. But was she, in some way, *wanting* it too? Maybe part of her felt uncomfortable or overwhelmed with how her online life had expanded so far into her real life. Maybe these guys from Alabama put her over the edge. Maybe she *wanted* to be reined in.

Whatever happened, however or why it happened, a new era is suddenly upon us: no MySpace, no IM, no Xbox LIVE. Miraculously, the hours once filled with these activities are quickly filled with other activities: track practice, phone calls, movies, The Sims, Tomb Raider, even reading. The change is so swift, so complete, and so seemingly painless that it's disorienting, like that other life was some kind of a dream we were living that we didn't know was a dream until we woke up.

Fast-forward three weeks to the semester report card: The C does not become a B, and the Internet ban is extended. She will have to get at least a B in math—and all her other subjects—by midterm grades in her first semester of eighth grade before she can get back online. That means no Internet all summer and halfway into fall. For a girl who throws a fit when faced with a sandwich I dare to prepare with whole wheat rather than white bread, Lizzie takes this news in stride. "Unpredictable" works both ways, I guess, and hooray for that.

ELEVEN

Lizzie and I are in the car on the way to a public pool I've arranged to rent, after hours, to host her thirteenth birthday party. "Thir*teen*," I say to her, emphasis on the teen, "how about that!" Lizzie gives me one of those smiles that says, Cool . . . but please don't launch into a whole long boring talk about this, okay? I can read her looks pretty well, always could. They're a lot like mine. So I keep my thoughts to myself as I drive. What I am thinking is: Today, June 2, marks the official beginning of Lizzie's life as a teenager. I am also thinking: Geez, it feels as if I've been living with a teen forever already. And I know, actual birth date notwithstanding, that Lizzie has considered herself a teen for quite a while. She has, after all, been presenting herself online as either sixteen or fourteen, which I see as part wishful thinking, part setting herself up to flirt with high school boys, and part a sense that she feels she really *is* a teenager. So this celebration, this circled day on our calendar, feels like a bit of an anticlimax.

Regardless, Lizzie and I have spent the last six weeks discussing party details, particularly the merits of various venues for the event—a bowling alley, a miniature golf course, a movie theater, a park, our house—the decision-making process being considerably tougher and more attenuated than I imagined. It's not that we fight about this. It's that Lizzie keeps changing her mind, one day bubbling over about one location, the next day (or maybe hour) railing about how she hates, hates, hates whatever idea it was that she had so recently and dearly embraced. The first half dozen or so times she did this, I made the mistake of being invested in each decision and each change of heart, and my patience grew thinner and thinner. I almost, I admit, lost my temper. But I pulled back at the last moment. It is her *birthday*, I chided myself. I am not going to yell at her about her *birthday*. What kind of an ogre would do that? And I re-minded myself—as if I needed reminding—that she was mercurial about absolutely everything else, so why not this?

As recently as two weeks ago she had been insisting on a girls-only sleepover, an idea whose appeal had everything to do with the nail-polishing, makeup-applying, pillow-fighting scenes of sleepovers she had seen in movies over the years rather than with reality. The reality is that Lizzie would probably hate a girly-girl sleepover. The reality is that most of Lizzie's friends are boys. When this dawned on her, she made a run at sug-gesting a coed sleepover, which was, of course, immediately and defini-tively nixed by both me and Tom. What followed was predictable: She set her mouth in a straight line, told us *fine*, now she didn't want *any* party, and stomped upstairs. The bedroom door was summarily slammed. Impos-sibly loud music was played. My husband and I exchanged battle-weary looks and went back to eating dinner. The next afternoon, as if the previ-ous blowup had never happened, she announced, with enthusiasm, that she wanted a pool party. Happily, luckily, there had been a cancellation, and I secured this Friday's eight to ten p.m. slot.

As difficult as the choice of venues was, it did not come close to equal-ing the complexity of compiling the guest list. Who beyond her three close friends would be invited changed daily depending on which way the middle school wind blew. One day she'd sit with a kid at lunch, a kid I'd never heard of, a kid not even on the radar screen, and she'd come home all excited about the guy and put him on the list. A few days later, he was history. Last week she had a tiff with Nattie—something about band practice—and Nattie was temporarily excommunicated. Evan has been a list stalwart, but whether his two buddies, on-again, off-again pals of Lizzie's, were on the list changed almost daily depending on whether they ignored her or paid attention to her in the cafeteria. I had no idea there could be so much drama in list making. If and when I am involved in wedding plans for this girl . . . well, the mind boggles.

But finally there is a list of fifteen, and we move on to the question of food. I want to bake a cake. I like to bake but rarely have an excuse to do so, and I love coming up with fanciful decorations: crushed Oreo "dirt" sprinkled on the frosting, concentric circles of color-coded jelly beans, gummy worms slinking out from between cake layers. Perhaps this is why Lizzie wants a bakery cake. It *is* her birthday, so bakery cake it is. It's in a box in the trunk along with a cooler packed with three half gallons of ice cream and five liters of soda. Lizzie has grudgingly allowed me to include a bowl of fresh fruit salad just in case someone besides me would like to avoid a diabetic coma.

In the car on the way over, Lizzie turns up the volume on one of those generic *American Idol*–style pop songs and sings along. I am silent, thinking. But instead of thinking about Lizzie and the official-as-of-today end of her childhood and what it means to have another "woman" in the house, I am thinking about how my thighs will look in the bathing suit I have brought along to wear at the party.

The weight I carry, that so many women carry, is not just measured on a scale. The extra five, ten, twenty pounds—whatever the number is that month, that year—are an emotional burden, a psychological burden that I have carried since I was Lizzie's age and even younger. In part, I inherited this burden from my mother, a woman who may—*may*—from time to time have carried an extra five pounds on her five-feet-two frame. But that's not how she saw her body. She frowned at herself in the full-length mirror in her closet—much as I look askance at my own image in the bathroom. She never left the house without first squeezing herself into an ultraslimming "compression undergarment." She denied herself all but the tiniest portions of the gourmet meals she painstakingly made for the rest of the family. She had a weight problem, all right—but it had little to do with excess poundage.

And she had a problem with my weight too. She didn't make many comments about it, only just enough. I was never fat as a kid, but I was, at times, what used to be called "pleasantly plump." (Ah, to live at a time when "plump" could be considered "pleasant.") Every year, I lost the same ten pounds at summer camp where I ran around all day and, in the cavernous mess hall, did not sit down to anything approaching my mother's Julia Child–inspired dinners. When I came home in August, she would always be delighted with the new, more slender version I presented to her.

She would admire me, praise me, take me shopping. I felt she liked me a little better at the end of August than she did at the beginning of July.

My mother was not, of course, the only one who taught me to be dissatisfied with my body. American pop culture—ads, movies, and most especially *Seventeen* magazine—showed me what a female body ought to look like. It was the model's body. It was the dancer's body. And I didn't have it. My ballet instructor, Andre Eglevsky, informed my mother, in my presence, that I was too heavy to ever go en pointe, that I should, after six years, quit taking lessons because I'd never ever be a ballerina. I was twelve. I weighed 110 pounds.

I lost weight. I gained weight. I lost it again. And so forth. I got older. I grew wiser about many things. But not *this* thing. Several decades of feminism, a true-partnership marriage, and a solid career notwithstanding, I was still—*am* still—a person who defines a "good" day as one with strenuous exercise and no indulgences and a "bad" day as one that involves a bakery item.

I am trying hard not to pass along this fixation to my daughter. But I am not doing a good job. She catches me frowning at myself in the mirror. I catch myself—as I did a few months ago—expressing my insecurities, my self-criticism in front of her. I don't think I'm going to change. But I can, at least, keep this particular monologue as *internal* monologue. I try not to talk weight or diet in front of her. I want her to grow up loving her body, dammit, and enjoying whatever shape she ends up being.

But now things are getting complicated. After hitting puberty early, Lizzie gained weight—a pretty normal occurrence, said her pediatrician. At first it was just a few unnoticeable pounds. Then, aided by cheese quesadillas, chicken fingers, and the end of soccer, the weight gain continued. It became noticeable, enough weight so that her clothes no longer fit well. She wasn't fat. She was strong and athletic and—just like I had been at her age—"pleasantly plump."

I will not talk calories with her, I had promised myself. I will not talk weight loss or diet. If I were to say something, she would be hurt. She would think—as I thought—that her mother's admiration and respect and love had something to do with her weight. Or, as I now know from my research, it would unfold like this: I would *mean* to send a "meta-message" of concern; she would *hear* a "meta-message" of criticism.

Is it possible this weight gain is already making Lizzie feel bad enough about herself? I read one report that said 80 percent of teen girls are unhappy about their weight. *Eighty percent.* I know that regardless of a strong ego—which this girl *does* have—she has, like I have, like all of us have, been inundated by images of female bodies, near-skeletal female bodies. In stores, she sees size 00 clothing. Even minus-size clothing. Last time we were shopping, I held up, in utter disbelief, a pair of jeans that would not have fit my skinny, hipless sons when they were eight years old. We weren't in the Boys' section; we were in Juniors. And I was not holding up the smallest size these jeans came in. I held them up so that Lizzie could see just how ridiculous they were, so that we could laugh about them together. I held them up so that I would have an opening to tell Lizzie a statistic I'd just read: Almost one-third of teen girls wear a size 12 or larger. Her size. She looked at the jeans, snorted, but didn't seem particularly disturbed or amused—or interested.

It occurred to me then that maybe this whole weight thing was more about me than about her. In fact, one of the toughest things about having a daughter is just that: parsing out what are her issues and what are actually our own. After all, it's impossible not to project. We mothers were once all teen daughters. We see ourselves—or look for ourselves—in our daughters. We project. We remember what we felt like at that age, and we perhaps too often assume that our daughters are going through the same thing. But maybe they're not.

At Lizzie's school, for example, there are a lot more "big girls" than there ever were at mine. Perhaps an ironic result of the increase in overweight teens is a wider acceptance of body types by the kids themselves. I think of Lizzie's friend Starr, who probably weighs 185 pounds. She is outgoing and upbeat, and is one of the more popular girls in the class. She is also a hip dresser. So maybe it's okay to be a plus-size teen these days. That would be great. Sort of. If it weren't for the health consequences.

Everyone knows the statistics. The headline-worthy, enduring health story of the day—of the past decade, in fact—has been the childhood obesity epidemic. According to the Centers for Disease Control figures, the percentage of obese teens has tripled in the last twenty years. The National Survey of Children's Health estimates that 26 percent of all teen girls are either overweight or obese. (The percentage varies astonishingly from state to state, with Colorado the leanest at 16 percent and Kentucky the fattest at 38 percent.) In Oregon, where we live, a recent report documented that one-quarter of eighth graders are overweight or obese.

The frightening issue is not the weight itself—it is the disease, or the increased risk of disease, that could follow in its wake. As everyone knows, there is now an epidemic among adolescents of type 2 diabetes, a disease directly related to excess weight, a disease that, until recently, afflicted only the middle-aged. I read a scary University of California study investigating the health effects of being overweight during adolescence. It projected alarming increases in the rates of heart disease and premature death by the time today's teenagers reach young adulthood. And Swedish researchers who fed mice on basically a teen junk food diet (high fat, high sugar) found evidence of Alzheimer's-like plaques and tangles in the rodents' brains after only nine months. Yikes. If Lizzie is setting herself up for health problems, how could I *not* intervene?

The message I really want to send is not about what she weighs but about what she eats. I think it is okay—it is my considered strategy—to talk about diet—but not *going* on a diet. This is not about size 4 jeans; it's about her health now and in the future. Her eating habits have tanked—despite (or perhaps because of?) living in a household where junk food is rarely found in the cupboards, soda is conspicuously absent from the refrigerator, and meals are made from fresh, often organic, ingredients. The food in the trunk of the car tonight—if ice cream, cake, and soda could be called "food"—is an aberration, a special-occasion indulgence, at least as far as I am concerned. For Lizzie, these items are, collectively, the Staff of Life.

She rarely eats breakfast. (We fight about this almost every morning, and she wins—because how can you actually force someone to eat?) She takes to school the wholesome—but not ridiculously wholesome as in seaweed and tofu—lunch I make for her and stashes it in her locker until it becomes a biohazard. She comes home ravenous, but says no to any snack remotely associated with the fruit, vegetable, whole grain, and protein food groups. At the base of her personal dietary pyramid is cheese, followed by anything deep-fried. Combining the two—an order of deep-fried mozzarella sticks at Chili's, for example—is, for her, a peak culinary experience. At home, she refuses to eat at least three-quarters of the dinners put before her, the exceptions being burritos (because she can add cheese), pizza (cheese), and chicken Parmesan (topped with, yes, cheese). This is also what she orders in restaurants. With fries.

These eating habits, I learn from my research, are only slightly worse than the average teen. Close to half the kids her age don't eat breakfast. More than a quarter don't get minimal servings of fruits and vegetables. And if you don't count French fries as a vegetable, *half* the kids don't get minimal servings. In a national survey of teens' favorite foods, pizza, ice cream, and chips top the list with cookies, French fries, and doughnuts not far behind. It is no solace whatsoever to learn this. I don't care if everyone else's kid eats like this, I don't want *mine* to eat like this.

In focusing on nutrition instead of weight, I am—*maybe*—not sending bad-body messages. But what I am doing, it is clear to me, is giving us a whole new reason to clash, a whole new arena in which to do battle. This has not been lost on Tom, who hates that the dinner table has become the Civil War battle of Antietam. Like a lot of guys who are six feet tall and have great metabolisms and have blissfully, mindlessly eaten whatever they wanted, food "issues" are alien to him. *Emotional* and *eating* are two words he would never think to put together. He eats when he's hungry, and he stops when he's full. Imagine that. It is a burden to live with someone who has no sense of guilt about food, to whom food is just food. Some of our most heated arguments this past year have been about my attention to the quality and quantity of Lizzie's food intake.

So, what is happening with my clever nutrition discussion strategy is that I have 1. created yet another source of tension between us, 2. made an enemy of my husband, 3. not managed to improve Lizzie's eating habits one bit—or bite. And, oh yes, 4. this has made not a dent in those extra pounds Lizzie is carrying. I am not sure how exactly one measures failure, but I am pretty sure this qualifies. Still, I have no other ideas, and in the face of this ongoing fiasco, I continue with my efforts to get her to read package labels and think trans fat grams, to befriend an occasional piece of fruit, to eat slowly rather than gobble, to care what she puts in her mouth.

But clearly, I am stuck. I don't want her to obsess about weight, but I do want her to care about what she eats. I don't want her to obsess about what her body looks like, but I do want her to care about her health. But these issues are interwoven—and then all shot through with my own body neuroses.

Perhaps it seems odd to be thinking about nutrition and diet and weight loss and body image on this day of all days—a party day, a day of celebration—but that's what I'm doing. That's where thoughts of wearing my Speedo in front of fifteen teenagers have taken me. I do not deliver a nutrition lecture in the car—even *my* obsession has its limits—but that doesn't stop me from trying to mentally tally the average glycemic index of the items I have stashed in the trunk. I am *such* a party animal.

Sitting next to Lizzie in the car this warm early June evening as we drive into the parking lot of the pool, I force myself to clear my mind of all this clutter. It helps to look over at my girl. She is doing just what I am not: inhabiting the moment. Her eyes are bright. She is singing loudly and slightly off-key. I squeeze her arm. She is out the door before I even turn off the engine.

The party, for all its supposed cultural significance (thir*teen*), for all its prefunction turmoil (venue, guest list), and for all the anxiety (mine), is just a party. I don't know what I was expecting exactly. Some end-of-childhood epiphany played out before me? A coming of age aha moment during which I see my daughter as the adult she will become rather than the child she no longer is? A kind of aquatic bat mitzvah? In fact, it's pretty much your standard kids' pool party. Lizzie and her friends swim, splash, throw beach balls, attempt to stand on kickboards, whip each other with Styrofoam noodles, push each other into the pool, get yelled at by the lifeguard, eat cake with their hands. Lizzie seems completely relaxed and utterly unself-conscious as she jumps in and out of the pool. She is wearing baggy, knee-length surfer shorts and a bikini top, her official swim outfit. I had thought—*projecting*—that her choice not to wear a regular swimsuit had to do with feeling uncomfortable about her body. Now, watching her, I see no signs of discomfort. Just the opposite. She, like her friends, is caught up in the moment, carefree, acting like a kid, like a ten-year-old. Hooray for childhood, I think. Let them hold on as long as they can. Let there be times like this when no one talks about the meaning of sixty-nine or describes the taste of vodka.

But the kids do eventually reveal some of their teenage selves. Weary of an hour and a half of horseplay, the girls cluster at one end of the pool and stage whisper to each other about the boys, and the boys gather at the other end of the pool and pretend to ignore the girls.

Happily, everyone ignores me. But just in case one of Lizzie's friends should happen to glance my way, I wrap myself, sarong-style, in an over-sized beach towel.

TWELVE

It is the Fourth of July, and as is our tradition on this day, we head out to Yoncalla, a downwardly mobile but still game little outpost about an hour south of here, for an old-fashioned day of celebration. This is not a research trip. This is family fun. It is only at the very last moment that I stash a spare reporter's notebook in my backpack. With us today is Damon, Lizzie's boyfriend du jour. They sit shoulder to shoulder in the backseat, silent, holding hands. Once or twice I catch Damon's eyes in the rearview mirror, but only for a nanosecond. As soon as he glimpses my gaze, he averts his, not sneakily or (heaven help him) guiltily, but with that potent mix of early teen snarkiness leavened by fear of authority with a dash of general disdain for anyone over the age of, say, seventeen.

When we arrive in town, we set ourselves up in a line, sitting on the curb of Main—and pretty much Only—Street, drinking blue Gatorade, and waiting for the parade. And here it comes: Boy Scouts and army veterans, semitrailers hauling elderly ladies from the local historical society dressed in gingham skirts and white bonnets, 4-Hers on their Appaloosas with braided tails (the horses, not the girls . . . the girls all sport eighties-era Farrah Fawcett big hair), baton twirlers, toddlers in wheelbarrows pushed by their mothers, and, bringing up the rear, an Elvis impersonator packed tightly into satin bell-bottoms. What more could one ask from a parade?

Everyone, with the exception of Elvis, throws candy at the curbside crowd. It's one of the traditions of this parade, and it has always been

Lizzie's favorite part. Normally she's running out into the road scooping up handfuls of Jolly Ranchers and Tootsie Pops and Dum Dums, then running back to stash them at the curb until the next group of paraders bombards us. At the end of the parade, she's amassed a two- or three-pound pile of candy, most of which I end up hiding at the back of a tall cupboard until she forgets about it (and I throw it out). That's part of the tradition too. But today, with Damon by her side, I see that she is trying to play it cool. No squealing when candy is thrown, no rushing out to grab it, no waving madly at the paraders to encourage more candy tossing. She just sits on the curb holding his hand.

Oddly, even though I have always hated the candy mania, this breaks my heart. I think two things, almost simultaneously. First, this is how childhood ends. This is how we know childhood has ended, when our kid no longer runs out to grab the candy. And second, isn't this just what women learn to do early on—moderate their behavior for their men, try to figure out (without asking) what pleases them, and do that, act that way?

Damon is not an excitable guy. He's quiet and laid-back, two adjectives one would never use to describe my daughter. And he is one year ahead of her in school, an eighth grade graduate soon to launch into high school and the big time. She is but a middle schooler still. Perhaps she feels she has to temper her exuberance. How cool is it, after all, to dash out into the street to grab cheap candy? And so, perhaps she has decided, subconsciously I am betting, to mirror his remove, to become more like him and less like herself.

It starts so early, this whittling away at what you are, this tempering, this watchfulness about what pleases, this submersion of identity until you become Mrs. Somebody Else. I did quite a bit of this in my earlier years, but I do very little of that nowadays. If Lizzie learns anything from me, I hope she learns this. At the moment, though, it appears that the siren song of sucrose is too enticing to ignore completely. Lizzie can't help herself. Halfway through the parade, she starts picking up candy and stashing it.

When the parade ends, we mosey over to the rodeo, the second reason we come here every Fourth of July. The event is big enough to be on the Northwest rodeo circuit—meaning at least some of the riders have not only guts but also talent—but small enough so that the bleachers have only four rows and you eat the dust of every horse that gallops by. Lizzie and Damon sit apart from the family, his arm around her shoulders, then her arm around his, staying close in the intense heat of this afternoon as only the newly smitten do. They slurp on Hawaiian shave ice and dig into deep-fried elephant ears and down a few rodeo corn dogs, the ingredients list of which, if I dared peruse it, would put me into cardiac arrest. Lizzie knows how deeply I disapprove of this kind of eating, but she's taken advantage of the situation to indulge one junk food fantasy after another. She knows I won't make a stink about it because Damon is with us. She knows I won't embarrass her. I have brought actual food for the family—turkey sandwiches, coleslaw, fruit—but this doesn't interest them. "Oh, Mom," Lizzie says, exasperated. "That's not what you eat at a rodeo." She does have a point.

We are sitting two rows above Lizzie and Damon, and I watch them more than I watch the show in the corral. They don't talk much. I've noticed that before, and I've asked her about it. I've even asked her, boldly, poking my nose where it doesn't belong, "What do you two talk about?" I'll say this for Lizzie: She may smart off more than I could ever have gotten away with, or ever dreamed of getting away with. She may slam the door in my face, literally and figuratively. But sometimes she tells me stuff. She tells me stuff I never told my mother. (Of course, my mother never asked.) So when I ask her what she and Damon talk about, she actually answers me.

She says, her voice all of a sudden quiet, that they really don't talk about much at all, just random stuff, like hey, look at that, or isn't that cool. I persist. But you're together a lot. You must talk about *something*. Do you talk about movies, about music, about video games? No, she says. About school or friends? She shakes her head. About your families? She rolls her eyes. Talking about families—how stupid and lame and pitiful our parents were, how they understood nothing about who we were or what we thought—this was the biggest single topic of conversation among me and my friends at her age. Well, second biggest. First was boys.

We just don't talk a lot, she says, again. Then she pauses and looks away. I can tell that she's considering whether to go on, but she doesn't consider for long. Once she starts talking, she doesn't do much self-editing. "Really, Mom," she says, "we just mostly kiss." She's pretty thrilled about the kissing stuff, I know, but I think she's also a little disappointed that they don't talk. I think it has maybe occurred to her that they don't actually have much to say to each other. I could be reading in too deeply to what really is a minor flirtation, a little crush that has temporarily caught hold, but I think, even as she is enjoying having this boyfriend, she is aware of the underlying flaw in the relationship.

And aren't we all? I mean, right at the beginning, from that first date, from that first heady rush into love, don't we see the chink in the amour? I've asked a number of my female friends about this, women who are no longer with their long-term partners. Did you just fall out of love? I ask. Did you just wake up one day and not want to spend another minute with that person? What happened? All these women say the same thing: I knew in the beginning that he (or she) wasn't the right one, but I overlooked it, I made excuses for it, I thought I could change it—whatever the *it* was (lack of ambition, the way he treated his mother, her aversion to dogs). They saw it coming, from day one. I make a mental note: Whenever and however this thing with Damon ends, I'll remind Lizzie about what she said, about how she saw Damon wasn't the one even while he was still the one.

This is the best and worst thing about being the mother of a daughter—the way everything she does reminds you of what you did or wish you did or wish you didn't do; the way everything she does brings back your own childhood, your own teen years. You understand. She thinks you're clueless. You want to save her. She doesn't want to be saved.

The rodeo goes on for hours, bucking broncos and bull riders, calf ropers and barrel racers, a clown who isn't funny, an announcer who is, Charlie Daniels blaring from the loudspeakers, former rodeo queens (more big hair) working the crowd, handing out signed photographs. We drive home, sweaty, dusty, and satisfied that we have once again had an authentic country experience. Damon stays for dinner, then we head out to watch the fireworks from atop Spencer Butte, a two-thousand-foot hill just a mile from our house. The view from the top is 360 degrees, so we'll be able to see the two big municipal fireworks displays plus whatever else, legal and illegal is going on below. The hike up the butte is lovely and well traveled, perhaps a mile up the forested hillside along a good trail. The four of us—Lizzie and Damon, my husband and I—tromp up there along with what looks like half of the under-twenty-five population of town. The mood is loud and boisterous, the air at the top sweet with the smell of marijuana.

Lizzie and Damon can't wait to get away from us. We give them one of the two flashlights we've brought along and tell them to meet us back at a particular rock outcropping when the fireworks are over. They head off, and we almost immediately lose sight of them. There are maybe two hundred people up here scattered in clumps along the narrow rocky spine of the butte, and everyone is in party mode. But the main attraction turns out to be anticlimactic. We are too high—that's elevation not inhalation—to experience the full force of the firework displays. They play out beneath us, colorful flashes, interesting but distant, with little impact or drama. The shows go on for more than an hour. It starts getting chilly, and we haven't brought sweaters. I'd like to start heading down, but, of course, we have to wait to meet up with Lizzie and Damon.

Finally, all is quiet below, and the crowd starts dispersing, one group after another passing around the last joint and heading down the trail. We wait at the rock outcropping. We wait five, ten, fifteen minutes. The kids don't show. Damon has a cell phone with him, but we don't. Unlike just about everyone I know, I haven't yet bonded with my cell phone. I view it as neither accessory nor necessity but rather just another gadget I have to worry about keeping recharged. Tonight, too late, I wish I had it with me.

My husband takes the flashlight and goes to look for them while I stay at the appointed meeting spot. He comes back ten minutes later without them. Then I go out looking, walking the length of the spine and clambering down the south-facing hillside where there are still pockets of onlookers. The beam of my flashlight catches couples, cuddling, kissing, playing guitar. But no Lizzie, no Damon. I am beginning to worry.

Back at the meeting spot, we wait another ten minutes. I am now moving from worrying to catastrophizing, constructing scary scenarios in which they have gotten lost in the woods or, worse yet, been injured. Another ten minutes go by. I walk over to the few remaining clusters of people still up top and tell them I need their help. Could they please, on the count of three, yell out "LIZZIE!" They do. Three different groups, several times each. No response. No Lizzie. It is now more than an hour since the fireworks ended, almost two and a half hours since we all climbed up the trail.

Maybe they looked for us in the wrong place, thought we left already and hiked back down? Setting aside my catastrophic scenarios, this sounds like a possibility. We decide to hike back down and check in the parking lot. Maybe they are there waiting for us. We sprint down the path in the dark, losing the good trail almost immediately. We are alone, there is little moonlight, and our flashlight batteries are giving out. Although I have been up and down this butte close to a hundred times during the twenty years I've lived here, I can't seem to locate the trail. We stumble over rocks, edge ourselves down steep side paths. I am both chilled and sweating.

There is no one down in the parking lot, no cars remaining except for ours. Maybe they came down already, waited, and then started walking back to our house. It's only a mile away, a straight shot down a good road. We drive home slowly. No one is walking alongside the road. Lizzie and Damon are not at the house. It's now eleven p.m. I want to call the cops, but my husband thinks we should give it a little more time.

We drive back to the parking lot below the butte. Empty. I think we should at least call Damon's father, but in my panic, I've forgotten to bring the cell phone from home. My husband jumps in the car and drives home to get it while I wait alone in the parking lot in case they show up. When he gets back, I am going to call the cops. I don't care what he says. Then I'm going to hike back up the butte.

Five minutes later, he's back with my cell phone and the news that there was a message on our answering machine at home. Lizzie called on Damon's cell to say they were at the top of the butte, couldn't find us, and were going to start heading down. The call came in maybe ten minutes ago, sometime between the first time we checked home and when my husband went back for the cell phone. They have been on top of the butte this whole time. Where, exactly, I cannot imagine. Didn't we look everywhere? Didn't we have people yelling for them? I am so relieved that I start to cry. It's dark. My husband doesn't see.

I call Damon's father, who shows up ten minutes later, looking calm and unruffled. I don't find this out until weeks later, but this isn't the first time Damon has given him a scare. And it isn't the most serious of issues he's had with his son. We wait another ten minutes, and still no one shows. It is now midnight. I can't wait any longer. We all start up the butte again.

About a half mile up the trail, I hear voices and see a faint light. I start running until I can make out figures on the path ahead. It's a small group, two women and three men in their twenties. The guy in front is holding an open cell phone in front of him, the light of the tiny screen dimly illuminating the path. No sign of Lizzie. I am about to lose it when I hear Lizzie's voice yelling for me. She and Damon are maybe twenty yards behind the other group. They are fine. Everything is fine. They didn't get lost, they tell us. They say they came looking for us when the fireworks ended and couldn't find us. Lizzie is crying now. They say they never heard us calling. I don't care at this point. I hug my daughter, hug her boyfriend, hug my husband, hug Damon's father, and we all troop back down the trail again.

Later, at home, when Lizzie is in bed, already asleep, the quick deep sleep of the innocent and the unconcerned, my husband and I sit talking in the living room, wide awake. He says this is just like some charming but frightening Mark Twain story, with Huck Finn and Tom Sawyer lost in a cave or wandering down by the river. Now that it's over, we talk about the evening's adventure as narrative. It is compelling in its simplicity. In this story, one fears losing a child to the elements—the dark trail, the moonless night, the deserted hilltop. There is the quick, reasonable fear and the quick, satisfying resolution. The situation is scary but uncomplicated.

But now the story—both the real one and its Twainian retelling—is over. Lizzie is safe. And really, was she ever in any danger at all? The whole situation would never have occurred had I brought my damn cell phone with me. I should just go to sleep.

But I can't. What happened these past few hours stays with me. I see it as a parable, a simple story fraught with meaning, a story meant to teach me some greater truth. For too long a moment tonight I believed I was in danger of losing Lizzie to the dark trail, an actual, physical, dirt and rock, dark trail. Now I see the trail as a symbol, the things we can lose a child to today: drugs, depression, eating disorders, unprotected sex, disease, a bad crowd.

A bad crowd. I think of Damon and wonder about his influence tonight, wonder where the two of them could have gone off to that they didn't hear the loud chorus of yells, wonder what they were doing wherever they were. Wasn't it just yesterday that I knew all her friends and all her friends' parents? I vetted their houses. I looked at their bookshelves. I peered in their refrigerators. Now she hangs out with a boyfriend I barely know. She is on the cusp of a life that is becoming increasingly invisible to me. I see myself waiting in the figurative parking lot for a daughter who never shows.

I know that letting go is part of being a good parent, that letting go is part of the natural, healthy progression of my relationship with Lizzie. But letting go is not the same as losing, is it? Tonight's cautionary tale seems to me a foreshadowing: Soon I *will* lose her—not, I hope, to the dark elements, but to high school and then college, to her own dreams and ambitions, her own life. This is a lot to think about sitting on the couch at two in the morning after a day like we've had, after three long hours in panic mode. But as my self-induced state of hypervigilance fades, it is replaced by a new resolve. There is a "lesson" in the exaggerated terror the incident has provoked: I need to work even harder to forge a connection between my daughter and me. I need to dig even deeper, make even more of an effort, push the envelope of intimacy. I need to find Lizzie, *really* find her, before I lose her again. Before I can let go.

THIRTEEN

I have a plan. I won't just wait for opportunities to get close to Lizzie. I won't just sit back and observe her life from the sidelines. I will start *creating* opportunities.

Maybe what I have is not so much a plan as it is a fantasy: a road trip. A mother-daughter cross-country trek, just the two of us. Wouldn't this be the ultimate, iconic bonding experience? We need something like this, some concerted, purposeful endeavor, to bring us closer. I knew this before what happened last week on Spencer's Butte, but now I not only know it; I feel it; this sense of impending separation, this ticking-clock sense that I have to get to know Lizzie before I really do lose her.

But it's not all doom and gloom behind my travel plans. My motivation also comes from a sense of unrequited celebration. My daughter has just entered her teens, and I think she and I should mark this passage with something more meaningful than last month's pool party. That party was nice. Lizzie had fun. Everyone had fun. Even I had fun, albeit wrapped in a beach towel. But the party felt no different from her twelfth birthday party, or her eleventh: lively kids, lots of cake. Where was the symbolism? The rite of passage?

I would love to take Lizzie on a road trip like the trek I made with my sons seven years ago, but I don't dare. She's not like the boys. She wouldn't disappear in the upper bunk of an RV for hours, lost in a book. She couldn't just sit and watch the landscape go by. She doesn't roll with the punches. And she wouldn't have a sibling sidekick for company. Besides, the sequel is never as good as the original. I need to think of something more appealing, some adventure that better suits her personality—and our relationship. Maybe a shorter trip? Maybe by train?

I am a great fan of long distance trains, even in these never-on-time, surly-service Amtrak days. During the past twenty years or so, I've ridden on almost every long distance train in America, meeting odd and interesting people (a 450-pound man whose only means of travel was the train, a woman with eight months to live, a poetry-writing former special forces marine, a Russian mafioso) and racking up enough experiences with a capital E to offset long delays and iceberg lettuce salads served by sullen waiters in bare-bones dining cars.

The train, I thought, would be just the thing for Lizzie and me. We could travel together but not so together, not stuck in an RV by ourselves twenty-four hours a day. On the train, she could snack at will (a major selling point), wander the cars, and, most important, socialize. She would love the socializing part. She specializes in making fast, temporary friends—at camp, at the beach, wherever we go—intense relationships that last a day or a week and then disappear without a trace. Not having to drive eight or ten hours a day would allow me to spend quality, not merely quantity, time with her. But just because I love long distance trains doesn't mean Lizzie will. In fact, considering all the things I like and she doesn't, and vice versa, I am just as wary of the train idea as I am enamored of it.

And so, I decide on a modest trip, not a long, meandering cross-country journey like the one I took with the boys. I scour the Amtrak schedule to find a train that goes to an interesting place just far enough away to give her a sense of the rhythm of long distance train travel. I decide on Monterey, California. There's a renowned aquarium there and a touristy boardwalk I think she'd enjoy. The trip is just long enough—we'd depart before dinner and arrive midafternoon the next day—to allow for several onboard meals and an overnight in a sleeping compartment.

I pick the dates, develop the itinerary, make the reservations, buy the tickets. I don't involve Lizzie in the planning at all—although she does sign off on the Monterey destination. The kindest interpretation of my behavior is that I am thinking of this trip as a welcome-to-your-teens gift from me to her. And so, I am buying it, packaging it, and wrapping it up to give her. Another way to look at it—which escapes me at the time—is that I am continuing to hog all the power. Lizzie will soon show me the error of my ways.

The journey begins in true Amtrak fashion, which is to say, late, very late, and with considerable confusion. In fact, this train we're catching, which runs between Seattle and Los Angeles—arguably the most beautiful route in the country—has the worst on-time rate in the system. The train is officially called the Coast Starlight but everyone who knows anything about trains calls it the Coast Star*late*. Apparently there is a freight train derailment in one of the mountain passes about fifty miles south of here, on the way to California, so although our train arrives just twenty minutes late from the north, it will have to sit at the station for as long as it takes to clear up the accident. We get onboard thinking we will stash our bags in our compartment, make our dinner reservations, and then get off again. We can wander around downtown, get a latte somewhere, sit in the park, and come back when the train is ready to leave.

But a few minutes after we get on, the conductor announces that the train is going to back up into the train yard and wait there. No one is to get off. The conductor tells us he has no idea when the train will leave, but it won't be stopping again at the station on the way out of town. Lizzie settles in with a bag of Cheetos and a manga book. I sit staring out the window of our first-class sleeping compartment. My view is the ass end of the county jail. The minutes turn into an hour, then two, and we go nowhere. I give in to the experience. You have to if you want to remain sane on Amtrak. Anyway, even though we have yet to move an inch, it's time for dinner.

Eating onboard is more than sitting down to a sometimes surprisingly decent meal—it is a social occasion. In the sixty-four-seat dining car, with its tables of four, the rule is "community seating." Lizzie and I are seated next to a sixtyish couple from Mystic, Connecticut, who have just spent a week in Seattle with their daughter who is—her mother says—"as high maintenance as the space shuttle." When I tell these folks that I am writing a book about mothers and daughters, the woman rolls her eyes, and her husband, who has said almost nothing throughout the meal, says, "You will absolutely have to interview my wife."

"It just never ends," she tells me, shaking her head and looking over at Lizzie, who is contentedly making her way through a piece of cheese-cake. "My daughter is thirty-four." Big sigh. If Lizzie is tracking the conversation, she doesn't let on. I think she is focused on her plate, just too thrilled right now that I didn't make a stink when she ordered the cheese-cake. I watch her eat out of the corner of my eye while I listen to more tales of woe from this mother of an adult daughter. I have, of course, heard many tales of woe from many mothers by now, but none have featured daughters quite this old; none have implied, like this one, that mother-daughter difficulties can go on forever. None, that is, except the tale of my mother and me. I don't like being reminded of that by this woman's story. My fervent hope is that Lizzie and I will get it all out of our systems now, and in ten or twenty or thirty years I won't be telling stories like this to strangers on a train.

After dinner in the dining car, finally on our way following a three-and-a-half-hour wait at the station, Lizzie and I sit in oversized, uphol-stered club chairs in the Pacific Parlour Car. I stare out the big, curved windows as a pink dusk darkens into a soft grayish blue, the color of Lizzie's eyes. She has her headphones on listening to Irish drinking songs (courtesy of her older brother) on her iPod. Her head is thrown back, and she is silently mouthing the words. There's a two-thirds moon against a denim sky. She sees it, points, and smiles. I squeeze her hand. Later, in our compartment, she takes the upper berth, and I fall asleep in the lower, to the sounds of the rails and my daughter's soft snoring.

At noon the next day, almost six hours behind schedule, we pull into Sacramento. Apparently, sometime during the night, the train sat on a siding for a few hours while freights passed us by. I love how ridiculously out of sync train travel is in this country with the way I live my life, the way so many of us live our lives: on a tight schedule, rushing from ap-pointment to appointment, efficiently ticking off items on the daily to-do lists. This is more like the way kids live, not the overbooked Upper West Side of Manhattan kids you read about in the *New Yorker,* but the millions of other kids out there in the hinterlands beyond the Hudson, kids like Lizzie and her friends, who don't own watches, who forget time. The rhythm of the train, I am delighted to note, seems to agree with her. She is up early this morning, wandering the train for a while, trolling for companions, then back to the compartment for a catnap. After breakfast, we sprawl on the bed watching an old episode of *Friends* on the little DVD player they give passengers in the sleeping cars. She listens to tunes on her iPod, goes for another stroll. When I catch up with her an hour later, she is in the parlor car deep in conversation with the woman we met at dinner last night, the one with the thirty-four-year-old, high-maintenance daughter. When Lizzie sees me, she drops the grown-up persona. "I'm hungry," she says, with that petulance I know so well. "I need a snack." It's a half hour until our lunch seating.

"There are muffins back in the sleeping car next to the coffee urn," I tell her.

"Oh, that's okay," she says, suddenly grown-up again. She smiles at the woman from Connecticut. "This is just me being a whiny thirteen-year-old." I am by turns astonished, delighted, and proud. Lizzie has a sense of herself I didn't know she had. She sees her crankiness—and by implication her nasty moods, her capital-A Attitude—as part of a teen persona. She is saying—isn't she?—that she sees these outbursts as symptoms of her age, not of the state of our relationship. I am grinning. The woman and I exchange warm looks over the top of Lizzie's head.

Finally, late in the day and twenty-five or -six or -seven hours after we first boarded the train, we're in Monterey. We eat dinner at a wharf restaurant with nineteen fresh fish entrees on the menu. I savor one of them as I silently congratulate myself for not commenting on Lizzie's menu selection of deep-fried chicken fingers and French fries. I know this won't last—my silence, that is, not her terrible food choices. We check into the hotel. Our room is gorgeous, with hardwood floors, a wood-burning fireplace, a window seat nestled beneath a bank of windows facing the bay, and, much to Lizzie's joy, a TV with a zillion channels. But there is only one bed—a huge, frothy, pillow-topped king bed—but just the one.

"I'm not sleeping in the same bed as you," she says. Everything was going so well up to this moment. Where did this come from? "No way am I sleeping in the same bed," she says again, almost snarling. She says she'll sleep in the window seat and goes looking for extra blankets. I take a deep breath and force myself not to respond. The hardest thing in life—or at least in mother-daughter relationships, or at least for me—is learning when to keep my mouth shut. I still always want to say something: counter her remarks, argue her out of her opinions, comment on her food and clothing and friend and entertainment choices. Even if I'm right—and of course I'm right—I've got to give it (her) a rest. I need to just brush off her surliness. She's tired. She's tired of so much mom time. But I'm stung. The tone of rejection in her voice still never fails to bring tears to my eyes, which I mask by turning my head away as I climb into the big bed and bury myself in a book. A few minutes later, she gets in too, gives me a withering look, scrunches over to her side, and promptly falls asleep.

The next day, all goes well—the aquarium is a hit, there's a Ghirardelli chocolate store down the street that gives out free samples—until we are seated at the restaurant for dinner. We're seated at the worst spot in the place, a tiny table sandwiched between a door to the kitchen and a serving station. I make a fuss until we are moved. She's disgusted with me, embarrassed to be seen with me. It dawns on me as I register all this in the elevation of her brow, the shaking of her head, and the snippiness in her voice, that my father used to do what I just did all the time, and I used to react just the way Lizzie is reacting (minus the snippy remarks). My father, the cranky New Yorker who went through life convinced that everyone (waiters, mechanics, sales clerks, dentists) was out to cheat him, always asked for a different table at a restaurant, regardless of where we were seated. It was a habit, I think, born out of a need to put everyone on notice that he was not a guy to be trifled with. This never failed to mortify me, so I am trying hard to give Lizzie a break. I am not exactly succeeding, but I am trying, which is a movement in the right direction. We've had a good day and everything was going just fine, and this situation is different. The table we got actually *was* terrible. I am not my father! And Lizzie, unlike me at her age, is an ungrateful little snot.

When we're served, my dinner is in error, so I send it back. She starts in on her plate of multiple deep-fried items immediately. "Oh, don't wait for me," I say sarcastically. I am pissed at her attitude. That's my excuse, I guess, for acting like I'm thirteen. "Just go right ahead."

"Don't worry, I will," she says, proving which one of us really *is* the thirteen-year-old. But then, thirty seconds later, she looks up from her plate and says sweetly, "Would you like a bite?"

It's "popcorn shrimp"—more deep-fried batter than crustacean. Of course I don't want a bite. I take one anyway and give her arm a squeeze. Maybe this is a peace offering? A thoughtful act? Or maybe it's just another sudden mood swing. I'm not sure, but I intend to enjoy whatever it is.

The next day I insist we go on a bike ride together. This has all the earmarks of a very bad idea: physical exercise (of my choosing) undertaken in the morning (Lizzie's worst time). Just to make matters worse, it will wrench her away from the multitude of TV channels we get in the hotel room.

What am I thinking?

I am thinking, Why not push the envelope? We've traveled together on a train for twenty-four-plus hours. We've slept in the same bed. We've eaten every meal in each other's company. Why not go for broke? The proposed adventure is a bike ride along the Monterey Bay Coastal Trail, a twenty-nine-mile paved path that runs from Castroville to Carmel, parts of which I've already run in the early morning while Lizzie stayed in bed and watched such shows as *World's Heaviest Man* (Manuel Uribe of Mexico at 1,200 pounds, in case you needed to know) and *Animal Cops*. This is what I will be taking her away from, and she won't be a happy camper. I propose to rent one tandem bike, because if we rent two separate bikes I fear Lizzie will either lag behind or decide to give up ten minutes into the ride. I am courting disaster, though, because riding a tandem bike calls for close teamwork and cooperation, not our strong suit.

When I tell her the plan for the morning she, of course, balks. Biking is, she says with a full measure of teenage disgust, just about the stupidest idea she can possibly imagine. "Lame," she says, not taking her eyes off the TV screen (*SpongeBob*). "Really lame."

A half hour later, after much bickering, the big threat of no more TV and, to soften the blow, the grand enticement of an after-dinner sundae at the Ghirardelli shop (yes, food as reward; yes, I know, I know), we are off. But as we steer the rental bike out of the shop and onto the path and mount the beast, I begin to think that she may be right about the lameness of this idea. I have never been on a bicycle built for two. I didn't realize what a balancing act this is, how even a subtle movement from the rider in back—that would be Lizzie—affects the entire operation. Remove a hand from the handlebars, or lean over to scratch a leg, and the bike goes haywire. It's just what can happen in a family, what happens in our family: You're rolling along just fine and then one person, with a single remark, changes everything, shifts the dynamic, puts everyone off-kilter. Lizzie is a master in this regard.

We have just started pedaling down the path. "Great," she says in that voice that clearly indicates this is not. "I'm gonna have to look at your butt for the next hour. That'll be fun." I would laugh if I thought she was trying to be funny, but she isn't.

"Roll up your pants leg or your jeans'll get caught in the chain," I order, my tone more strident than necessary. For unknown reasons she has refused to wear shorts. She ignores me. Three minutes later, the hem of her jeans does, in fact, get caught in the chain, and we almost topple as I struggle to stop the bike. I turn my head to give her my best withering look. She rolls up her pants, and we soldier on.

It is not our only close call. Once she leans back, shifting her weight, which jolts the bike to one side. I stamp down my foot, jamming my ankle as I try to maintain our equilibrium. Another time, she stops pedaling, which puts sudden double pressure on my pedals, and as I lean in to keep our forward momentum, the bike wobbles ominously. Then, a few minutes later, I steer us down the wrong path for a few yards, riding into a parking lot instead of curving with the bike path, and as I try to turn the bike in a wide circle, we come close to tipping over once again.

"I wanna go back," Lizzie says, for the fifth or sixth time. I have lost count. I ignore her and concentrate on the extraordinary scenery: the soft layers of cloud and fog, the deep blue bay, the tangy ocean air.

Several miles down the path, we stop the bike to turn around. We're struggling to get back on at the same time while keeping the bike upright. The ocean air is cool, but I am sweating.

"Put your right foot on the pedal," Lizzie orders me from behind. Her tone is measured and authoritative. I pay attention. "Now push off with your left," she says. We count together without planning it: "one, two, three," and then launch the bike perfectly, no wobbles, for the first time.

We pedal, silently, for the next twenty minutes. I am taking big, deep breaths of this glorious ocean air and thinking about what just happened: My daughter took control. She transcended annoyance, exasperation, and attitude (hers and mine) and moved us forward, literally and otherwise. I would never have had the presence of mind or self-confidence to take the reins, even for a moment, from my mother's hands. How amazing that she did this, as simple as the act was. She is different from how I was— and in a good way, and I am different from how my mother was. Part of me feels light and liberated as I embrace these happy thoughts, the other part thinks: Gee, isn't this a bit too much to read into a five-second exchange on a bike?

"I'm taking my hands off the handlebars," she says, many miles down the path. She knows now to warn me. She stretches her arms out to the sides, closes her eyes against the ocean breeze and starts singing: *Today, while the blossoms still cling to the vine* . . . I sing along. We bicycle out to Lover's Point that way, pedaling hard, Lizzie hands-free, both of us singing, the sun burning up the fog.

By the time we come out of the restaurant that evening, it is almost nine, late but not late enough to go back to the hotel. I don't want to be subjected to any more hours of mindless TV than absolutely necessary, although I have to admit I am, disturbingly, curious to know if the 1,200-pound Fattest Man in the World lost weight on the Zone Diet. "Let's go watch the sunset," I say. "I think we can see it from the pier up there." But it turns out that we can't. Monterey Bay opens in a northerly direction, so although we are standing on a West Coast beach staring out over an ocean-like body of water, we are not looking west. No sun. "Maybe if we go down the trail a little there'll be a clearing and we can see," I say. The sky is turning sherbet colors. This is going to be a spectacular sunset.

Lizzie, full of surprises on this trip, gives me another one: She gets into the spirit of the quest. You just never know with her. We find the path— the same one we were biking on this morning—and start walking in a direction that feels like south to me but is actually west. We walk fast. It doesn't take us long to reach a clearing, but we see that a point of land is obstructing our westward view. Maybe, if we can just get around that point, we can see the setting sun. "Let's give it one more try," I say. "We still have time." We walk even faster. The point of land is maybe a quarter mile ahead. The sky is darkening, but I think the sun still must be above the horizon because it is illuminating a jet overhead, its glinting silver body leaving a blazing white contrail. We lengthen our stride. Finally, we reach the next point, climb out over the rocks, and see . . . another jetty of land obscuring our westward view. Lizzie looks back toward where we've come from.

"Look," she says, "the moon is following us." It's true. Behind us, all this time, has been a big, gorgeous, almost full moon, the pearly, slightly pink color of an abalone shell. I have to laugh. Here we are, the two of us chasing the sun while the moon has our back. This scores a perfect 100 on the woo-woo meter. We turn around and walk back toward Cannery Row, our faces illuminated by soft moonlight.

On the train back home, we have exhausted our togetherness, which is fine with both of us. Lizzie befriends an excitable eleven-year-old boy whose father gives him a fifty-dollar bill to spend in the snack car and an exquisitely bored, stringy-haired goth girl who accompanies them wordlessly and unhappily. I walk back to the parlor car where I nestle into one of the overstuffed chairs and start flipping through a book I've brought along but have been loath to open, *50 Great Tips, Tricks & Techniques to Connect With Your Teen,* which promises "Fun! Simple! Tools any parent can use." (The exclamation points are mine.) Books like this make me feel stupid. If there really are so many Fun! Simple! ways of connecting, how lame am I for not thinking of them myself?

When Lizzie finds me a few hours later, I've long since abandoned *50 Tips* ("Enjoy bridge or complex card games. Take your teen to historical landmarks." I can hear Lizzie groan. I can hear myself groan.) I am now making my way through a day-old copy of the *Sacramento Bee*. I look up to see that she's applied eyeliner, part of a recent foray into makeup to which I have given my tacit approval. I must admit, she does look great in eyeliner. And I've got to admire her application skill—on a swaying train, no less. I have never learned to use cosmetics. The front of Lizzie's black Killers T-shirt is dusted with Doritos crumbs, and she has the wild eyes of someone who has downed one too many Cokes. Her two friends got off the train at the last stop, she tells me. Now she is out trolling for a new buddy.

She doesn't have to look far. At the end of the parlor car is a string bean of a kid sitting alone, nodding his head vigorously to whatever music he is mainlining into his ear canals. A few seats away is someone who looks like a long-suffering mother. Lizzie sits down right next to the mother and starts chatting her up. It pleases me—and pains me terribly—to see her be so charming with adults other than me. This woman is clearly charmed. I see that she is introducing Lizzie to her son, which is just what Lizzie wanted. She and this boy—who, it turns out, will be on the train all the way to our stop—spend most of the rest of the trip talking about their favorite bands; their favorite video games; the relative merits of Xbox 360, Nintendo Wii, and PlayStation 3; laser tag; and the fine art of paintball. This is the advantage Lizzie has growing up with two older brothers. She can more than hold her own in the arcane world of the slightly geeky teen boy. When she and the kid run out of things to talk about, they arm wrestle. Lizzie wins. I love that she doesn't know—or better yet, doesn't care—that she's not supposed to. It's strength of character I see, and confidence, just those traits she exhibited when she took over on the bike path. This has been a good trip.

FOURTEEN

I n the car on the way home from Lizzie's first week at summer camp she is in high spirits, ebullient, talkative. It has been two weeks since we've returned from our mother-daughter trip, and I am still basking in the residual warmth of our adventure. Lizzie, however, has moved on. To her, summer means one thing: camp. This morning, her face is flushed with a combination of excitement and sunburn. She's wearing ripped jeans, a cherry-red camp T-shirt, and a bead and hemp necklace that has "arts and crafts activity" written all over it. She looks wonderful.

"I'm in such a great mood, like really, really great," she tells me, beaming. She loves camp just as I did. Camp, in fact, was the apex of my childhood, adolescence, and teen years. It was where I learned how to be someone's best friend, where I learned to play every sport I know, where I got my first kiss. I spent every summer, from age six to seventeen, at a camp in the Berkshires of Massachusetts.

Summer camp is different on the West Coast, or at least in the Northwest, than it is in the East. Here you don't have to go far to get to camp-worthy country, and the experience is decidedly egalitarian. Lizzie goes to a no-frills, yurts-in-the-woods camp on eighty densely forested acres in the foothills of the coastal mountains just a half hour from our house. There are no tennis courts, baseball diamonds, or soccer fields. There is no waterskiing on the lake (there is no lake). There are just winding paths through fragrant fir, pine, and cedar to a semi-scummy swimming hole and little clearings with activity tepees. The sessions are a week long, with campers coming home Saturday morning. Those who re-up return for the next week Sunday afternoon. Most kids sign up for one or two sessions. Lizzie is signed up for all six. She wishes there were more, and I know just how she feels. At camp, untethered from family, she has the ability (the challenge, the fun, the power) to be exactly who she wants to be, to remake herself from year to year, or even session to session. I loved who I was at camp, and it's easy to see Lizzie feels the same way about herself.

On the thirty-minute drive back home, she talks nonstop about her week: She has a new camp name, Hawk, of which she is very proud. (The staff and helpers all have self-chosen camp names that range from the sweet—Rainbow, Cottontail, Donald Duck—to the edgy—Captain Bones, Shark Bait). She placed first in the toilet paper toss in the Camp Olympics. Snickers, her counselor, is very cool and showed her how to apply liquid eyeliner, which, Lizzie says knowledgeably, is way harder than the pencil she had been experimenting with. There was a bear sighting that freaked out everyone. Cinnamon, a cute boy counselor, accidentally started a fire by the horse corral when he tried to burn out a wasp nest. She shows me the bruise where Maggie, her horse, bit her. "She was just pissed off about something," she says, matter-of-factly. I love that my daughter is tough like this. I have always loved this about her—and she knows it. I don't know what I'd do if I had one of those *eeek*-it's-a-spider kind of girls.

"So, you're coming as a counselor next week, right?" she says to me.

"Yeah," I say cautiously. We'd started talking about this idea several months ago. It was to be part of my research for the book, a way for me to see Lizzie in a different context, to watch and listen to other teen girls in a relaxed, nonschool setting. It would not work, given the rhythms of camp, for me to simply observe from the sidelines, as I did at school, so I had volunteered my services as a counselor. I would be, in the lingo of cultural anthropology, a participant-observer.

But I knew it wasn't going to be as simple and clear-cut as that. Since my aha moment the night of the Fourth of July misadventure, I had been thinking of this upcoming week at camp as not just an opportunity to observe but also as an opportunity to bond. Lizzie loved camp. I loved camp. We would find each other in deeper ways, connect in deeper ways through this shared love, this shared experience. That meant I was going to be cultural anthropologist and mother simultaneously, that I was looking for both perspective and intimacy simultaneously, keeping my distance and working to *close* the distance simultaneously. As if this were not enough to make my head explode, I also understood the irony of what I was about to do: invade the very territory I knew—and had celebrated in my own life—as hallowed, parent-free ground. But I didn't want to—I couldn't—dwell on *any* of this. I had to stop overthinking. I was committed to this next adventure, and I had to *just do it*.

"We were talking about what a good camp name would be for you," she says. I am surprised—and delighted—that she's been talking about this with her yurt mates, that she's even *mentioned* that her mother is coming to camp next week. "We like 'Lotus' better than 'Sunflower,'" she says. These were the top choices we came up with a few weeks ago.

"Great," I say. "Lotus it is." Then I ask the question I am not sure I want the answer to: "So, now that it's actually going to happen, how do you *really* feel about my being a counselor?"

"Well, at first I thought, gee, we'll, like, get into fights, and I'll be tired of seeing you because, you know, camp is where you go to get away from parents." She smiles, almost apologetically. "And maybe you wouldn't like the way I'd act, and you'd start giving me looks. You know . . ." she pauses for dramatic effect, "'The Look.'" Yeah, I know. She's the third child. I've had time to perfect The Look.

Lizzie has long been a recipient of The Look—little good it has done me—but this is the first time she's named it or joked about it. It's a testament to her blindingly sunny mood that she makes this joke. But also, I think it is a clear indication of her maturity, her ability to see a situation as well as live it, a kind of refined and sophisticated judgment. Her powers are growing. I shoot her The Look, and we both laugh.

"So," Lizzie says, continuing her thoughts about my upcoming tenure as counselor, "I figured maybe it wouldn't be so bad, like hey, my mom is going to be a counselor, and how cool is that, because you could give me the inside scoop, like when the counselors send all the campers away and talk about them. So I could find out all this stuff about what happens behind the scenes." I love this reciprocal idea. She is allowing me to be a fly on the wall. In return, I will be her mole.

I ask her if she will help me pack for camp next week. I do this for two reasons, the first of which is practical: She knows this camp, its activities, its microenvironments, and the appropriate clothing. But the second reason is more important: I have learned a lesson from our tandem bike experience. I am giving her an opportunity (small, yes, I know) to exercise her power, to show she knows more than I do, to take the reins. I can tell she is thrilled. Usually I am the one telling her to go upstairs and change out of the Killers T-shirt because we're going to a restaurant with tablecloths and that's just not how one dresses. I am the one telling her to wear shoes, not flip-flops, because it's thirty degrees outside.

Now she gets to dictate to me, and she warms to the idea immediately, offering tips and advice, telling me which jeans to bring, which sweatshirt to leave at home, that my flip-flops won't work, that I better remember extra batteries for the flashlight. She's in control. I vow to let this happen more often, to create appropriate opportunities for it to happen. Camp Wilani is her turf. I am going to try to acknowledge that every chance I get.

The next day, we're back in the car driving out to camp. Despite our conversation yesterday, it is still hard for me to believe that Lizzie is okay with this. (And, despite yesterday's resolve, I continue to struggle with the idea that *I* am okay with this.) When I told my friend Sarah a few weeks ago that Lizzie had agreed to my stint as a counselor, she was aghast. "She *what?*" Sarah said, practically yelling. "I can't have heard that right. She's letting you come to camp with her?" I nodded, smiling a little smugly. Okay, *a lot* smugly. "I would have *died* if my mother came within fifty miles of my camp," Sarah told me. My sentiments exactly.

As we drive out the winding highway west into the hills, I consider why exactly Lizzie is going along with this. And I think it's more complex and interesting than her desire to get a behind-the-scenes peek of camp operations through me as a counselor. After all, camp is where she is proudest and most confident about herself, and it thrills me that she wants to share this aspect of her identity rather than hold it close and separate from me as I wanted to do at her age. Clearly she trusts that making herself known, and thus making herself vulnerable, will be okay.

And this gives me hope: If she and I *had* been on the same path my mother and I traveled, maybe we were not on it now.

At camp, Lizzie heads off to her cabin with her sleeping bag and stuffed duffel. This week she will be what's called a TIA (teen in action). It's one rung below CIT (counselor in training) but one rung above Wrangler, which is what she was last week, which is one rung above regular, ordinary camper. I remember well how important the intracamp hierarchy can be, the doling out of rights and privileges, the status conferred by each successive rank as one moves up the ladder. The TIA position confers the following benefits: a cabin without a counselor, lights-out an hour later than regular campers, free time for several hours in the afternoon, and—best for last—a license to flirt with the male CITs. In exchange, TIAs are essentially kitchen grunts. Lizzie is not actually old enough to be a TIA—the girls are fourteen and fifteen—but because she's been a camper for four years and a Wrangler for two, the camp director has waived the age requirement.

I watch her disappear up the path and then I drive back home. I've decided to give her a day to settle in before I make my official appearance. Midmorning the next day, I am back meeting with Gecko, the assistant director, who greets me with enthusiasm and assigns me to a rotting, spider-infested little A-frame set in the woods. I grab my gear, kick open the door (the wood has swollen from years of rain, the hinges are loose and rusty), and breathe in the heady scent: carpet mold and damp towel mildew with base notes of dead mouse and western red cedar. It's awful but also familiar and endearing. Maybe not *that* endearing. I open the window to let in fresh air, but the screen is torn, and a squadron of mosquitoes, who appear to have been waiting for the opportunity, fly in. I drop my sleeping bag and leave before more than eight or nine of them can suck my blood. Back at the HQ, I am given an official counselor neckerchief and handed a printout of the weekly schedule.

I walk up the gravel path to the mess hall, where Gecko tells me he has scheduled my yoga classes, the first of which will begin after lunch today. Yoga was not my first choice when I was thinking about what I could offer as a counselor. But it turned out that my expertise (or rather, the things I still remember how to do)—tennis, softball, volleyball, water sports, horseback riding—were either not offered or already covered. That's when I came up with the rather unlikely idea of yoga counselor. I figured it was something campers could do, rain or shine, with no special equipment or dedicated space. My own yoga practice is barely a year old, so the notion of teaching others is (pun intended) quite a stretch. I try to keep in mind that an expert is just someone who knows a little more than you do.

In the lodge-style mess hall, the TIAs are finishing breakfast cleanup. Lizzie is in the dish pit with two other girls emptying stacks of clean, scalding plates from a dishwasher the size of a gorilla. She's trash-talking with one of the girls, her hair matted, her face flushed from the steam. The girls are busy; Papa Roach is blaring from a boom box. No one notices me as I stand in the doorway and watch. A good three minutes go by. Finally, Lizzie looks over and sees me.

"Mom!" she yells over the din. "You're here!" She gives me a spirited high five with her warm, moist palm. At this moment, I am exquisitely aware of the privilege she has conferred on me, and I don't want to mess up in any way. I keep quiet and wait for her to make the first move. She nudges me out of the kitchen and into the dining hall. I give her a quick hug, which she graciously accepts.

"I'm kinda scared about this whole yoga thing," I tell her. I am not being disingenuous—I *am* truly concerned—but I also want to make a point about my vulnerability, to emphasize my newbie status compared to hers as an old hand, to show her that I recognize her power. Here I am, not even an hour into this camp experience, blurring the lines between journalist-anthropologist and mom. But it feels okay. It feels, well, inevitable. I can't say no to the mother part of me, the part that wants to reach out and bring her close.

"I mean, I do know how to teach, and I do know a little yoga, but I have never taught yoga," I say. She gives me a grown-up look.

"You can do it, Mom," she says. "I have confidence in you."

That afternoon, my first yoga class with the six CITs goes well. They are four girls and two boys, all high school juniors, and they are more serious and obedient than kids would reasonably be expected to be at summer camp. That's because being a CIT here is part of a leadership program, and the kids get community service credit (necessary for high school graduation) for their participation. I guide them through the easy poses I know while offering the lilting, evocative instructions I've learned from my own teachers: Open the windows of your heart, let the sunlight of your breath shine through . . . The kids think I know what I'm doing— "Thank you, Lotus," one of the boys says after class, "that was awesome"— which is a relief. I feel I have established a camp identity.

After class, I walk down a forest path with no destination in mind. I hear the *whoosh* of the wind through the trees, smell damp earth and cedar, listen to the *thwack* of arrows hitting hay bales over at the archery range. I wander between the arts and crafts cabin, what is known as "the bald meadow" (a dirt parking lot), the tepees and the small cold swimming pool, where I listen to and participate in the same kind of fragmentary, desultory conversation I remember from my own camp days. How lovely not to be listening to adult talk about book tours or bathroom remodeling but rather who made the biggest splash with a cannonball and how mean Squirrel was to last year's TIAs and whether Captain Bones's tattoos are cool or kinda scary. I run into Lizzie several times during the afternoon—she's painting a sign at arts and crafts, she's walking a young camper out to the horse corral, she's flirting with a counselor—and I play it cool. I smile and nod. She does too.

At seven the next morning, there's a soft rain falling as I make my way from my A-frame to the mess hall. I can hear the rain, but I can't feel it. The tree canopy is so dense that very little rain gets through to the forest floor.

"Good morning," says Donald Duck. Donald Duck is a Gulf War vet with PTSD and Tourette's syndrome who is serving as camp nurse this week. He's a big guy who sweats a lot. He is also a very nice guy. The kids seem to take his clicks, blinks, and twitches in stride.

Lizzie walks in, slightly bleary-eyed. The rest of the TIAs file in. They have already formed cliques—a few came with friends, the others have formed twosomes or threesomes—and I see Lizzie is not included. A year or two difference means a lot at this age. Lizzie, who looks mature to me with her eyeliner and her straight hair slicked across her forehead, looks like a little kid next to these girls. Her face is soft and round, her skin unblemished. She has braces. It's obvious that she hasn't found a place among these fourteen- and fifteen-year-olds. I know that must be painful, and I know I can't do a thing about it.

Lizzie comes to her own defense, though. She starts hanging out with the girl CITs who go to the same high school as Lizzie's older brother and think he's cool. They treat her kindly, indulge her like a little sister. I listen in, without seeming to, as they talk for fifteen mind-numbing minutes about earlobe stretching and the relative merits of hard-cartilage and soft-cartilage piercing.

Lizzie has also found another niche to inhabit this week. Courtesy of my counselor status, she begins showing up at the staff table after meals, sitting next to me, joking with the staff, pretending not to eavesdrop on their conversations. In the mornings she is sleepy and sometimes sullen—the TIAs stay up past midnight in their cabin and are awoken at 6:30 a.m. to start their kitchen duties. After lunch and dinner her mood is better. But it doesn't matter, really, what her mood is or if she talks to me. I figure she's here mostly to breathe the rarefied air of staff and to impress her peers with the fact that she can sit at the staff table. I don't care. What matters to me is that she is not only okay with being seen with me, she is going out of her way to be seen with me. This is different from when she allowed me to sit in the back of classrooms at school. This is an open acknowledgment, a kind of public proclamation of our relationship. Donald Duck dubs her "Little Lotus." She chucks me on the arm. "Cool," she says.

Captain Bones is in charge of the TIAs. He's a short, burly, talkative, multitattooed twenty-year-old who dropped out of high school at fifteen, the same year he (illegally) acquired the first of his thirty tattoos. He has swirls of bone in his ears, the holes of which have been stretched to half-inch openings. He has a nose piercing, a lip piercing, an orange-tinted Mohawk, and one of the few day jobs (other than tattoo artist or body piercer) that a person who looks like he does can have: He is a part-time barista at an edgy urban coffeehouse. You wouldn't think, by the look of him, that he would be counselor material, let alone a counselor for a dozen teenaged girls. But you'd be wrong. I have watched him with the girls. He is relaxed and offhand but also thoughtful and interested. Lizzie, who is *very* interested in the fact that Cap'n, or Bones, as he is also called, and I are engaged in spirited conversation at the staff breakfast table, says he is "awesome." My detached self takes careful note of his role-model position, while my mother self silently prays Lizzie doesn't want to stretch her earlobes, not to mention drop out of high school.

Cap'n wants the girls ("my girls," as he refers to them) to be a team, which they aren't. He tells me this with a sense of concern and an earnestness you would simply not expect from a guy who looks exactly like the guy you never, ever want your daughter to date. He has given the girls spiral notebooks and asked them to keep journals. "Write anything you want," he tells them. "Don't be afraid to say what's on your mind. I won't judge you. I'm not your parent."

The arts and crafts picnic table is, I am discovering, a very good place to hang out. The TIAs congregate there when they aren't setting up or cleaning up in the mess hall. It's pleasant and shady, and the arts and crafts counselor, Squee, a laconic eighteen-year-old boy, is, for reasons I cannot fathom (perhaps because I am not a teenage girl), hot stuff. The little kids go to their next activity, but the TIAs remain. Lizzie ambles over. She is at arts and crafts whenever she doesn't have to be elsewhere. A whiter-shade-of-pale TIA, with the same matte black dyed hair as half the other TIAs, sits on the bench next to Lizzie. She has brought her spiral notebook with her, the one that Cap'n gave out to all the TIAs. I ask her what she thinks about keeping a journal. What I'm hoping is that she and maybe one or two of the others sitting around the table— and maybe even Lizzie—will start talking about what they've written in their journals. Write about whatever is on your mind, Cap'n told them. What a coup that would be, my finding out what they think. But no such luck.

"I don't write what I'm thinking about," Pale Face tells me. "If I wrote what was really on my mind, Cap'n would just think I was crazy."

"I don't write anything in the book," another girl says. "Ya know why?

I, like, lost it, like five seconds after I got it." The girls laugh. I catch Lizzie's eye. I wish she would say something. I wonder—okay, I am dying to know—what, if anything, she has written in her notebook.

My fourth day as Lotus. I am in front of the mess hall on my rubber mat with eighteen kids—TIAs and CITs—in front of me, and they are all doing yoga! Amazingly, astonishingly, Lizzie has asked whether she can be at the head of the class with me. I am not sure what to make of this. Is she not only *not* embarrassed to have me around but actually *proud* to be associated with me?

Maybe some switch flipped, and for a moment she saw me not as her mother but as a competent adult woman, a woman whom other people (teens! her cohorts!) seem to respect. And then the switch flipped back and she realized, hey, this is my mother, and I can go right up there and be part of what she's doing. Or maybe my counselor status confers status on her, which she needs if she is to hold her own with these girls who are one or two years her senior. Or she woke up in a terrific mood, her brain awash in dopamine. I am going to go with the "proud to be associated with me" interpretation. I don't want to hope for too much, or expect too much, but this morning it feels as if we've come a long distance from the days of icy stares and slamming doors.

I must remember this, burn this image into my mind: Lizzie in her black tank top with hemp and bead necklace, black gym shorts, eyes closed, going through asanas on my right. My eyes are focused on the group in front of me. I think she likes that. I am not making her feel self-conscious. I do sneak a peek every once in a while. She is looking at me, studying the pose, mirroring my stance. I almost can't concentrate because of how elated I am, how good it makes me feel to have my daughter by my side. In this moment, my disparate roles come together effortlessly. I observe her yet I also feel close to her.

We end with a long savasana. I bring them through progressive relaxation, talk them through breathing. "You can come to this place of peace any time you want," I tell them. "This place is within you and within your control. If you are angry, you can come to this place. If you are upset, you can come here. Here is where you can let go of whatever you need to be free of." I listen hard to my own words.

The afternoon stretches on forever, the sun streaming through the trees, the soft insistent heat. I wander. I sit at the arts and crafts picnic table and watch. I teach another yoga class. And still it is only four p.m. At home the afternoon goes by in a blink. I answer e-mails, run an errand in town, and that's it. Here I forget time, and it forgets me. This afternoon, right now, this is what it feels like to be a kid, what it feels like to meander without thought or plan, to just let the day unfold, to just be. I have been focusing on how close to grown-up Lizzie is, but this week at camp reminds me that she still has some childhood left. Lucky her. For maybe the first time, it occurs to me that everything about these early teen years is not melodrama and conflict, temper and mood, storms and skirmishes. There is, in fact, something special and precious about being thirteen, about inhabiting that narrow space between girl and woman. I am seeing Lizzie in both roles here at camp, and I remember—of course, I knew this!—what it was like to straddle adulthood, to move without thinking between the simple joys of childhood and the challenges and confusions of growing up, to be both and neither, to exist in a near-constant state of confused exaltation.

It's my last afternoon at camp. I go to the general store—a little shack staffed by a brooding nineteen-year-old who goes by the camp name Shark Bait. I go to buy two friendship bracelets, one for Lizzie and one for me. They are flimsy, cheap things, fifty cents apiece, braided hemp with seven little beads woven in. There is a choice of five different bead colors. Red is for love; yellow is for peace. The amethyst stands for strength, the little booklet says. I buy two amethyst bracelets and carry them around in the pocket of my cargo shorts for the rest of the afternoon, thinking about what the best time would be to give one to Lizzie. The bracelets will seal our camp bond, commemorate that part of our week together that was mother-daughter. I envision a little ceremony, with me tying the bracelet on her wrist, and with her doing the same for me. I get sweaty just thinking about how heartwarming this will be.

I wait until just before dinner. I can't bear to eat another camp meal, so I am heading back home early. Lizzie and I walk to her cabin to gather up some dirty clothes for me to take home. There are no shelves in the cabins. The kids just throw the clothes on the floor, wet swimsuits or towels on top of jeans, grimy socks tossed on top of clean underwear. The air inside my A-frame may be rank, but her cabin smells worse. I figure taking the damp and dirty clothes home with me will make packing easier for her tomorrow.

But as we walk up the rickety porch steps and into her cabin, I make a mistake, a mistake I don't realize until it's too late: In the blink of an eye—my eye that is, my eye taking in the heap of filthy clothes by Lizzie's cot—my two roles collide, and mom easily aces out detached observer. I should be looking at the mess in front of me and thinking about how I will later describe it in words. Instead, I am looking at the mess in front of me and thinking about how I will have to triple wash it when I get home. I am no longer the cool counselor Lotus who Lizzie likes being around. I am no longer the objective onlooker studying teen girl interactions. I am the judgmental mom.

The shift is seamless, unconscious, unnoticeable to me. But had there been a surveillance camera in the cabin that early August afternoon, I am sure it would have caught me with a disapproving look on my face picking through the damp, dirty pile of clothes, lifting each piece with exaggerated delicacy, thumb and forefinger pinched, so as not to sully myself. The audio would have picked up a deep, discontented sigh. And I'm betting I probably said something like, "I can't believe this mess," or "How can you even think about wearing these clothes?" or maybe just "Oh. My. God."

I was on autopilot. Or, to switch metaphors, I was reciting lines by rote, not thinking about their meaning or impact, not even thinking about the play—the too-familiar play—I had, without realizing it, started to act in again. When I think this through later, in the car on the way home, I realize that my reaction had little to do with the dirty clothes. Dirty clothes are dirty clothes. What did I expect after a week in the woods? The pile of clothes was just a trigger. The thought process it triggered—so quick I didn't catch it—went like this: dirty clothes . . . more work for me . . . she has no idea how hard I work . . . ungrateful kid. And, dirty clothes . . . that means back to doing laundry . . . and shopping and e-mail and to-do lists . . . which means the end to this magical time for me. That's a lot to read into a pair of jeans, muddy sneakers, and a few soggy pairs of socks.

At the moment, though, stuffing the clothes into a big plastic bag and lugging it out onto the porch, I am oblivious to how I am acting, and why. I am just pissed. I set the bag down, sighing (I bet), offering a final tsk-tsk (I am sure). Then I remember the bracelets.

"I've got something for you, Liz," I say, reaching into my pocket for the two friendship bracelets. Although I have barely caught my breath after ragging at her, I am determined to play out this scene I've mentally rehearsed, this sweetheart ending I've imagined. I put the bracelets in the palm of my hand and show her. "They're from arts and crafts," I say. "I'll tie yours on if you tie mine." She glances at my palm, then quickly away. Her face is stony. It's payback time.

"Oh," she says, not making a move to take one. "They are, like, really, really cheap. I would *never* wear one of them."

I cry in the car for the first ten miles. For the next ten, I replay the scene in my head and curse myself for blowing what had otherwise been an incredible week.

Driving back out to camp the next morning to pick up Lizzie, I rehearse my apology. But it turns out that both my overreaction and hers are, for her, already ancient history. I hardly get through my "I was such a jerk yesterday . . ." preface when she interrupts. "No problem," she says. Her tone is part dismissive, part forgiving—but mostly uninterested. She wants to talk about the funny skits the counselors performed at the final evening campfire. She wants to talk about bringing more makeup with her for next week at camp, another session as a TIA. She wants to stop at Starbucks for an iced mocha.

FIFTEEN

Another week of summer camp is almost over. I'll pick up Lizzie tomorrow and find out how the session went for her, how well she adjusted to her second stint as a TIA kitchen grunt, if any of the one- and two-year-older girls befriended her, if she missed me. (Okay, I don't actually wonder about that last one. I am not *that* self-deluded. And really, I wouldn't *want* her to miss me.) But I do hope she retains a few memories of our week together—up to, but not including, my laundry meltdown. I am thinking happy camplike thoughts when the phone rings. The camp director, Goofy, is on the line. "Lizzie is okay," she says, quickly, correctly assessing that I will think bear mauling or snakebite as soon as I hear her voice. I wonder why she's calling. Maybe she wants me to come back for another yoga week? But no, this call is about Lizzie. She's not hurt. She's in trouble.

It turns out that she was out after curfew, missing from her cabin for several hours the night before. This is a major no-no. As the TIAs have no counselor in their cabin and no bed checks, her sin would have gone unnoticed had not two of her cabinmates ratted her out to Captain Bones this morning, saying that she didn't get back to the cabin until maybe two a.m. No one knows when she returned, really—the girls were just guessing—and no one but Lizzie knows exactly where she went and what she did. Goofy tells me that Captain questioned her first, which was quickly followed by a series of interrogations by other staffers. Lizzie told them she wandered around the camp and fessed up to visiting three places during her meanderings: a group of cabins for younger kids where she hung out with the on-duty counselor, the counselor's retreat cabin (off-limits to all but the staff), and the horse corral, where Lizzie said she went "to have alone time and look at the stars." These late-night wanderings would be bad enough in the eyes of the camp staff, but there is more.

It turns out that right around the same time Lizzie was missing, two male counselors were also MIA for a few hours. One of the counselors, Goofy tells me, was the kid who calls himself Squee. I am not happy to hear this. I know this kid. I observed Lizzie and this kid all week when I was Lotus. Most of Lizzie's free time—sometimes as much as two or three hours a day—was spent at the arts and crafts area where Squee presided as counselor. Lizzie would sprawl on one of the picnic table benches watching the little kids paint wooden plaques and make lanyards, or she'd joke with the slightly older kids who, uninterested in the planned projects, would paint each other's forearms with tempera or construct elaborate traps for spiders. Sometimes she joined in or helped with the activities, but it was obvious that she was there for another reason, this boy. At first I thought that he just put up with her. He was bored, and she was company. But as the week progressed, I began to see that it was not boredom—or at least, not just boredom. He was complimented by the attention she was paying to him. And, although he hid it well beneath a thick veneer of teen taciturnity, he was interested.

I was not thrilled. It did not inspire confidence that this kid's nom de camp was Squee, a fictional character in a distressing goth comic book series called *Johnny the Homicidal Maniac.* I know this cultural reference not because I am preternaturally hip, but because, like all the other instant experts out there, I Googled it and read the Wikipedia entry. Anyway, the comic book character Squee's mother is addicted to prescription pain meds, and his father hates him so much that he declares him mentally unstable and commits him to the "Defective Head Meat Institute." Nice clean fun. Makes you wonder about the counselor Squee's family life. I didn't want to read too much into his name selection, but, knowing Lizzie's penchant for kids with issues, I certainly took note. But I did not shift into overdrive about all this. Camp activities are supervised, all out in the open and good clean fun. If Lizzie had a little crush on a slightly sketchy older guy, so what? It could not develop into anything I need worry about—and camp would be over in a few weeks anyway.

But now, when I learn that Squee was missing for the same hours Lizzie was missing, I begin imagining . . . no, not imagining, but once again catastrophizing. I am already most of the way to statutory rape before I tune back into what Goofy is saying. She doesn't think anything bad happened, but she is very upset about what she so carefully calls Lizzie's "poor choices." There will be consequences.

Her voice is grave. This is a big deal. Squee has already been fired. Lizzie, Goofy says, will not be allowed to come back to camp for the final two weeks this summer. We talk for a half hour, then talk again later that afternoon. I want to get the complete story from Lizzie—assuming she will tell me—but the more I think it through, the less I am concerned that something truly bad happened to her last night. Maybe it's because I trust in her strength and common sense. Maybe it's because I perceive Squee as self-conscious and relatively nonthreatening, certainly not a predator. At the end of the second long phone call, I am more angry than concerned. I am angry at the camp for the lack of supervision that allowed this to happen. I am angrier at Lizzie for abusing the privilege she was given, the opportunity to be a TIA a year early. And I am embarrassed that she was so irresponsible. These camp people know me. I am not some invisible parent of an errant daughter. I am—I was for a week—a member of the camp family. Wait 'til I get my hands on her.

Underneath the anger, though, and the knee-jerk response, I am deeply conflicted about how to handle this situation. I remember all the stunts I pulled at summer camp—the midnight raids to the boys' cabins, the clandestine rendezvous with the boy du jour at the rifle range, sneaking smokes behind the social hall, going AWOL to a secret spot by the lake. My daughter's infraction is, truth be told, nowhere near as heinous as some of the things I did (and got away with). But I can't tell her that, can I? I mean, I *could* tell her, and it would momentarily bring us closer, but wouldn't it also abrogate my responsibilities as a parent? In fact, bonding over our mutual bad behavior at summer camp seems to me a classic "Best Bud" Mom move—the misguided mother who wants to *share* the teenage experience with her daughter—pulled from the pages of that book I read last fall, *When We're in Public, Pretend You Don't Know Me.*

In my efforts to draw closer to her, I can't be a teenager myself. I still must be her mother.

I am struggling with the fact that I want honesty from her, but I am not prepared to be honest in return. It's not at all that I want Lizzie to think I am flawless. She knows I'm not. I point out my own weaknesses for her to see. I apologize for bad moves. It's more that I don't want her to think that if bad behavior was okay for her mom—after all, I survived—then it's okay for her. I want to be a role model, but not *that* kind of role model. So I will keep my checkered past to myself when Lizzie and I talk about what she did or did not do last night. Meanwhile, Goofy calls a third time, and we work out a compromise: Lizzie cannot return to camp next week, but she can come back the following week—just not as a TIA. She will be demoted back to her own age group, a Wrangler.

In the car the next afternoon, Lizzie is unusually silent—not contrite exactly, more like holding her breath waiting for the big wave to hit. But the big wave is not going to hit. I now understand that I am my worst self in attack mode, and Lizzie is at her worst when put on the defensive. The challenge right now is to hold her responsible, to have high expectations, to enforce rules but not to act out of anger. The challenge is to be both strong-minded and loving. I am working on it. I take a deep breath. "So," I ask, "what happened? Tell me what happened the night before last."

Lizzie is taken aback that I'm not yelling. Good. I haven't pushed her to the battlements. But she recovers quickly, and within seconds is close to copping an attitude. She swears she just wandered around alone. She swears she never saw Squee that night. "Anyway, Mom. He's just a friend. Like we're brother and sister. That's all." She knows, she says, that leaving the cabin after curfew was the wrong thing to do. "Blah, blah, blah," she says, shooting me a sidelong look to see if she exceeded the bounds. (She did, my hard squint tells her.) But she just doesn't consider it a big deal. She doesn't know what all the fuss is about. "I mean I walked around. That's it." I am not going to get anything more out of her, assuming that there is more to get. But I am left unsatisfied, left imagining my daughter, who doesn't like the dark, who doesn't like things that scurry around in the dark, meandering along little dirt paths through the forest at midnight. It does not compute.

But I will not spend the rest of the drive home interrogating her. If I do, I will get nowhere. No. That's not true. I will get *some*where: I will get frustrated and angry. Then she'll lash out and make a particularly cutting remark, and I'll go from angry to wounded. And when this melodrama ends, I will have failed to discover what happened at camp. But I will have succeeded in opening up an emotional space between us. So I turn on the radio, and we drive home the rest of the way without conversation.

Meanwhile, my husband has gone ballistic on the subject of Squee, on even the remote possibility that something happened between them during Lizzie's after-hours adventures. "What would an eighteen-year-old boy want with Lizzie?" he asks me that night after she is in bed. "I *know* boys that age. *I* was a boy that age."

But I have one very sharp, very clear memory that prevents me from conceding his point. I was a year older than Lizzie is, when, during a brief vacation with my family, I met and developed a mad crush on Wayne, an Atlantic City hotel pool boy. And by "boy" I mean a nineteen-year-old, out-of-high-school guy. I was in ninth grade, but Wayne thought I was sixteen. That could have been because I told him I was sixteen. When we left for home, Wayne asked for my address and then he proceeded to write me letters.

About a month and a half later, he showed up at the door of my parents' house having driven from Atlantic City to Long Island just to see me. I was beside myself with joy. My father was not. "This guy only wants one thing," he said as a prelude to why he wasn't going to allow me to leave the house with him. I knew my father was wrong. If Wayne wanted "one thing," he could easily get it back in A.C. from any of the girls who hung out at the pool. I was deeply, deeply offended that my father thought so little of me—or at least that's how I took his remark—that he figured there was only this one reason a guy would be interested in me. (For the record, he was wrong. Wayne and I had long talks and a few chaste kisses. We corresponded for almost a year.)

And so, I am quick to counter my husband, to defend Lizzie's integrity and thus, not meaning to, Squee's honor. I sound more sure of myself than I am, which is often the case. We talk about this—okay, we argue— for at least an hour. In the end, though, we agree that we don't have to take any action. Lizzie is already being punished by a week's banishment from camp. Squee has been fired. The chances that Lizzie will ever see him again are slim.

In the car two days later while we are out running errands, Lizzie asks me to put in the CD of "that girl who wrote all those songs only she didn't sing them other people did and got famous." She means the new Carole King CD I bought on impulse at Starbucks last week. Halfway through the first song, she asks me what I think about younger girls and older boys dating.

"What's so bad about an age difference?" she asks.

"Well," I say, *very* interested to see where this is going, "how young is the girl?" She doesn't answer. "Like maybe, um, thirteen?" I say. She nods. "And how old would the boy be?" I ask. Silence. "Like, say, eighteen?" She nods. Now we're getting somewhere.

I tell her not that an eighteen-year-old boy has only one thing on his mind, because truthfully I don't know and never did know what was on the mind of an eighteen-year-old boy (or, for that matter, a forty-year-old man). But I tell her that some eighteen-year-old boys have had consider-able experience dating, that a lot of them have had sex already, and that the way they look at girls is affected by this. The thirteen-year-old girl probably hasn't had those kinds of experiences and really lives in a dif-ferent girl-boy world. She is listening.

"I don't mean that it's all about sex," I say. "I know there are many reasons a guy, whatever age, would be interested in a girl, whatever age. But there could be problems you—I mean, this thirteen-year-old girl we're talking about—haven't thought of."

"Like what?"

"Well, like how this younger girl might really look up to and respect this older guy and might be swayed by things he says. Like trying weed, for example. Or drinking." She considers, or appears to consider, this.

"So," I say, ready to get real, "this whole younger girl, older boy thing . . . is this a hypothetical question or is something going on?"

"What does that mean . . . hypothetical?" she asks. I explain.

She is quiet for almost half of one of Carole King's songs. "Um, well, yeah, something's going on," she says, finally. I am on instant alert. She senses this and immediately backpedals. "Well, not *really actually* going on, but, well . . ."

"But, well, *what?* So you and Squee are not 'brother and sister' like you said?"

"I told you that because I thought I'd just ease you into the idea," she says.

"What idea?"

"Um, like last night, on the phone, he asked me out."

I make myself take two full deep belly breaths, Lotus-style. Then I say, as calmly as I can and with what I hope is resonant finality, "That's just not going to happen." Lizzie is silent, but I can tell by how she squares her shoulders that she hasn't given up.

All this long week of Lizzie's exile from camp, she and Squee are apparently talking on the phone. I don't monitor her calls or quiz her afterward, but I know there is contact because every day she offers a new piece of information about him: He lives with his grandparents. He has an older sister. He's going on a trip to California. And I know it because, several times this week, she floats the idea of going to the movies with him. And several times this week, I say no. Tom continues to rail about what eighteen-year-old boys want. I continue to struggle with ambivalence, wanting to protect my daughter but also wanting to believe that some older guy could like her just because she's likable and not because of all the nasty things he thinks he could do to her.

Thankfully, as the week progresses, the intensity of the situation diminishes. Lizzie is in contact with other friends. She plays Ultimate Frisbee with her brothers. We all see a movie. Life goes on. I shift my focus, just as Lizzie does, from the week that was to the upcoming week. Although the camp director and I have reached an agreement that Lizzie may return, I tell Lizzie only that Goofy will *consider* allowing her to return if she receives a letter of explanation and apology. Lizzie is not much of a writer, and she isn't as repentant as she might be, so it takes several days of increasingly pointed suggestions—also known as nagging—to get her to write it. But she does, and in doing so I think she comes to terms with why Goofy and the folks at camp saw her transgressions as serious business, even if she didn't. Now we're set: Lizzie is off to a full week in the woods away from the siren songs of inappropriately aged boys.

I am off on my own adventure, six days of alpine hiking in remote eastern British Columbia, trekking ten to twelve miles a day along ridges and through glaciated canyons, up and down traverses, along the sides of mountains, climbing twenty-two hundred vertical feet my last day. It is part of an intense fitness, detox, boot camp experience that, for reasons that elude my family and every one of my friends, I adore. I return invigorated, severely bruised, and ready to dive back into the much more strenuous life of being the mother of a teenage girl.

The morning after I return home, I drive out to pick up Lizzie from her final week at camp. This was the week she had to prove herself, to show how hardworking and spirited she is, what a great camper she is, how that last week was an aberration. She has grand plans for being a counselor at this camp someday, so getting back in their good graces is important. There are important life lessons here too: Actions have consequences. People judge you by what you do. Taking responsibility for mistakes is important. I promise myself not to deliver any lectures. She needs to learn this herself—and I think she is.

When I drive up the steep dirt road to the dining hall where she is waiting with her gear, I can see, immediately, the week has been good. She wears her emotion on her face and carries it in her body just like I do. With us, there's no pretending. She is filthy and beaming, leaning over the railing on the dining hall porch, chatting with a girl who I assume was a cabinmate. I drive past slowly, waving, then watch her from the rearview mirror as I pull into a spot past the building. She is hugging her counselor, Snickers. As I walk toward them, I hear Snickers say, "That was an awesome week, Liz. You were great." Captain Bones, lazing on the steps, stands up and gives her a hug.

In the car, Lizzie is ebullient. "This was the best week ever," she tells me. She was one of nine Wranglers—twelve- and thirteen-year-old girls—who worked with the horses, saddling and grooming them, mucking stalls, holding reins and walking the little kids around the corral. Miss Patty, the horse owner, loved her, Lizzie says. And she really got along with the girls in her cabin. What a difference it makes that she was with girls her own age this week. Placing her with the TIAs—only a year older but out of her league—was, I can see now, a mistake. In fact, her wandering that night might have been a "see how cool I am" response to feeling alienated from the group. I hadn't thought about motivation before, but this makes sense.

I listen delightedly as Lizzie regales me with camp tales. The night before, her cabinmates had done up her hair with a curling iron for the final dance party. There was a silly intrigue. A seven-year-old boy, the cousin of her counselor, had a big crush on her, a fact that was communicated with much giggling and whispering and ended with Lizzie graciously asking him to dance. Apparently, his head came to the bottom of her rib cage. "He was so cute," she says. Another night all the girls in the cabin stayed up until two a.m. evaluating the hotness quotients of all the male counselors. And best of all, she stepped up. She took on extra work. She volunteered. She redeemed herself, and, even though she might have thought she didn't need redemption, she is very proud.

I am too, and I tell her so. She is a joy to be with this morning. We are two high-spirited girls who've just spent great weeks outdoors; we're strong, healthy, and feeling our oats. She says she is getting excited about starting eighth grade in a month, and she's going to do better in school, and her braces will be off soon, and maybe we can buy a curling iron, and the day she gets her braces off she can go to school with a new hairstyle and new clothes, maybe even—here she looks meaningfully at me—a skirt.

"I need a new look, Mom," she says, my fashion queen who wore the same pair of grungy jeans with interchangeable black T-shirts and cheap silver jewelry (the earrings turning the holes in her ears green) all through seventh grade. She talks nonstop. Now she's talking about her future, about college, and that maybe she wants to go to vet school after or maybe she might be a counselor for teens because, she says—no irony felt or intended, no sense of our tumultuous history—"not everyone can talk to their mothers like I can talk to you." Whew.

I know the exuberance will fade, and that tomorrow or sooner she will forget about the new hairstyle and the new clothes and the plans to go shopping. She will insist that she never said she would work harder in school. We've been down this road before. If she were not a teen, this gush of uberenthusiasm, this hyperbolic outpouring of good will and great intentions (inevitably followed by surliness and ill temper) would qualify as proof of mental illness. I know I am hearing the unedited outpouring of her incompletely wired work-in-progress brain, but I am learning to love it. I love hearing about her big dreams and great ideas. It's okay that this glorious mood will fade. I intend to enjoy it as long as it lasts.

When we get home, she runs upstairs to flop on her bed, and I begin unpacking her duffel. The jeans are so matted with dirt that they are actually stiff. I have to throw away half the socks. Below the mildewing towel, I find an empty can of men's deodorant, a black tie, a red ribbon, a large Tupperware container with Oreo crumbs, and an envelope with photos of the week, including one with Lizzie beside her favorite horse. Lizzie is leaning against the horse's long neck. The smile on her face is so blissful that I stand there and stare at the photo for a full minute, transfixed. There's a big envelope at the bottom of the bag, and, without thinking much about it, I open it. Inside, there's a note from her counselor, Snickers ("You go girl. Great week!"), printouts of several e-mails my husband and I sent to her that week, and the thin spiral notebook that Captain Bones gave all the TIAs at the beginning of camp. I (shamelessly) open it and see that the first few pages are covered with my daughter's sloppy printing. I am about to (shamefully) close it and throw it on the pile with her toiletries bag when my eye catches the first sentence:

"When I was eight, I got raped behind my elementary school." What? My knees almost buckle. I have to sit down on the boot bench. I feel sick.

"When I was eleven, I got molested by my best friend Evan." Evan? I know Evan. I feel hot and cold at the same time. I run to the bathroom to throw up. Then I sit back down on the boot bench, spread the book open on my lap, and read the rest.

"Just a month ago, I had a crush on Moose at day camp, and I guess he knew so he took advantage of that and molested me. I wonder to myself, 'Are all guys like this?' Why aren't they just interested in getting to know me? I haven't met many guys who just want to sit down and talk. It's like they all want to take advantage of the girl and feel their power. Yesterday I did strange marks on myself with a knife so I can remember what pain bad boys gave me. I can't tell anyone this because whenever I think about it, it feels like I can't speak, like I don't know how to talk all of a sudden."

It goes on like this for a while. I want to stop reading so I can catch my breath, so I can think, so I can pull back from the panic I feel. But the sentence at the top of the last page grabs me, and I read on.

"Is weed bad? My friends do it all the time at school. Should I do it? The answer is NO but I do it anyway. I just got so tired of people asking and asking. Am I bad? I have no idea, and I don't really care if I am good or bad. It's my life and I get to do whatever I want with it. It's nobody else's business."

I finish reading and close the notebook. I feel light-headed, my skin sharp and prickly, like I've just downed a triple shot of espresso. What should I do? I think about doing nothing, about keeping this information close to the chest, waiting for a time to slowly draw out Lizzie in a conversation. I think about calling my friend Sarah and unloading on her. I think about walking out to my husband's office and showing him the pages.

But I don't do any of those things. I do what I have to, what I must, what I knew I would do the moment I started reading. I bolt upstairs, notebook in hand, calling to Lizzie. She comes out of her room, looking soft and pink. She's taken a shower, and her hair is clean and straight. I ask her to sit down on the steps next to me. I try to keep my voice steady, but it starts to crack. I search for words but find I don't have any. I hand her the notebook and look at her, searching her face, her eyes, for something, I don't know what.

"Lizzie," I hear myself say, "Lizzie, honey, is this true?" I don't pause to give her a chance to answer. Now that I found my voice, I can't stop talking. "I found this in your bag from camp and I'm sorry but I read it and I don't know what it's all about but I am so scared and worried and please tell me what's going on, please talk to me." I stop only because I've run out of breath.

"Oh, Mom," she says, putting a hand on my shoulder, "that's a story I'm writing. It's a story."

"A story?" This had never occurred to me. "Since when do you write stories?" My brain attempts a 180 but can't quite manage it. "You mean this didn't all happen to you? You weren't raped behind the elementary school? Evan didn't molest you?"

"Geez, Mom, it's a *story*," she says patiently.

"But you write 'I.' You write like this happened to you."

"Well, yeah," she says. "Um, Mom, like it's called *first person?*"

"Okay, so you mean this *didn't* happen to you?" I am still in shock, still not comprehending. Now it gets through to her what I was thinking when I read these pages, and she pats me on the shoulder, our roles reversed.

"See," she says, "I had this idea for a story, a book, really, for teenage girls because so much stuff can happen. I mean all these people tell me at camp about things that have happened to them, but they haven't told anyone else. And I think maybe I could write about it, and then lots of girls could read it and not feel so alone in what they are thinking."

I am half listening while surreptitiously checking out her arms and legs for cut marks. I see none. Now I am able to focus on what she's saying. She tells me her idea: a book with three main characters, two girls—one troubled, one supposedly perfect (but it turns out her parents are all screwed up)—and a boy who is just figuring out that he's gay. Each chapter will be in a character's voice, all first person, but three different people.

She is full of ideas, narrative twists, subplots, supporting characters. If I had a twinge of doubt that she was making all this up, telling me she was writing a story when really these pages are about her and her own experiences, I do not doubt now. She has so obviously thought through this whole idea. She even has names for the characters. Not only has my daughter not been raped, mauled, or molested; not only is she not smoking weed with her friends; she is imagining and working on a project that will help kids who confided in her—kids with issues, the kids she seeks out and who seek her out.

Maybe it's because my brain is bruised from the workout it just got. Maybe I'm in a suspended state because of the emotional distance I've traveled in the course of the last fifteen minutes—panic, shock, numbness, confusion, pride. Or maybe I am overcome by her earnestness, her compassion, the force of her intelligence. Whatever the case, I forget for a moment that this book is undoubtedly another temporary enthusiasm, a manic phase idea. This notebook will probably sit, unopened, in one of her desk drawers. But really, does it matter? Her sensitivity toward others, her inclination to nurture and help—these are not part of a transitory mood. This is part of who she is, who she is becoming. I see the "friends with issues" issue in a different context. I want to tell her this. But I don't want to bury her under my own insights. Anyway, she knows. I was the one who didn't know.

I give her a long, hard hug.

SIXTEEN

I t's the dog days of late August, those endless, hot, dry afternoons, the sky bleached white around the edges, oak leaves brittle on the trees, pavement that burns feet through sandals, that big, bright, unrelenting, energy-sapping sun. Vacation trips have been taken, camp is over, school has not yet begun. It's the dead zone, a week or two that feels as if all the juice had been sucked out of it. I am caught between wanting to hold on to the fading magic of the season and wishing that the temperature would drop and the rains would come and we could all settle into a fall routine. Lizzie is, as I was at her age and at this moment, at loose ends. But where I would have been trying to lose myself in a book, Lizzie is tethered to the phone and the computer.

With camp over, the memory of Squee is (thankfully) fading, although I know there is still some communication going on. Lizzie makes occasional, increasingly halfhearted attempts to persuade me—she has completely given up on my husband—to allow her to go to the movies with this boy, but her attention has clearly shifted. She is thinking about the future. She is not thinking about school—eighth grade begins in a week—she is thinking about boys. Or rather, boy. Damon, her sweet-faced boyfriend from last school year, will be starting high school. Lizzie, of course, will still be in middle school. Because of our trip to California followed by the camp season, Lizzie and Damon have spent hardly any time together since their top-of-the-butte Fourth of July misadventure. But a few days ago, we ran into Damon and his father at Trader Joe's, and now he's on the front burner again.

They begin talking on the phone most every night. As I have not yet sunk so low as to listen at the door (although, I admit, I think about it), I don't know what's going on. I ask Lizzie if they have any plans to get together before school starts. Maybe he can come over and watch a movie, I say. No, she says, after the third night of long talks behind closed doors. Damon is "grounded forever" and won't be able to do anything with her this weekend or next weekend or any time in between. I feel bad for her. I think Damon is a nice kid. One time, months ago, when Damon spent an afternoon at our house, I walked in on him and Lizzie as they were watching a movie. Damon's arm was around Lizzie's shoulder. With his free hand he was brushing a strand of her hair from her face. It was such a gentle move, so endearing. I have liked the boy ever since.

"So, why is he grounded?" I ask Lizzie.

"I don't want to tell you," she says.

I have learned that sometimes it doesn't matter how earnest and well meaning, or how open-minded and accessible, or how nonjudgmental, or even how lighthearted and quirky I think I am being, she just won't talk to me. But then other times, it doesn't take that much coaxing to get her to talk. I believe I've discovered the secret: She'll spill the beans if I stay cool and nonchalant, if I pretend not to care too much. I offer her a half smile and tilt my head—subtle, but I hope encouraging, body language.

"Well," she says, eyeing me closely, "his father found a bag of weed in his backpack."

Shit. I think this, but don't say it. A big reaction will shut her up.

"So," I say, not casually, because this isn't casual, but not in full Reefer Madness panic either, "he smokes weed?"

"Yeah."

"He's smoked in front of you?" Do I want to know the answer to this?

"No," she says. "But remember when we ran into him and his dad at Trader Joe's? Well, he was high then."

"He was?" I am trying to remember exactly what transpired during that thirty-second encounter in the sushi aisle. Was he acting goofy? Spacey? Were his eyes bloodshot? I have no idea. I can just picture *my* mother consulting the official "Clueless Parents' Guide to How to Tell If Your Child Is High on Marijuana" checklist back in the day, the difference being—and it is a big difference—that I was eighteen, not thirteen. And, of course, there's the other difference: I am not clueless. I have my own weed-smoking credentials, which give me a far different perspective from what my mother had: I don't think marijuana is a gateway drug. I don't think it's addictive. I don't even think it should be illegal. And there is one more don't: I don't think a thirteen-year-old (or fourteen-, fifteen-, or sixteen-year-old) should be smoking it. Like my misdeeds at summer camp, my adventures with illegal substances are part of what I consider an appropriately checkered past that I am not at all ashamed of but that I do not want to reveal—at least at her age—to my daughter. It is the classic "do what I say, not what I did" approach.

"Yeah," she says, "Damon was high, and he was trying to be so cool so his father wouldn't catch on."

"He told you this?"

"Yeah. On the phone."

"So," I say, real casual "where does he get the stuff?" She rolls her eyes. Like how could I not know. She sighs and decides she'll give me a break and enlighten me.

"There's this whole, like, system," she says. "All the kids at my school get it from the kids at Roosevelt." Roosevelt is the district's most upscale middle school. I'd like to know how the middle school marijuana cartel works, but I have much more important questions to ask.

"Has he ever asked you to smoke with him?" This baby-faced boy who smoothed back a lock of my daughter's hair, this shy kid who has eaten dinner at my table and ridden in my car. Yeah, I know somewhere there are nine-year-olds smoking crack and twelve-year-olds having babies. But this isn't somewhere. This is here. On my watch.

"No," she says. She says it both matter-of-factly and emphatically. No guile, no hesitation. I believe her. I'm relieved, but I'm not finished with the topic.

"Why do you think he smokes?" I ask. I'm not so much interested in

Damon's motivation—I'm already trying to figure out ways of jettisoning him from my daughter's life—but rather in how Lizzie might be thinking about drugs.

"He says it makes him feel great. Really happy. Like, no worries." How do I counter this—I who smoked for years and quit only because I quit tobacco and couldn't risk inhaling anything lest I fall off the wagon? Do I lie and say smoking marijuana actually makes you feel terrible? Do I deliver the doomsday lecture? Do I go down the "not until you're eighteen" route? Rather than jumping in with something, I decide instead to check in with her. Ask questions. Don't make pronouncements. That's what Kinlen, the wise woman/shaman told me months ago.

"What do you think the reasons would be *not* to smoke weed?" I ask. She has had years of antidrug messages pounded into her head at school, entire classes, the DARE to say no curriculum, take-home pamphlets, friendly cops who visit the classroom and tell scare stories, posters plastered in the hallways.

"Um, I can't think of any," she says after a long pause. Wow. *I* better think of a few pretty quick.

"Well," I say, "for one, it's illegal, and you can go to jail for it." I can see that Lizzie sees this as such a remote possibility that she need not consider it. She's right. A middle school kid thrown in jail for smoking a joint? Hardly.

"And think about all that gunk getting deep into your lungs. You're inhaling who knows what. It's like smoking cigarettes."

"Oh," she says. "I would *never* smoke cigarettes. Cigarettes are really, really bad for you." Ha. I guess at least one antidrug message got through to her.

Meanwhile, what to do about Damon? Now that I know he gets high, how can I let Lizzie keep seeing him? Isn't it just a matter of time before he smokes in front of her, or she gets curious, or an opportunity just presents itself? How can I sanction this relationship? Or more to the point, what can I do to break it up?

As I consider strategy, it occurs to me that I may not need to take drastic measures. In less than a week, they will be ensconced in their different schools, immersed in their separate worlds. If there is contact, it can easily be limited to carefully supervised, marijuana-free Saturday afternoons here at our house. I could even rush to answer every phone call and make sure they never, or rarely, talk to each other.

But is this what I want to do? I have, right now, in this instance, the power to protect her. But I can't really protect her, even now—and certainly in the future—from every kid with a baggie in his backpack. I *know* there will be other kids, other temptations. I go online to check out Oregon's annual Healthy Teens Survey, where I find that more than 12 percent of eighth graders in our county say they smoke marijuana (a number that doubles once the kids are juniors in high school). But from the stats, what I should really be concerned about is alcohol. Almost a third of eighth graders say they've had a drink in the past month, and 14 percent admit to binge drinking. It's scary out there, even in our protected little corner of the world. And so, maybe I can control access to this one kid who has told Lizzie that weed makes him feel "great" and "happy." That's good. But it's temporary. And maybe even harmful.

If I take away her power to make decisions by stepping in and taking control, what is she learning about how to evaluate temptation and risk, about what she values, about how to act responsibly? What happens the next time, or the time after that, when I'm not there to police the situation? I am struggling with this terrible tension between how much to hold on and how much to let go, and I am still struggling when three days later Lizzie announces that she and Damon have broken up.

"He has another girlfriend," Lizzie says. I listen closely to the tone of her voice. I study her face. How is she taking this? "Yeah," she says, "her name is Tyra, and she drinks and goes to parties and stuff." Lizzie says she knows this because—violating the no-Internet rule still in place—she went on Damon's MySpace page where Tyra has a link to her MySpace page. We are upstairs in her room having this conversation. She wants to show me. She clicks closed the game she was playing, and I nod okay. On MySpace, she finds Tyra's page, and there she is: heavy eye makeup, pouty lips. We both take a long look. Neither of us says anything.

"So, how are you feeling about all this?" I ask. She's already told me about Damon's getting high. She's told me about the breakup. She's told me about the new girlfriend. Maybe we're on a roll here. I stop to relish the thought, as I have many times in the past year: My daughter talks to me. Not always, and sometimes with an astounding lack of civility, but she talks to me.

"Are you okay with this?" I ask again. Lizzie looks over at me and shrugs. "Yeah, it's fine," she says. "I mean, we wouldn't have seen each other at school or anything anyway." She smiles a brave smile that broadens, right in front of my eyes, into a real smile. I marvel at the transformation. Is this whimsy or resilience or ambivalence? Is she actually okay with being dumped or is she pretending not to care? Maybe her reaction is proof of her emotional strength, a testament to her self-esteem. Maybe it's a sign of her growing maturity. Or it could be plain old teenage fickleness. I don't know.

And right now, I am too delighted to care. Damon's exit means Lizzie will be spared at least *this* potential introduction to marijuana. And it buys me more time to process the hold on–let go dilemma that I can see will be the leitmotif of these teen years.

After the high drama of last week—from the heart-stopping, first-person story in Lizzie's notebook to the Damon marijuana revelations to the breakup—you would think clothes shopping would not even register on the emotional Richter scale. And you would be wrong. What I've been dreading most about the end of summer, I realize as Labor Day weekend comes and goes, is *shopping*, the annual back-to-school, full-day-at-the-mall ritual enacted by harried mothers and insolent daughters in cities and towns all across this great land. The main issue Lizzie and I have is style—which, I am embarrassed to admit, is the same issue I had with my mother. My mother firmly believed she knew what was appropriate for me and what I looked best in. This was the woman who dressed in heels to go grocery shopping and accessorized every outfit with dramatic neck scarves. I, on the other hand, tended toward jeans and my father's old army shirts. Obviously, my mother was off base and I was in the right. And now, obviously, I am in the right once again—isn't it wonderful to be right so often?—and my daughter is off base. Believe me, I see the problem here, but I can't help myself. I truly believe—as I now understand my mother truly believed—that the kind of clothes my daughter wants to put on her body are objectionable.

I do not wear heels to go to the grocery store. Or anywhere. And my idea of accessorizing is to put on a wristwatch. I am not my mother. On the other hand, I am *a* mother, and I care what my daughter looks like when she goes out in public. I care that the inseams of her jeans are not so long that she steps on the pants legs all day, fraying and dirtying the hem so that within a day or two a new pair looks as if it came from the Salvation Army bin. I care that her T-shirts are not so tight that you can read every seam of her bra through them. I care that these same shirts are not billboards for statements like Hot to Trot, Just Lick It and Leave, or Everybody Loves a Little Beaver. I am also not a big fan of shirts with skulls, vampires with blood dripping from fangs, or barbed wire. Lizzie and I are not pink-and-frilly people, but there's a lot of fashion space between that extreme and the I-am-a-teenage-runaway look. That's the space I would like my daughter to inhabit, dammit.

And so, I begin this excursion with both opinion and attitude, and I'm betting Lizzie does too. While it's true that not that long ago she was bubbling over with enthusiasm about a "new look" for eighth grade, I've learned to see these bursts of zeal for what they are: fleeting and soon forgotten. I don't hold out much hope that this shopping trip will be much different from any of our other shopping trips. I am sure Lizzie thinks I should butt out of all clothing decisions, that I am hopeless and clueless when it comes to knowing what thirteen-year-olds wear, that I am a control freak and a general pain in the ass. And she may even be right about some of this. But how can I *not* care about the image my daughter projects to the world? At any rate, we've already battened down the hatches and gone to battle stations as we head off to the mall one sultry afternoon between Labor Day and eighth-grade orientation. New look or not, we have to buy some clothes for eighth grade, and this day is our only chance. I steer her toward Macy's where she stands twenty feet away from me as I go through racks and hold up a succession of jackets, none of which she looks at. She has her earbuds in listening to her music so loud that I can almost make out the words. She won't even go over the threshold at the Gap. Ditto, American Eagle Outfitters. At Aeropostale she tries on several pairs of boys' cargo shorts, the kind with pleated pockets big enough to hold several porterhouse steaks. Lizzie and I are both generously proportioned in the thigh area. The pockets, even sans steaks, are, well, unflattering. Yes, I say as much, realizing the moment the words are out of my mouth that I have broken my vow not to talk about weight except in terms of health and nutrition. It seems I am not the only one without a fully functioning frontal lobe this afternoon. Lizzie storms out of the store, I trail in her wake.

As I have now been stupid and insensitive enough to bring up the thigh issue, Lizzie defiantly makes her way to Torrid, the store specializing in plus sizes for teens. She scans the racks and quickly picks out a half dozen streetwalker-worthy dresses. Happily, the smallest size is too big. I consider this interlude a win-win. Our final stop is Hot Topic, where Patti Smith would have shopped had the store been around back in the day. Three-quarters of the inventory is black. Pretty much all of the inventory could double as Slutty Schoolgirl Halloween costumes. The stuff is so egregious that I wouldn't know where to begin to comment, so I don't. Which turns out to be a smart move in an otherwise dumb day.

Lizzie scans the racks, grabs a black bustier and a red-and-black plaid micromini kilt, and disappears into the dressing room. I stand by the door. A few minutes later, she emerges wearing the kilt, and I can see that it covers as much of her body as a wide belt would. She motions me in— which I consider my reward for not railing against the articles of clothing she chose to try on—then turns her back to the mirror and looks over her shoulder, seeing what everyone else will see. "Whoa!" she says, her eyebrows raised. We catch each other's eye in the mirror, hold the gaze for a moment, and then both burst out laughing. I relax for the first time since we motioned ourselves through the automatic doors into this climate-controlled, fluorescent nightmare of a mall.

We're now into our third hour with nary a shopping bag to show for the effort. "Don't you need shoes?" I ask. Shoes will be easy, I think. Or easier. My mistake is asking this while we are still in Hot Topic. I didn't even know they sold shoes here. Lizzie knows, though. She walks over to a shoe carousel half hidden in the corner of the store and picks out a pair of canvas slip-ons with alternating black and white skulls. They have the heft and quality of craftsmanship one would expect from the finest Southeast Asian sweatshop. She loves them. Of course. I decide not to put up a fight, because, unlike everything else in this store, the shoes don't expose parts of her body that should be bared only when showering. Also, I figure the shoes will self-destruct in six weeks or less.

We buy the shoes and call it a day. Both of us, from our separate places of wisdom, know it's time to leave. Her eighth grade wardrobe will have to wait.

SEVENTEEN

Mr. R. is the world's coolest eighth grade teacher—or so says Lizzie after her first few weeks in his class. I hadn't planned to embed myself in middle school again this year, but now I am curious about Mr. R., curious about what constitutes "cool" in Lizzie's mind and, of course, curious about whether Lizzie—and her cohorts—have changed since the end of seventh grade. And so, at least for a while, I am back at school.

Mr. R., it turns out, is a small, wiry, hipster of a guy who could be Elvis Costello's much younger brother. With his black-rimmed retro glasses, gelled up hair, and pegged jeans, he looks more like the musician Lizzie tells me he is in his spare time than a veteran middle school teacher. Lizzie thinks he's cool because he plays jazz, New Orleans–style blues, and klezmer with bands around town. He even invites his classes to his all-age gigs. I think he's cool too—not to mention talented—after going to one of his shows with Lizzie. And I really think he's cool when, by the fourth week of school, he is instructing the kids to create podcasts, teaching them how to edit in GarageBand, and talking to them about the mocumentaries they will be writing and filming later in the semester.

What I remember about eighth grade is plowing through *Great Expectations*, which, unsurprisingly, are hard to have when you are thirteen and reading Dickens.

But what really sells me on Mr. R. is a conversation I overhear one morning between him and one of the more challenging girls in Lizzie's class. This girl acts like Lizzie can sometimes act when Lizzie is at her absolute worst, which is to say obstreperous, attitudinal, and snotty. I have never seen Lizzie act this way with a teacher or any number of other adults. Like most kids (say the experts), she saves the worst of her bad behavior for home. I do think things are improving at home—less attitude, more communication—so what I really mean is that this kid talking with Mr. R. reminds me of Lizzie's nastiest behavior last year. It's hard to watch. But on the other hand, it shows me how far we've come.

The girl is giving Mr. R. some serious lip. I am watching the scene unfold thinking about how I would react. I'm thinking, Trip to the office to see the vice principal. I am thinking, Detention. Mr. R. listens, lets her run out her string. Then I see him take a small step backward.

"That's just *excellent* female attitude," he says, nodding his head, smiling a half smile. "If I need some female attitude, I'll know who to ask. Today, you are the go-to girl." She is momentarily speechless. Then she laughs and goes back to her seat. I feel I am in the presence of a master. Too bad I didn't sign up for lessons from this guy eight months ago when I needed all the help I could get.

I am not spending all that much time in classrooms this time around, but I do sit in on a dozen or so of Mr. R.'s classes, and I attend a few math classes where the formidable Mr. Z.—Lizzie's seventh grade and now her eighth grade teacher—presides. I am in math for no other reason than to work my strategy of shifting the balance of power. Math class gives me an opportunity to put Lizzie in the driver's seat. She is, contrary to what last year's mediocre grade would suggest, pretty good at math. She actually *likes* math. I'm not, and I don't—and she knows it. One day after school, I ask her to explain a concept Mr. Z. was talking about that day and that I completely missed. Another day I attempt to take a math quiz with the class. Lizzie has—gleefully, I might add—encouraged me in this pursuit and is very interested in the result. She wants me to hand in the test to Mr. Z., but I am too embarrassed. This delights her. What delights her even more is comparing our two tests. I save mine, and when she gets hers back (only two out of twenty wrong), we go over them at home. I have managed to come up with four correct answers, which I consider a minor triumph.

"That's okay, Mom," she says consolingly. "You can't be good at everything, you know." Believe me, I know. And I'm glad she does too.

Visits to math and the hip Mr. R.'s room aside, I mostly tag along behind Lizzie in the halls, hang out in front of lockers, and listen in on lunchtime conversations during the fall. I am interested in Lizzie, in her evolving eighth grade self, but that means I am also interested in the context in which she operates for so many hours five days a week. What I'm seeing during these first few months of eighth grade, what is most startling to me, is the persistently juvenile behavior of boys her age. As Lizzie spends a lot of her time with boys, their behavior interests me deeply.

Parents, doctors, and psychologists all acknowledge that the maturity gap between boys and girls in the middle school years is significant, even laughable. But I've most often thought of this gulf as physical because that's the most visible and startling of the inequalities: sixth grade girls who tower over sixth grade boys; seventh grade girls with womanly figures chatting with baby-cheeked, smooth-faced seventh grade boys. Now, by eighth grade, many of the boys have caught up in height with the girls, their voices have deepened, and a few hairs have sprouted, but meanwhile the girls are wearing heels and full-on makeup, and most look as if they should be babysitting rather than dating the boys their own age.

Lizzie doesn't look as old as some of her female classmates, probably because most days she still dresses in jeans, T-shirts, and flip-flops. But, like pretty much all the girls now, she has a woman's body, not a girl's, and her burgeoning skills with cosmetics give her face a new sophistication.

But the boy-girl differences I am observing are far more than skin-deep. I listen to the girls—Lizzie, Nattie, and Allie, and dozens of other girls too—talk to each other. I hear talk of divorced mothers who are dating again and what the girls think of the new boyfriend. I hear talk about a kid's "two moms" not in the context of making a gay joke (that would be what the boys do), but rather to puzzle out what it might mean for two women to love each other that way. I hear talk about body dissatisfaction, about a girl they know who has started to cut herself. Their talk is intimate and melodramatic, compelling, addictive even, like the soap opera you don't want to admit you watch. The boys, on the other hand, are telling each other fart jokes. Lizzie seems poised in the middle. With Nattie and Allie she is very much the empathetic, drama-loving girl. With Evan and his friends, her talk is both superficial and scatological. She seems to move between the two spheres effortlessly, almost unconsciously. I am in awe of this, the seamless transitions she makes—often several times within the five minutes between classes—between the emotionally resonant talk of the girls and the trash talk of the boys. Maybe I'm wrong, but I see this as a sign of her social sophistication—although, wow, the boys' conversations display everything but.

This is an example of boy talk, a conversation I overheard last week between two of Lizzie's friends:

"Hey, like Mr. Dubik is so pissed today," one of Evan's buddies says to the other. They are grabbing books from their side-by-side lockers between classes. Mr. Dubik is the fearsome enforcer-style vice principal.

"Yeah, Mr. Dubik. I mean Mr. *Pubic*," says the other kid. They both guffaw. A third kid saunters by. The first boy elbows him, and gets elbowed in return.

"Hey, dude," boy number one says to boy number three, "like, did you see *Mr. Pubic* in the hall this morning?"

"Mr. *Pubic*?" The kid laughs. It sounds just like the snarky "heh-heh" I remember from *Beavis and Butt-head*.

Today, the same trio is discussing a coach with the unfortunate surname (in the world of middle school, that is) of Cox. They have fun with that one for a full ten minutes, which is really hard—heh, heh, *hard*—to do if you think about it.

I am telling my friend Sarah about the middle school jokes one morning during our usual five-mile run. She expresses astonishment—not about the scatological hallway patter, but about the fact that Lizzie is continuing to let me shadow her. I don't think she's quite gotten over the fact that Lizzie allowed me to go to camp with her this past summer.

"She's *still* okay with you going to school with her? I mean, this is eighth grade now," Sarah says, her tone incredulous. "Leah would be so embarrassed."

Lizzie's continued openness *is* pretty amazing. It makes me proud to have such a daughter. And it makes me realize how much both of us, in our different ways and for our different reasons, want and need the connection the book is giving us the opportunity to forge. Sure, Lizzie likes the attention, and that's one reason she is cooperating. My research puts the spotlight on her. It illuminates her life and makes it important. Her friends notice and make comments. But there's more to what is happening than that.

Ever since we stopped playing dress up together when she was in third grade, I have looked for ways to connect with her. If she were a reader, we could connect through books. But she isn't. (I do not count manga.) Lizzie has to be the only literate thirteen-year-old on the planet who has read not a single Harry Potter book. I wish she liked any of the athletic activities I like—running, swimming, cross-country skiing, hiking—but in middle school she has gravitated toward two sports I know nothing about: wrestling and discus. I am an avid vegetable gardener. My idea of a perfect summer afternoon is squatting between raised beds, yanking weeds, and pinching back suckers. She finds this dumb and boring which, in all fairness, I think most people do. Coming up with activities we can do together has taken planning, negotiation, and, often, bribery. Now, however, the book is our joint endeavor. Going to school with her or, back before the Internet ban, going online together or our train trip or attending camp together—all activities shaped by the artifice of me as journalist-anthropologist, her as subject—give us this common enterprise, providing us with a way to be together that is outside the daily drama of our lives as mother and daughter.

But despite our many triumphs, despite the fact that I've learned to keep my cool at least 30 percent more often than I did eight months ago, most of our days still begin with a fight. She refuses to eat breakfast. She suddenly remembers, at 7:30 a.m., about homework she was supposed to do. I pass by her room and see no open floor space, only a tangle, a mountain, of damp towels and dirty clothes. It doesn't really matter what the trigger is, there is always a trigger. And more often than not—although *less* often than before—off we go. I make a comment. She comes right back at me. And although I know both of us see clearly what is happening—how could we not . . . I've been writing about this for months—we dig in our heels and go for it. Her excuse is that she is definitely not a morning person, and she is most definitely a teen girl. My excuse is that I can't stand it when people don't do what I want. And right away.

Sometimes the ugliness of the early morning continues in the car to school. I switch on NPR. She heaves a sigh that could blow one of the little pigs' houses down. "I can't believe we have to listen to *that*," she says. I turn up the volume. Or she beats me to the punch and puts on BOB FM, her favorite radio station. If I don't jump in and say something—and occasionally I don't—she amps up the volume to a level she knows I can't handle this early in the morning.

But then, when we enter the school building, our life as mother and daughter takes a backseat to our life as researcher and subject, and both of our moods improve. She'll shoot me a knowing or an amused look during class. She'll grab my arm, companionably, in the hallway. I'll ditch a class and bring her back a latte. The time we spend together like this is healing. Sometimes it just binds our wounds so that we warrior women can go back out into the mother-daughter fray. But other times, we experience moments of connection that I know, I *feel*, are bringing us closer together. What will happen when this time in our life is over, when the immersion project has ended, when the book has been written . . . I am not sure. But I am hopeful, very hopeful, that we won't lose what we've found together.

Meanwhile, the project has many months to go yet, and I have much to explore. And so, I continue to go to school through the fall, continue to observe without being too obvious about it, continue to take copious notes. What I see, in addition to the stark boy-girl divide, are the changes between Lizzie's seventh grade, twelve-year-old self and her thirteen-going-on-fourteen, eighth grade self. The first change is that, like a lot of the other kids in her class, she now has an air of privilege and cockiness about her, that I'm-at-the-top-of-the-heap strut that comes from having figured out what there is to figure out about middle school. She knows which teacher stashes a bag of pretzels in her desk, which teacher look the other way when you chew gum, the best bathrooms to run to between classes. She is the special pet of (and official assistant to) the PE teacher. The janitor knows her by name. The lunch ladies know her by name. I want her to enjoy this. I want to protect her from the knowledge that next year she will be bottom of the heap again at a school with

almost ten times the student population of her middle school in a sprawl-
ing building whose main hallway is reputed to be a quarter mile long.

She is also, as a thirteen-going-on-fourteen girl, learning how to be an
enthusiastic consumer of beauty products. A year ago, I had to force her
to take two showers a week. Just this past summer on our California trip
I was wishing for her to be as interested in personal hygiene as she was
in applying eyeliner. Now my wish has come true. Her daily morning
showers are almost twenty minutes long, barely time enough to choose
among the astonishing array of plastic bottles that line the rim of the bath-
tub and crowd the three-tier corner shelf: four different brands of shampoo, separate conditioners to "fortify," "restore," and "clarify"—plus a
just-purchased "anti-humidity smoothing milk"—three kinds of body
wash, two body scrubs, and two razors. On the bathroom counter is a hair
straightener, a hair curler, a hair "designer," hair gel, hair putty, antistatic
hair spray, heat-protector hair spray, and a big plastic tray with five eyeliner pencils, six little boxes of eye shadow, three lipsticks, two glitter pots,
and a collection of brushes, applicators, sponges, and pads. In seventh
grade she could go from alarm clock to out the door in twenty minutes.
Now she spends three quarters of an hour just in the bathroom.

Her fascination with beauty products doesn't come from me. I've been
using the same shampoo for a decade, and a natural-bristle brush is my
one and only hair tool. It's also a mystery where she has learned to apply
makeup as skillfully as she does. The thing is, she is not only highly skilled,
she is experimental, and not in a weird Halloweeny way, but more like
how I'd imagine a model or a cosmetologist to be experimental. She'll
spend ten minutes working on a new cat-eye concept, or decide to blend
two eye shadow colors you wouldn't think would mix, or brush glitter just
beneath her lower lashes. It all looks good. My idea of makeup is, on special occasions, applying a bit of mascara and a swipe of lip gloss. Now
when I want or need to be ultrafancy, I have Lizzie do my makeup. I do
this for practical reasons—I mean, she's *good*—but also for the togetherness, for the ten intimate minutes it gives us. How can we not be close in
those moments when her fingertips are feathering blush on my cheeks,
when I can feel her warm breath on my face as she leans in with the mascara wand? Our most convivial moments, as I've learned, take place when
she knows more than I do.

The other big change from seventh to eighth grade is that Lizzie is fully integrated into what she calls her posse—the previously all-male group that includes Evan and his two buddies. This year it seems that they have finally accepted her as one of their own. Last year she was on the fringes. Last year they seemed ready at any moment to expel her from their midst (and often did). Last year her long-standing friendship with Evan had earned her a tryout on the team—but not an official spot. The boys, Evan included, more than occasionally could (and did) make her life miserable in seventh grade by closing male ranks. But I think she slowly proved herself, mostly by dint of her formidable Halo and Guitar Hero abilities, which at first netted her grudging "pretty good for a girl" comments. In fact, she is pretty good, period, and eventually they had to acknowledge that.

I think she also proved herself—and I'm less happy about this—by this year accepting and then joining in on their juvenile behavior. Other girls, Lizzie tells me, think Evan and his buddies are "jerks." Their jokes are gross—and *everything*, says Lizzie, is a joke to them—and their antics, childish. Lizzie either appreciates, or pretends to appreciate, their humor, and at least occasionally participates in their rowdy behavior. Just recently the four of them got in detention-earning trouble for violating a hallway rule.

The group even has a name—courtesy of the janitor—"the Hawks." At first, I think that's kind of cool, not to mention oddly coincidental. "Hawk" was Lizzie's camp name this past summer. But then Lizzie tells me *why* the janitor has named them that. It is because the janitor, as well as the lunch ladies and Vice Principal Dubik/Pubic think these four need to be "watched like hawks." That said, it is clear that Lizzie is happier this year because she is part of a group. She still has Nattie and Allie as friends, but these relationships are, as they have always been, somewhat mercurial in the way many teen girl friendships are. Nattie still hugs her one day and avoids eye contact the next. Allie will invite her over two weekends in a row and then disappear from her life for the next three. The boys, however, are unchanging. They can be counted on for being loud and gross and obnoxious every day. What you see is what you get.

I would be more worried about this, about Lizzie's adopting the posse's rowdy ways to curry favor, if she didn't also have Nattie and Allie in her life and if, one recent afternoon at school, I didn't observe this scene:

I was sitting in the bleachers watching Lizzie's PE class, but only half paying attention. All of a sudden I see Lizzie race across my line of sight toward a group of five girls sitting cross-legged on the polished wood floor, so close their knees are touching. I scoot twenty feet down, still in the bleachers, so I can see (and hear) what's going on. Lizzie is kneeling down next to one of the girls, Blair, who is crying so hard I can see her body shake. Lizzie hugs her, and from over Lizzie's shoulder I see Blair's blotchy, swollen face. She is gasping and hiccupping and wailing all at the same time. Is she hurt? I scan the room quickly to see if the PE teacher sees what I see. He does, and he doesn't seem concerned. I am, though. I get up quickly and walk over to the group of girls.

"My mother is gonna *kill* me," Blair is wailing. "I mean, she's *really* gonna kill me. I just don't *get* detention. I'm not *supposed* to get detention." Her sobs echo through the gym. Wait a second. This over-the-top weep-fest is about *detention*? (Yes. It turns out that Blair, high-achieving, perennial honor roll, teen girl role model Blair, just got detention for talking to her girlfriends while the PE teacher was taking attendance.) Blair is so worked up about this that she is scaring her own circle of friends. I see that the girls, once a tight knot, have moved several feet away, leaving Lizzie and Blair alone together. Lizzie is patting Blair on the back. They have been classmates since elementary school but never really friends.

"Your mother will love you just the same," Lizzie is telling her. "She's still going to be proud of you. Don't you worry." I listen, and I have to blink back the tears. To see my daughter in this role, to hear the empathy and maturity in her voice, and to listen to her say essentially the same reassuring words I have said to her when I stress that there are no strings attached to my love (although, sure, I would like to see that B- become an A)—this qualifies as one of the finer moments for me.

I've forgotten entirely about poor Blair. I am thinking only of Lizzie. She has heard me! One of the core messages, maybe the single most important message a mother can send to a daughter—*I love you no matter what*—has gotten through. This was the one my own mother never could manage to send. Or maybe she sent it in a code I couldn't decipher.

Whatever happened, I didn't grow up knowing she had my back, and the emptiness that left inside me is still inside me. I listen to Lizzie reassure Blair about unconditional mother love, and I know—*I know*—my daughter must feel it herself.

After I finish patting myself on the back, after I beam a megawatt smile at Lizzie, I consider for a moment if Blair's mother will take the news of her daughter's detention as hard as Blair thinks she will. Maybe. Blair is an only child and a superachiever. Her mother is an impressive, prosperous (and very attractive) businesswoman who sets the bar high.

As do, I think, all of us educated, professional women who are the mothers of today's teen girls. Lizzie and I have never talked about this directly—what it means to be the daughter of a successful mother—but it's hard to imagine that this fact of her life goes unnoticed. She has sat in audiences when I've read from my books. She has seen my byline in magazines. Although most of the time I am just the woman who washes her clothes, makes her meals, and transports her from place to place, I know she knows there is more to me. And this is different, very different, than how I viewed my own mother.

Growing up, I never knew my mother as a person, as someone separate from her prescribed role in my life. Whether she purposely kept herself from me, as I did from her, or whether it was just how mothers of her day were taught and expected to behave, I don't know. I do know that the glimpses I had of her as a person were so few that I remember them vividly.

One time, when I was just about Lizzie's age, my mother was the costume designer for a community theater production. She had designed and sewn my clothes for years, a fact I not only did not appreciate, but I hated. I longed for a real label inside my skirts, not those "made for you by . . ." tags she hand stitched inside the waistband. I viewed her flair for sewing as my personal burden. But when she took this volunteer gig as a costume designer, I saw that other people thought she was talented. Several of the actors came over to our house for fittings. She got phone calls and messages. When the play opened, she was called onstage to take a bow.

Another time, much later, when I was living in San Francisco just after graduating from college, she flew west, supposedly to visit with her younger sister, who had long ago made her life in Southern California. My mother and I met for dinner in San Francisco, an event about which I have little memory. But I do remember quite clearly the phone call I got from my aunt a few days after my mother had returned home. My aunt confided in me that my mother's trip had another purpose. While in San Francisco, she rendezvoused with an old flame, a man with whom she had an affair before she met my father. I thought this was so incredibly cool. I had never thought of my mother as someone who had, old flames.

Of the many mistakes I have already made and will probably continue to make with my own daughter, this is not one of them. She *does* know me. I work at that. I want her to see me as an adult woman who has a life outside of motherhood, who has gone places and done things (well, *some* things), and might actually be, mom issues aside, an interesting person, a person you wouldn't mind getting to know.

And yet, coming on too strong is to intimidate or maybe even inhibit. Given that the mother's job is to be a great role model, and the daughter's job is to forge her own identity, having an accomplished mother can be a mixed blessing. My therapist friend, Joyce, thinks it may take the daughter of a successful mother longer to figure out what she wants to do. If mom is a top executive or a symphony musician or an accomplished medical researcher, how does daughter navigate around all that success to find a unique path? The bar is already so high, the expectations already so great. A slight misstep—getting detention, for example—takes on mammoth proportions. Yet Joyce says (and the research agrees) that ambitious mothers can significantly boost their daughters' self-confidence and that this can directly influence the daughters' later success. That's the result I'm hoping for.

A week or so later, Lizzie is helping me get ready for my annual "Come As Your Book Party," a social event I throw for the folks enrolled in a writing seminar I teach. Everyone must come in a costume that in some way illustrates the project they've been working on in the class. I've had ecosaboteurs and clowns, ghost hunters and lesbian brides, famous painters and diner waitresses. I dress up too. Today I am dressing up like the main character from my book in progress. Today I am dressing up like Lizzie.

She is thrilled. She has laid out special clothes for me on my bed: her favorite black low-slung jeans, the two-inch-wide black and silver belt she wears pretty much every day, a skimpy black T-shirt with a hot pink swirly design, three silver necklaces, and hoop earrings with the circumference of coasters.

"Hey, looking gooooood," she says when I emerge from the bedroom to model the outfit. She raises her hand for a high five. Then she steps back, squinting her eyes as she subjects me to a full-body scan. She shakes her head slowly. I can tell that my approval rating has just plummeted.

"What's wrong?" I ask.

"You don't look anything like a teenager!" she says.

"Well, I am, like, *way past* being a teenager, so I'm not surprised."

"Naw. I don't mean how incredibly old you are," she says, jovially. "I mean, you need something else." She grabs my arm and leads me to her bathroom. "Hair first," she says. Before I can object—I don't really like things done to my hair—she sprays my head with an overly sweet, floral-scented mist. "That'll protect it," she says.

"Protect it? What do I need protection from?" She grabs the hair straightener and brandishes it in front of my face. Fifteen minutes later, my slightly wild, wavy hair is shiny, slick, and stick straight. This is not something I'll ever do again, but I have to admit, it looks kind of cool if you go for the Morticia Addams type. Lizzie runs into her bedroom, grabs an old boom box she inherited from one of her brothers, and brings it into the bathroom. These few minutes without music have obviously been a strain on her. She puts in a mix CD and cranks up the volume. She sprays my neck and the inside of my wrists with her favorite perfume, Brown Sugar. I smell like a cookie. And as she ever so carefully applies eyeliner (upper and lower lids), eye shadow (three colors), blush, glitter, and Snicker's-flavored lip gloss, we listen to "This One's for the Girls," the chorus of which goes: "This one's for the girls/Who've ever had a broken heart/Who've wished upon a shooting star/You're beautiful the way you are." Third time through, we are singing together so loudly—"You're beautiful the way you are"—that I almost don't hear the doorbell. My costumed guests have arrived. I run down the stairs with Lizzie trailing behind.

"You're me!" she yells at my back. "Like, you're totally me."

EIGHTEEN

Just when I think I'm finished tagging along with Lizzie to school, an opportunity presents itself that I can't pass up. A community educator from Planned Parenthood is going to be taking over one of Lizzie's regular morning classes to talk about sex—a full week of sex ed, eighth grade–style. Unfortunately, it turns out that I am out of town for the Monday and Tuesday sessions. But when I make it to the class on Wednesday, Lizzie fills me in.

"Yesterday was puberty," she tells me. Yes, I think. Yesterday *was* puberty. That's what it seems like to me, as in *just yesterday* we were shopping for Lizzie's first bra . . . *just yesterday* we were having the pad versus tampon discussion. Now, like every other girl in eighth grade, she is solidly postpuberty. Virtually all these girls were postpuberty last year; most of them the year before, and many even earlier, in elementary school. When Lizzie started "budding"—the lovely term for the beginning of breast growth, known in medical circles as Tanner stage II—in fifth grade, I immediately made an appointment with her pediatrician. Surely there must be some hormonal imbalance, I thought, something awry in the endocrine system. Or worse, a tumor somewhere. Who starts to get breasts at nine and a half?

The answer is, today, lots of girls. After I calmed down enough to do some research, I was amazed to discover that half of all U.S. girls show signs of breast development by their tenth birthday, and 14 percent grow breast buds between ages eight and nine. New recommendations for the age at which puberty should be considered "precocious" and therefore, perhaps, related to an imbalance or disease have been lowered from eight years to seven years for white girls and to six years for black girls. *Puberty at six years old?* What happened to childhood? I know it was an invention of the nineteenth century, but it was a damned *good* invention.

Lizzie was well within the normal range for budding, the first stage of puberty, her pediatrician told me. Still, it was disconcerting. From my elementary school years, I remember only one girl who "developed," a tall, quiet, homely kid named Eleanor. We, the flat-chested girls—which is to say, all the other ten-year-old girls—alternately pitied and envied her when we weren't otherwise busy giggling. The boys whispered behind her back and, while there, took turns snapping her bra strap. Eleanor and her breasts were *the* focus of attention. Now Eleanor would be lost in the crowd.

Fifth grade—Lizzie's (and Eleanor's) budding year—was also Lizzie's first official, school-district-sanctioned sex ed class. ("AIDS awareness," with a focus on blood and needle sharing and scant mention of semen, was taught in third grade.) Fifth grade sex ed was an innocuous week-long "puberty sure is weird but everyone goes through it" curriculum taught with both humor and sensitivity by a much-beloved male teacher. Parents were notified by e-mail and mail about the class and given the opportunity to shield their ten-year-olds from the news about breasts, pubic hair, periods, and erections that most of them undoubtedly already knew (firsthand). If I remember correctly, none of the parents opted out. We didn't—one of the results being a forever-memorable dinner conversation during which Lizzie sweetly asked her two older brothers whether they had wet dreams.

Now, in eighth grade, she and her classmates are sex ed veterans, with extensive "teen health" sessions in both sixth and seventh grades. I know that some school districts in the country teach no sex ed at all, usually because parents object. In other places, sex ed consists of a stern abstinence-celibacy lecture. Of course, there are also those schools that distribute free condoms in the hallways. Lizzie's school is on the progressive end of the spectrum—we live in a progressive town in a progressive state—and so far, Tom and I have been just fine with that. It doesn't mean we forgo discussions about bodies and fluids and procreation (not to mention affection and infection) at home. We talk plenty. But sex ed at school seems to take the embarrassment out of the subject and make the conversations at home easier.

The community educator from Planned Parenthood standing in front of Lizzie's first-period class is a no-nonsense thirty-something woman in jeans and a slightly frumpy blouse. Her hair is pulled back in a bun that makes her look a little schoolmarmish, but her stylish Tina Fey glasses help a little. It does seem a bit odd to me that she's here, in an eighth grade class, with the sex ed message. I mean, haven't these kids been educated *enough*? What *don't* these kids know already?

I find out right away when the community educator says she will answer one of the questions a kid left in the question box yesterday after class. She unfolds a scrap of paper and reads: "Can lesbians get STDs?" At Lizzie's age, what I knew about STDs came from graphic illustrations in my friend's mother's nursing textbook, including a hideous photo of a blind man with his upper lip eaten away by syphilis. At what passed for sex ed in school—more about that in a minute—we were told that Benito Mussolini and Ivan the Terrible had suffered from syphilis. Syphilis drove you crazy! The only way to avoid getting syphilis and going crazy was to not have sex (until you were married).

Sitting in this sex ed seminar this morning, looking around at the astonishingly well-behaved (no giggling or snickering) group of twenty-eight eighth-graders, I remember my school's foray into this topic. It was about as unenlightened (and unenlightening) as could be imagined—not so much because the times were different then (the innocence of the pre-AIDS era), but because a vocal group of conservative parents in the district did not want the school "teaching sex." So, sex ed was a single, two-hour, gender-segregated session. At the girls-only event, we were lectured from the auditorium stage (with accompanying slides and transparencies) about fallopian tubes and uterine walls, about squiggly sperm and descending eggs. How the sperm got anywhere near the egg was never broached in sex ed. It was, instead, a topic discussed and debated at sleepover parties and after lights-out at summer camp.

The sex ed "talk" I got at home was no more enlightening. After dinner one night—this would have been a few months before the school-sponsored session—my mother took me aside in the kitchen and whispered that she wanted to talk to me. She would meet me in the bathroom upstairs after she finished the dishes. *The bathroom?* I assumed she was going to yell at me for leaving a ring around the tub. Or scold me for the hair in the sink.

A few minutes later, there we were, standing side by side in front of the bathroom vanity. My mother had locked the door behind her. She was holding a big manila envelope. From it, she removed a folded poster that she spread out on the counter and then taped to the mirror. It was a full-color illustration of the female reproduction system, courtesy of (I could see the logo in the corner) the Girl Scouts of America. She was a troop leader, my troop leader, and I'm guessing this was part of an education and information packet she was supposed to share with the girls.

After a brief, clinical explanation of menstruation—I think she was more uncomfortable than I was, if that was possible—she folded up the poster and put it away. The locked door, the bathroom venue—the message was clear: This female body stuff was weird and secret, awkward to talk about and so disgusting that conversation about it belonged in that one room in the house where other gross bodily functions took place. The best thing about that experience, in retrospect, was that it taught me what not to do with my own daughter.

Now, thirteen-year-olds like Lizzie are savvy enough to ask about lesbians and STDs. I don't know if I'm pleased about that or disturbed. Information is good. Ignorance is bad. But does my child really need to know about dental dams right now? I listen from the back of the room as the Planned Parenthood educator matter-of-factly lists the varieties of sex: penis to vagina, mouth to penis, mouth to vagina, penis to anus, mouth to anus. These are the words she uses. She speaks without affect, as if cataloging items on a shelf. I am impressed and appalled. I don't want to go back to the days when a girl could believe that a condom might float away and get lost up near her small intestines. (Yes, this is what I believed.) But, on the other hand, I wonder if there might be some advantage to talking about sex as if it were something more than part A inserted into part B.

I fear there's a danger that Lizzie and her generation of girls will think sex is no big deal, that it's so matter-of-fact they'll just do it if the opportunity presents itself. When I ask her about this later—yes, I know it's both ridiculous of me to be so brash and amazing of her to answer—I get a response that would warm the hearts of every member of *The 700 Club*'s audience: "They make sex sound so bad in that class," she tells me, "that I wouldn't want to do it." I don't know what to say to that, but she does. She has big opinions on the matter. "I mean, all they talk about is infections and sores, getting pregnant, HIV. It's like, you have sex, something awful is gonna happen to you. So why would I want to do it?"

Okay, so this isn't the healthiest of attitudes, but I can't help it if I'm just a little pleased to hear her say this. A vow of celibacy at thirteen is a *good* thing. Still, I have to say something mildly corrective. "Of course sex is not just about disease, but it's good to realize just how careful you have to be," I say. She nods distractedly. Old news.

"So," she says, looking at me all innocent-like, "how often do you and Dad have sex?" Interesting how comfortable I am prying into her life and how aghast I am when she pries into mine. She sees how disconcerted I am and starts to laugh. "I don't really want to know, Mom, *believe me!*"

In the classroom the following day, the matter-of-fact lady in the Tina Fey glasses asks the class to guess how many kids their age have already had sex. There's a yearly study conducted by the state, so she has the actual statistics for eighth graders in this county. The kids call out numbers: 42 percent; 55 percent; 99.9 percent. They all laugh at that. There are one or two guesses below 30 percent, but most of the kids guess higher than 50 percent. They think more than half of their classmates have had sex.

The Planned Parenthood educator puts a transparency on the overhead projector and reveals that only (only!) 16 percent of eighth-graders in this county say they have had sex. By eleventh grade, it's 44 percent, she says. (The class guesses, on average, 85 percent.) One reputable study of teen sexual behavior found that the median age for girls having intercourse for the first time is seventeen. Other studies have set the figure between fifteen and seventeen and a half, depending on ethnicity and family income. (Girls who come from upper-middle-class Asian American families wait the longest.)

I wonder why these kids have so overestimated how many teens are having sex. I think it may be the sex-saturated media environment, their collective exposure to so many images, so many words, so many hidden and not-so-hidden messages. Sex and sex talk are so pervasive, so casual that they don't shock, or even call attention to themselves. Maybe all this talk, and all this action, doesn't make today's teens want to have sex—as so many fear—as much as it makes them think everyone else is having it.

After school that day, I ask Lizzie her opinion about the matter. Why does she think the kids overestimate how many teens are having sex?

"Well," she says, "maybe they aren't. I mean, like, it kinda depends on what you mean by 'having sex.'" I don't understand, I tell her.

"I mean there are three kinds of virgins, you know."

"There are?" I say.

She looks at me indulgently. Clearly, I need to be educated.

"Well, yeah. There's a vagina virgin, a mouth virgin, and an anus virgin."

I am so glad she cleared that up for me.

The next day, the subject is "delaying sex." (What *kind* is not specified.) The sex educator opens a discussion about peer pressure—the kids are *very* knowledgeable about the lines used to coerce and cajole—and then asks them to pair up to brainstorm possible responses. I see that Lizzie is conferring with the boy who sits to her right. She says something, and he laughs a little too loud. I wonder what she said to him. I find out a few minutes later when the kids start sharing their responses. Some of them are amazingly sophisticated, thoughtful, and articulate statements you cannot imagine a thirteen-year-old in the throes of teen passion saying to another thirteen-year-old in the throes of teen passion.

"I do trust you, but I trust myself more."

"If you really loved me, you wouldn't want me to do anything I didn't want to do."

Lizzie has not spoken up in class today and didn't yesterday, but now she raises her hand.

"Yes," says the instructor, "what would you say if someone tried to pressure you?"

"I'd say . . ." here Lizzie pauses, inhales a deep breath, then shouts, "NO!" She can't see me, but from my seat in the back of the room, I am beaming.

The fact is, any fears I might have had about Lizzie's being sexually active are on hold. I am presently not at all worried about which of her three virginities she might be asked or tempted to forfeit. This is not so much because of her bold "just say no" attitude—which I applaud and respect—but because for the first time in more than a year, she does not have a boyfriend. Or rather, she does not have a traditional boyfriend, a guy she met at school, a kid she could invite over to the house. No one has appeared, in person, to fill the void left by the exit of Damon at the end of the summer.

But someone *has* appeared: Marcus. Marcus is her virtual boyfriend, a kid she met on IMVU back before the Internet ban at the end of seventh grade. After a week or so of cartoon-bubble conversation in exotic environments, their relationship migrated to MSN Chat, where they could more easily instant message. I was keeping a close eye on this. Cyber relationships have their own set of hazards. If I let my mind wander, I could imagine the two of them talking dirty, watching porn, baring their bodies in front of webcams. In fact, nothing like that happened. (I will admit that, after she went to sleep, I checked the sites she visited. Also, the webcam "disappeared" from her room one day. Just in case.)

But I needn't have been concerned. Marcus was mostly interested in telling Lizzie his troubles—difficulties living with his divorced mother, problems with an on-again, off-again girlfriend—and Lizzie was thrilled about offering the sage advice of a then twelve-year-old. As befits a drama-loving teen girl, Lizzie immersed herself, or allowed herself to be immersed, in the theatrics of Marcus's life. For several weeks, her online chats included lengthy exchanges with Marcus's best friend and the girl Marcus was having problems with and the best friend of the girl Marcus was having problems with.

After a summer hiatus—and a shift in technology (with the phone replacing the Internet)—the relationship has recently reemerged. Marcus's girlfriend issues have disappeared; his romantic regard is now directed at my daughter. He is currently calling almost every night and, for the moment, Lizzie is delighted with the attention. At the beginning of this new phase in their relationship, I sometimes rushed to answer the phone before Lizzie could pick up so I could engage the kid in conversation, find out some basics, make sure he knew an adult was paying attention. Other times, I have hovered close to the phone (but cleverly out of sight) so that I can catch at least Lizzie's side of the conversation. It all seems innocent enough—lots of talk about friends and who likes whom and who used to like whom but no longer does, with occasional references to music and computer games. The kid is age appropriate and lives a good 1,500 miles away. What else could a mother ask for?

The latest with Marcus, as of two days ago, is that he wants to come out here for a visit. This scheme is so far-fetched, involving as it does his getting a driver's license (he is barely fifteen), a car (fat chance), and parental permission (I can't imagine that) to drive two-thirds of the way across the continent to visit a middle school girl he's never met. I love how completely out of the question this is because it relieves me of the burden of taking it seriously. I don't have to ask any questions. I don't have to bring up any objections. I don't have to initiate a dialog with Marcus's mother. I can just let the two of them talk about this for as long as they want to. I know nothing will come of it. I am going to enjoy this while it lasts. (Which, of course, it doesn't. Fast-forward two months and Marcus is old, old news.)

NINETEEN

The next excitement—if you consider a week of sex ed exciting—in Lizzie's eighth grade world is the mentorship project, one of the most talked about and anticipated undertakings of the school year. The idea is for each kid to explore a job or occupation by hands-on investigation, by becoming both an apprentice and a fly on the wall. It's not so much a "what do you want to be when you grow up" assignment—Mr. R. is careful not to frame it in such weighty terms—but rather a way to explore, up close and personal, the world of work.

The choices the kids make range from journalist (Blair), lawyer, and architect to glassblower, rock band drummer (Evan), and barista. Lizzie decides, early and emphatically, that she wants to work with a veterinarian. But then, two days before she has to hand in her choice to Mr. R., she changes her mind. It would be "way more fun," she tells me, to work in a bakery. I have to remind myself that this is just an eighth grade project, not a career choice. My friend Mazzi has recently opened an artisanal, wood-oven Italian bakery that Sarah and I frequent every morning after our run. I ask him if he will take on Lizzie, and he generously agrees to let her apprentice to one of his early-morning bakers.

It's the first day of the mentorship, the first of six Monday mornings she'll spend at the bakery. Lizzie has set her clock radio for 4:30 a.m., but she sleeps through it. I am in her inky black room at a quarter to five jostling her awake. She is, in equal parts, excited and terrified. What will she do? What will Audrey, the twenty-something baker to whom she has been assigned, allow her to do? How will she manage to both work and scribble notes about the experience? (Mr. R. is requiring a full written report.) Suppose she messes up? We talk it through in whispers. It's fun being up with her predawn, the house dark and still, both of us too sleepy to engage in our usual morning combat.

I walk her into the bakery through the back door at 5:15. The lights are blazing, the Cranberries are blasting from speakers set high on the wall, and five-feet-tall Audrey is elbow-deep in dough. The place smells of cinnamon, coffee, and wood smoke, just like I bet heaven smells, if there is one. Audrey looks up and smiles at Lizzie and points to a big white apron. I tie it around her, scrape her hair back in a ponytail, and watch as Audrey shows Lizzie how to measure flour for a batch of scones. Lizzie forgets her anxiety—and me—in less than a minute. I slip out the back door.

When I return three hours later to take Lizzie to school, she is covered in flour, her hair dusted, her nose smudged, her shirt powdery, her black shoes whitened. She's flushed and grinning.

"Hey, Mom," she says when I walk in the front door. "Can I make you something?"

"Sure," I say, not knowing what to expect. Then my daughter proceeds to the gleaming stainless steel imported Italian espresso machine and makes me an entirely incredible twelve-ounce, moderately foamy latte. Apparently, in between measuring flour, cutting slabs of butter, shaping scones, folding croissants, and packaging ciabatta, she has learned to make espresso. Not bad for three hours' work.

For the next five Mondays, we repeat the drill: up at 4:30, at the bakery's back door by 5:15. Each session, Lizzie learns something new and not always about baking. "Do you know some people need five-shot lattes to start the day?" she asks me, incredulously, when I come to pick her up one morning. Another morning, she tells me all about Teresa, the cake decorator with the Mohawk and the face piercings, who looks like a nineties grunge band reject but in reality is a serious culinary school student. "It's funny how sometimes people don't look like what they are," Lizzie says as we walk out the door. "You really have to talk to people to know them." Lizzie tells me about how hard the people at the bakery work—the early hours, the long hours, the weekend shifts, the time spent on your feet, the lifting of heavy sacks—and how they all love it. Mazzi is a great boss, she tells me. He's funny. He's relaxed. He cares about people. "You can be a boss without being bossy," Lizzie says. She is talking about Mazzi, but when she says this, and then hears herself, it occurs to her that the remark has broader (and more personal) applicability. I can see the realization in her eyes and in her sudden big grin as she elbows me. Another morning she waxes poetic about the art of baking. "It's not just work," she says, offering me a lemon poppy seed scone she helped make earlier that morning. "Mazzi doesn't just knead the dough, he folds in pockets of love."

Meanwhile, Lizzie is developing quite a following at school owing to the box or two of bakery rejects she brings in with her on Monday mornings: blueberry turnovers that didn't quite turn over, banana bread that stayed in the oven a minute too long, slightly misshapen chocolate chip cookies, doughnuts with the holes closed up, perfectly lovely croissants and pain au chocolat that don't quite meet Mazzi's high aesthetic standard. She doles out the pastries, one to Mr. R., one to the eagle-eyed (and sweet-toothed) band teacher Mr. Black, and then to friends, Nattie, Allie, the Hawks, and a growing group of hangers-on. One boy she barely knows actually runs after her in the hallway. Others gather around when she walks into class, peering over her shoulder at the open box in her hands, patting her on the back, telling her how lucky she is to have this mentorship, commenting on the delectability of various items. Did you really make that? Wow. She loves the attention. I see her grinning. I see her playing Lady Bountiful. I also see that she is getting smarter and smarter each week; that she is seeing who her real friends are and who pretends to be a friend when there is something to be gained. That's a lot to learn in six weeks. It's almost beside the point that her written report and an accompanying video shot with Mr. R.'s camera both earn As.

A week after Lizzie's last morning at the bakery, on a cold and rainy Sunday, I plan an afternoon of making bread at home, something Lizzie, with all her experience, has never done, and I haven't attempted in probably twenty years. I am shamelessly piggybacking on the wild success of her mentorship, thinking that baking might be a shared activity for us, a mother-daughter moment.

Finding commonality continues to be a challenge. Some promising attempts have gone badly: a lovely picnic in the park that ends in a fight because I made the sandwiches on whole grain rather than white bread; another park outing ruined because someone (I) forgot to bring the right Frisbee; a planned Saturday night of popcorn and watching movies that is scuttled because none of the five envelopes from Netflix contain the one show she decides she will watch.

But this Sunday, Tom is off to Portland, and Lizzie and I are on our own. We often get along better when we're on our own. Partly it's because she can't play me off against my husband. Partly it's because she doesn't have him as a Halo 3 partner, so she *has* to interact with me. And, I think, partly it's just the "girls-only" vibe that animates us both.

We are not strangers to each other in the kitchen—we've made batches of cookies together from time to time—but today is different. Making bread takes more skill, more time—and more togetherness. The afternoon unfolds as a high-energy, full-bore culinary adventure, four flour-dusted hours of mixing, kneading, baking, and sampling. Lizzie has chosen the music we bake to: REM, Queen, AC/DC, Green Day. We dance around the kitchen, gyrating our aproned hips, using wooden spoons and spatulas to tap out the beat on the counters. We do the twist, the Macarena. I attempt a split. While we wait for the dough to rise, we somehow find ourselves on the floor doing stomach crunches. We both have so much energy we don't know what to do with ourselves. Where does the energy come from? I think it's all the energy we aren't using to fight. It's freed now . . . and wow.

The loaves emerge from the oven perfectly risen, pillowy, with tawny, golden crusts. The scent is intoxicating. The afternoon is a gift, pure and simple.

TWENTY

With the mentorship over, eighth grade marches on, the pace, it seems to me, ever accelerating. I'm running out of time. I need to focus my attention on one of Lizzie's endeavors I have not yet explored, at least not in my role as journalist-anthropologist. The endeavor is athletics. From late fall through midspring, after-school sports are a big part of Lizzie's life. Neither of my two sons was much interested in sports, so my first foray as Soccer Mom—so to speak, as the sport is not soccer—has been with Lizzie. Through her first two years of middle school, I have, of course, been involved in her athletic activities but as a parent, which is to say I have shopped for specific sport shoes, provided Gatorade, laundered uniforms, picked her up from practices, and, on alternating shifts with my husband, watched her matches and meets.

Her winter and spring sports schedules have often defined (and limited) family time. But I think it's been a small price to pay. The revolution wrought by Title IX, the federal legislation that prohibited sex discrimination in school sports (among other programs), has had an extraordinary effect on the lives of girls. I've read the research: Girls involved in sports have higher self-esteem, a better body image, fewer eating disorders, and lower teen pregnancy rates than their sedentary sisters. I cared very little about whether my boys participated in athletics. I care very much that my girl does. And so I plan to spend the next few months tracking her progress, watching her up close and personal, trying to understand what sports mean to her, being a more focused, more active, more interested observer than I was last year or the year before. She cares about the sports she's involved in, and I think, by watching closely, I can learn more about who she is through her participation. And maybe we can grow closer in the process. It is a good start that we share a love of competitive sports.

Lizzie's fall-winter sport is wrestling. Yes, that's right: grabbing on to someone else's sweaty body and maneuvering him down onto a mat teeming with who knows how many classes of bacteria while dressed in a skintight singlet that shows everything, including goose bumps. That's what my daughter likes to do. Chin locks and camel clutches, half nelsons and body scissors. And did I mention that middle school wrestling is a coed sport? Coed it may be, but few girls go out for it. Since sixth grade, Lizzie has almost always wrestled boys, in practice and in meets.

None of that—sweaty male opponents, second-skin singlets that show panty lines, germy mats—sounds like great fun to me. But here's the worst part: You have to *weigh in in public* before every meet. A guy actually shouts out your weight to someone with a clipboard. *Shouts it out.* For me, getting on a scale in the privacy of my own bathroom is an event so fraught with fear and self-loathing that I have to psych myself up for days to do it and allow myself a weeklong recovery period. I am the one who was wrapped in a big beach towel at Lizzie's thirteenth birthday party to avoid being seen in my Speedo by a bunch of kids. There is not an alternate universe that could be imagined where I would subject myself to weekly public weigh-ins. It is amazing—and inspiring—that Lizzie is not fazed by this. It's a blessing that she has not inherited my body issues.

As I've watched her wrestle for the past two years, I've tried—but in retrospect, not that hard—to figure out what was appealing about the activity. Back in sixth grade and through part of the seventh grade season, it seemed to me, the parent, the casual observer, that what was appealing to Lizzie about wrestling was that she was winning. She was good, and she brought home ribbons and medals to prove it. Back then, at the beginning of middle school, she was in the midst of a puberty growth spurt and was taller and bigger than many of the boys in her class. And so, sometimes Lizzie won because she was stronger. And sometimes she won because the boys she wrestled—and she almost always wrestled boys—

didn't want to hurt her. But when those same boys who let her win began to see how tough she was and started actually wrestling her, she won because she was better. She had the moves. That changed the landscape. The boys began to bring their very best game to the mat. They didn't want to lose to a girl. It would be an embarrassment to lose to a girl. So they went at it. But she had three or four inches on them, and a low center of gravity, and six months of aikido, which she took back in fourth grade, and many of them couldn't bring her down.

I watched that change last year, in seventh grade, when the boys started catching up in height. Last year it was much harder for her to win matches. I am betting that this year it will be almost impossible. The boys now have shoulders and backs, biceps, delts, traps, and lats. Meanwhile, Lizzie has been busy growing her 36B. And so, as mysterious as it has been to me that she likes this sport, it is now even *more* mysterious that she is going out for it in eighth grade when her chances of winning any matches are slim.

This *really* interests me. I am a fierce competitor, one of those hard-to-take types who believes that it *is* whether you win or lose—and yeah, yeah, I know, how you play the game—that's important. I hate losing. I am a bad loser. I quit playing after a while if I lose too much. Before I met my husband, I was the SCRABBLE champ of my crowd and loved playing. But I soon discovered that he was much better at the game than I was. After I lost big a half dozen times, I opted out of the competition. Lizzie is not opting out as I did. I want to understand why. I want to see what this means about what kind of girl she is, what kind of woman she might become.

And so, as the season starts, I begin quizzing Lizzie about the attraction of wrestling (especially in the face of almost-certain defeat—a detail that, of course, I do not include in my conversation). She is, it turns out, quite articulate about her love of the sport. "It makes me feel powerful," she tells me. "And it's mental too, like figuring out what someone is going to do before he does it so you can do something first." She tells me wrestling is about balance and movement, position and strategy. One day she comes home talking about a former high school wrestling champion who had come to her PE class to demonstrate some moves. She talks about this guy using words like "graceful" and "elegant." It is the first time I hear her use the word "elegant" in any context. She says, when this guy wrestles it looks as if he were "dancing with a partner."

I want to see wrestling this way, and as long as Lizzie is talking about it, I do. But when I've gone to her sixth and seventh grade matches and seen her actually do it, circle a boy opponent, grab arms, shoulders, torsos, thighs, knees, writhe around on the mat trying to escape a hold, grimace in pain when she's in a headlock, I think, Why can't she dress in a cute little skort and go play tennis like I did at her age?

Today—Halloween—is Lizzie's first day of practice. I arrive a few minutes after the final school bell and meet up with her in front of the girls' locker room. She is wearing the costume it took us two very long hours to find at the mall last week: a deep scoop-necked, miniskirted, ultraformfitting, red and white half-angel (wings, halo), half-devil (tail, horns) outfit. Compared to the naughty nurse, sexy nun, saloon slut, tavern wench, and pirate girrrl costumes she tried on—and tried to persuade me to buy— outfits one might expect inventive sex workers to wear, this one is tame. She gives me a quick smile, grabs a power bar from my hand, and disappears into the locker room to change into her singlet. The uniform singlets that the school provides have been used hard for five, six, maybe seven seasons. Once upon a time, they must have been brilliantly colored and vibrantly elastic. Now, they are dingy and so stretched out that the kids have to constantly tug on the shorts to keep them from riding all the way up their thighs. It was painful to watch last year, so I went online and bought Lizzie her own sleek, spandex singlet, black with gold chevrons, to wear this year. I may not like wrestling, but I'm a sucker for outfits.

I am sitting on the floor in the big gym, my back against the wall, when she comes through the door. She is wearing the black and gold singlet. She is also wearing the red fishnet stockings from her half-angel, half-devil Halloween costume. It's hard not to stare. I don't even try. She's like a living, breathing exegesis of twenty-first-century girlhood, a big, audacious statement that says: I'm not sure who I am yet, but I'm having a helluva good time finding out. There's also the in-your-face subtext:

You think it's weird? Well, that's *your* problem. I was no shrinking violet, but I was never this fearless.

The coach, Mr. C., takes a look, and I see him smile the subtlest of smiles. Mr. C. was Lizzie's seventh grade history teacher, the one who enthralled the class with anecdotes about Aztec human sacrifices, and we know each other pretty well. He walks over to me, squats down, and tells me, whispering, that he has chosen Lizzie to be the captain of this year's wrestling team. "She's never missed a practice or a meet," he says, as if I, chauffeur and cheering section, didn't already know this. "She's got guts," he says. "And I think she could be a great team leader." He doesn't say—he can't say—that she's the star of the team. We both know that day is gone.

My friend Sarah has a theory about Lizzie's attachment to wrestling. One morning, running on our usual route, I tell her about the wrestling meet I watched the day before, the first one of the season. Lizzie wrestled four guys, big, beefy, eighth grade boys with meaty shoulders and broad backs, and she lost every match. She put up a tremendous fight in two of the matches and managed not to get pinned. I watched her from the sidelines, wincing every time she was thrown to the mat, watching the effort (and the pain) play across her face, yelling encouragement as I tried to block the thoughts that made a beeline from wrenched shoulder to broken neck to full-body paralysis. I counted the long minutes until the matches were over. And those were the *good* matches. The bad ones included a bout with an opponent who pinned her within five seconds, a stunning takedown that left her breathless and dazed, and a final match where she managed to stay on her feet for close to fifteen seconds and left the mat limping and in tears. I tell Sarah this story and explain my confusion about why Lizzie likes, and continues to like, wrestling.

"I see it," Sarah says, panting along beside me. "It's just her brand of feminism. She's following in your footsteps—just taking a different path." We both laugh at the nonsense, and the sense, of that remark. "When you think about it, it's really quite amazing," Sarah says. "She is a feminist like you but she gets to rebel at the same time, choosing something she knows you don't like. It's perfect."

This is one of the reasons I love running with Sarah, why I endure all those mornings she regales me with the extraordinary accomplishments of her extraordinary daughter (last week, Leah's stunning performance in a high school play; this week, her 790 PSAT score). Sarah really does listen, and she cares enough to think about what I tell her. I'd been so busy being mystified by—and, I have to admit, being kind of repelled by—the whole idea of my girl wrestling that I hadn't looked at it this way. Sarah may be right. Lizzie may have found a perfect solution to being my daughter.

I show up for after-school practice later that week. As the newly appointed captain, Lizzie leads the team in warm-up drills and stretches. I told her that I would like to participate in the prepractice drills. After a long day sitting in front of a computer screen, writing, I would welcome some late-afternoon activity. Of course, I have an ulterior motive: By joining in, I am creating one of those happy situations in which she is the boss. She is enthusiastic about the idea. The chance to show herself as a leader while simultaneously ordering her mother around—that's heady stuff. I come to school wearing sweats and an old tank top and make my way to the gym. It is very bright and very loud. It smells of floor wax and BO, not in that order.

Lizzie sits in the middle of the big mat with the team circled around her: twenty-three boys and two girls. She acknowledges me with a nod, then starts the stretches, showing and cuing for the next ten minutes or so. She is intent and intense, totally and completely in her body and in the moment. It's lovely to watch. Most of the kids follow her lead—as I've seen them follow the coach's lead—uncomplainingly if not enthusiastically. The two girls clearly admire Lizzie. She knows this. She can't help but know it. I've seen how they hug her before every practice, how they defer to her. To the boys she wrestles, the older, bigger boys, she is just another team member, another practice opponent. Maybe at the beginning, back in sixth grade, they thought it was weird wrestling a girl. Now it isn't weird; it's just unusual. For many of them, Lizzie is the only girl they have ever wrestled. They think she's cool—although not cool in a girlfriend-material kind of way. Except for Micah, that is, back last year.

He was a teammate, and their mutual crush began at wrestling practice. Micah is the one I dubbed the Phallus from Corvallis.

After warm-ups, Lizzie organizes the kids for sprints across the gym, skipping backward, grapevine, crab walk. I do everything but the crab walk. There are just some positions into which I will not (okay, cannot) contort this body. When the wrestling begins, the kids pair up to practice the latest moves.

I stand on the side of the mat watching Lizzie tussle with one of the girls on the team, a sweet-faced, six-feet-tall, 200-pound mountain of a girl who doesn't wrestle well but doesn't have to. She just plants her feet, and she stays planted. She feels uncomfortable wrestling with boys, and the only other girl on the team besides Lizzie is a small, thin sixth grader who Mountain Girl could pick up and toss across the room. Not that she would. Mountain Girl is soft and gentle. The only thing threatening about her is her size. When she and Lizzie wrestle, Mountain Girl often substitutes tickling for the holds and moves they are supposed to be practicing.

I'm watching the two of them as the assistant coach walks up to me. His name is Kenny. He is the former top-notch high school wrestler and national champion who Lizzie has told me so much about, the one who came into her PE class, the one who wrestles as if he were dancing. Kenny is now volunteering with the team. He looks like a wrestler from the neck down, with a compact, muscular, no-nonsense body. But he also has a full head of taffy-blond hair pulled back into a big, bushy ponytail and an innovative display of facial hair that makes him look half–born-again hippie, half–*The Lion King* cast member. He introduces himself and asks if I would like him to show me some moves. What can I say? I certainly hadn't planned on anything like this. I just wanted to do warm-ups with the team. But I'm standing there; everyone else is rolling around on the mats, and Kenny seems like such a sweetheart.

He tells me to take a position on my hands and knees. Then he crouches over me, wrapping one arm around my rib cage and grabbing my wrist with the other. In an instant, he has flipped me on my back. The move was fluid, almost balletic. No pain, no grunts. We reverse positions, and he shows me how to use my weight and balance to flip him. Then he flips me again, but instructs me to keep rolling, to use the momentum of his initial push to bring him down. Lizzie has stopped wrestling Mountain Girl and is watching.

"Go, Mom!" she yells. She's grinning.

Kenny goes off to work with the real wrestlers. I go back to watching Lizzie. After a few minutes, Mr. C. tells the kids to circle up again. They form a big ring around the perimeter of the mats, lining up in weight order. Then, two by two, starting with the lightest, they come to the center of the circle to wrestle. The winner gets to stay to wrestle the next in line until he loses or the weight differential becomes too much.

Lizzie and I stand side by side, watching. She is pointing out moves to me, explaining holds, telling me who weighs what and who has taken home what ribbons at which meets. Here we are, once again getting along famously, because she is the teacher and I am the student. As another wrestler comes into the circle, she elbows me in the ribs, winks, then walks over to Mr. C. She leans in to say something to him, meanwhile looking at me with a sly grin. I can't hear what she's saying over the chatter of her teammates, but I do hear Mr. C.'s booming voice.

"You want to wrestle your mom? Sure!"

Several of the kids hear it as well and steal glances over at me. This one supercharged runt of a kid, maybe seventy pounds, races over from the opposite side of the circle. "You should totally do this," he says, beaming up at me.

"Yeah," Lizzie taunts. "You should totally do this."

I guess I have to totally do this.

I give more than a fleeting thought to how ridiculous I might look. "Might" is an overly optimistic auxiliary verb. But Lizzie has set this up. This is her thing, her turf, and she has gone out of her way to include me. Another kid might be embarrassed by her mother's presence. She might avoid her mother, pretend she didn't exist. But Lizzie is trying to engage me. How can I say no?

We move into the center of the circle. The kids are hooting and clapping. Lizzie crouches down, elbows to her sides, forearms at ninety degrees, head up, eyes squinting. I mirror the stance. We circle each other, alternately trying to look fierce and breaking out in grins. She takes swipes at my knees, trying to grab on, to pull me off balance. I keep moving, staying on the balls of my feet. I swipe at her too, her elbows, her knees, her calves. I connect once, but she pulls back, and I lose control. We are not evenly matched for a variety of reasons, not the least of which is that I don't know what I'm doing. Then there's the little matter of the more than three decades that separate us. Still, I am in good shape, and I am determined to put up a fight. I'm not concerned with embarrassing myself anymore; I'm concerned with embarrassing her. She has given me this extraordinary opportunity to be part of something she loves. It's a gift, really, and I want to be worthy of it.

I swipe at her legs again and manage to get her off balance for a moment. She goes down on one knee, but I don't know what to do. I hesitate just long enough to give her time to get up. I'm still thinking about what I should have done—lunged? thrown myself on top of her?—when I find myself flat on my back. Lizzie had locked eyes with me and, keeping my gaze, had moved in quickly to grab my right ankle and bring me down. No hesitation on her part. She is on top of me before I have the good sense to roll to my stomach. Her torso is crosswise over mine, her hands gripping my wrists, the pressure of her shoulders mashing me into the mat.

Mr. C. is circling us. He gets down on his knees and bends all the way over so his head is down on the mat. This way he can see the moment that both of my shoulder blades touch the mat. The pin. He doesn't have to wait long. I struggle, really I do, but Lizzie has me. I can't work against both her and gravity. I don't know the moves, and she does. I'm down. Mr. C. calls it. The kids are hollering. I lie there for a moment, looking up at my daughter.

How must that feel—besting your mother? What a triumph. And how unique. There are all these father-son moments, from mythological tales to shooting hoops in the driveway, catching the bigger fish, moments when the younger gets the better of the older, when the younger feels his power, and the older feels the rich ambivalence of pride and fear— fear of losing status, of being replaced, of aging. For lots of women this plays out in front of the mirror, the smooth-skinned, shiny-haired, cellulite-free teen daughter showing the mother—who is now none of these things—that her physical peak has passed, that she needs to make way, to cede her status. It is still about power for men and beauty for women.

That's why this moment is so extraordinary: It is not about beauty; it is about power. Lizzie and I, minus the Y chromosomes, have engaged in a physical battle, but it has a different meaning for us than the male contest. It's not about physical strength. It's not about who the new alpha will be. It's about power, all right, but not the kind that comes from muscles. It's about her power to be different from what I am.

Lizzie extends her hand and yanks me to my feet. She raises her right hand, offering up the palm for a high five. I want to hug her, but I hold myself back. I slap her palm, a vanquished opponent, a proud mother.

TWENTY-ONE

Track-and-field season follows hard on the heels of wrestling. It's an easy transition for Lizzie—and for me too. Paying attention to her life as an athlete has, so far, been quite a bit more fun than I imagined it would be, considering my initial antipathy toward wrestling. And it's been enlightening to see Lizzie in this other role, to see those qualities that can sometimes make her so difficult to live with—fearlessness, stubbornness, pride—play out in such positive ways. It's also been a surprise to me, a very pleasant surprise, that—although her choice of sports and my athletic proclivities couldn't be farther apart—we can bond over our love of physical activity. I am looking forward to immersing myself in spring track season.

Lizzie's forte is discus, and so she moves from one power and strength sport to another. Here, though, in track, she is a bona fide star, having earned the title of district champion in both sixth and seventh grades, the best girl thrower among the top competitors in all the eight area middle schools. Of course, as with wrestling, I watched her compete through sixth and seventh grades. I saw and applauded these track victories. But I was not "studying" Lizzie's life in sixth grade, and last year I was too busy shadowing her in the classroom to also pay attention to her life on the field. And so, when I went to the meets, I was just another mother watching from the sidelines. I didn't observe with the intensity of an anthropologist. I didn't ask the penetrating questions of the journalist. This season will be different.

I have never thrown a discus, nor, before Lizzie took up the sport, had I ever even seen one thrown. When I've watched track and field events on TV—the occasional Summer Olympics over the years—I've watched track, not field. I've watched sprinters, hurdlers, and steeplechasers. I have seen some sinuously graceful men use fifteen-feet poles to vault themselves into the air as if gravity were a choice they decided not to make that day. But that's about it for my previous interest in field events. It may be, as I read on an overheated sports blog the other day, that "running is the oldest sport, but throwing heavy things is the best!" However, flinging weighty objects has never interested me.

When Lizzie announced her intention to go out for track in sixth grade and then came home from the first meeting all enthused about discus, I was taken aback. I thought of the sport as a strictly male endeavor, a sweaty world inhabited by beefy guys with linebacker shoulders and thunder thighs. Later I discovered that women had been throwing the discus in Olympic competition since they were first let into the track and field games in 1928. I also learned that discus throwing had a classic pedigree: It was a gymnastic exercise of the ancient Greeks. Both *The Iliad* and *The Odyssey* make mention of it.

But what eventually made me begin to appreciate the sport—this was toward the end of Lizzie's sixth grade season—was coming across a photograph of a famous marble statue, *Discus Thrower,* which is a Roman copy of a lost Greek original cast in the fifth century BC. The statue is of one of those gorgeous Greek men with a perfectly proportioned, elegantly muscled (do I need to add, naked) body. He is standing, knees bent, torso twisted, right arm fully extended behind him, a discus in his hand. Any second he will uncoil his body and hurl the discus in the air. How there can be such a sense of movement and power in inert stone I don't know. The statue is a miracle.

It is also a mistake. As Lizzie told me—her tone dismissive—when I showed her the photo: "That's *so* wrong. No one throws that way." Then she went on to critique the guy's stance, head position, arm position, and grasp of the discus. She was, by then, an expert. Okay, so the statue doesn't stand as a coaching tool. It will just have to be enough for me that it is a gorgeous naked man.

Because of the gorgeous naked man and because of Homer—this is the kind of sports snob I am—I have had an easier time relating to her track efforts than I did to her love affair with wrestling. Although I know, of course, that wrestling has a Greco-Roman ancestry, the sweaty-bodies-of-strangers thing was (until I actually tried it myself) a deal breaker for me. I like Sarah's take on Lizzie's unorthodox sports choices, the idea that she has found her own way to be a strong woman, a way that both follows my lead and blazes its own path. But that's Sarah's perspective, and Sarah is a forty-something women's studies professor. I am willing to believe that this is what's happening with Lizzie on a subconscious level. The explanation makes perfect sense to me. But I want to learn more about Lizzie's eye view. On a *conscious* level, day to day, what's behind her attraction to yet another power and strength sport?

We're talking about this very subject a lot these days, as the new season begins to unfold. I am attending her practices, watching carefully. The first meet is still a few weeks away. If I hit her in the right mood—undistracted, expansive, upbeat (a glorious state of being that generally lasts a few minutes less than our conversation)—I can find out quite a bit. I can find out, for example, that she thinks of the hard work of daily practice and the stress of competition as rewards. "It's like, I do something I really don't like—school—and then I get to do something I love," she tells me. She is lying on the floor on her stomach in my writing office in one of those rare expansive, upbeat moods.

"Like, let's say I fail a test." She sees my frown. "Okay, so I don't actually *fail* it, but I get a C or something." There have definitely been Cs. "So then I can go out in practice and just chuck the discus and get all that energy out, that bad feeling." I nod silently. And I think, Maybe that's been part of her attraction to wrestling too, the pure physicality of it. It is certainly the *doing* rather than the *winning* that has kept her coming back to that sport. And then I think, How smart: to use the body to quiet the mind. People pay $200 an hour for advice like this, and my daughter has come to it all by herself. She has a strategy, a healthy strategy, for dealing with disappointment, with feelings of failure or lack of competence. She knows how to take care of herself. I say none of this out loud. If I stay silent maybe she will talk more—an interviewer's trick I learned long ago, and one I should use far more often as a parent.

"I like the feeling that I am better at something than everyone else," she says, and then catches herself. "I know that sounds bad, but . . ." She trails off. "I'm not bragging. It's really true. I *am* better." She is. Through the sixth and seventh grade seasons she not only threw farther than all the other girls, she threw farther than the boys too. I mention this, and she smiles broadly. "People are amazed at how far I throw," she says. "Some of the kids think that's really cool. Some of the girls really like it that I'm better than the boys. But . . ." She trails off again. Again, I am silent. "But some of the kids, they don't like me because I'm so much better than they are."

"And so how does that make you feel?" I ask, hearing myself sound like some two-bit therapist. I am remembering how, at her age and too many years later, I would hide or underplay my achievements when I thought they'd affect my popularity, especially with boys.

"There's nothing I can do about it," she says. "I mean I could say to them that they could be good too if they worked harder, but really, it's like their problem if they're jealous of me." Okay, then. No therapist needed. Self-confidence is a beautiful thing to behold.

But, of course, no one—not even my strong, powerful, (sometimes overly) assertive daughter—is self-confident all the time. Like so many teen girls, Lizzie wants to both fit in and stand out. She wants to be accepted, one of the crowd—maybe not the *in* crowd, but some crowd, some group— but she's also intent on establishing a sense of personal style. Watching her closely this past year and a half, seeing her in action in her own world, not just at home, it seems to me that she ping-pongs between the two extremes. One minute she will flatly refuse to wear a just-purchased pair of Vans because "no one wears those anymore"; the next minute she is dressing in red fishnets for wrestling practice.

It's not just superficial style, either. Her choice of wrestling and discus shows the same dynamic. At school, she is not a member of the popular crowd or the drama geeks or the goths or the emos. But she wants to be, needs to be, a part of some crowd. The Hawks, her guy friends, give her a sense of inclusion, but during the winter and spring sports seasons, she also finds a place among the jocks. Sort of. Her choice of the two least female-friendly sports at school means she has few girl teammates, and while some of the boys clearly admire her abilities, others are intimidated and stay away. It's a difficult dynamic to insist on individuality even as you work for inclusion. I think this is part of negotiating life—not just the teen years—for those of us who crave both distinction and acceptance. For Lizzie, it is also one of her signature personality traits: the duality, the entanglement of paradoxes, the easy (and sometimes exasperating to me) acceptance of opposites. She is not only the archetypal mercurial teen, she is also the ultimate Gemini.

And a rebel with a specific cause: to be what her mother is not. Aside from, and more significant than, her choice of sports in which to compete, there is the fact that she chooses sports as the arena for her best efforts, not academics. And it *is* a choice. I don't think she lacks the brainpower to excel academically. What she lacks is the desire to do well. She knows that I was an A student, on honor roll, a National Merit scholar. She knows I went to grad school. She knows that academic achievement is part of my portfolio, and that's a good enough reason to *not* make it part of hers. Of course, it could be that all this is less about me than I think. In general, whatever happens out in the world is less about me than I think. But this mother-daughter push-pull thing is just so intense that it's hard not to see it as underlying every part of our lives.

Lizzie stands up to me within the limits of the household. She stands up to me, challenges my authority (my strength and power—the two most valued assets in the sports she has chosen, I hasten to add) in ways my sons never did, never had to. She pushes the limits, pushes way beyond the limits, which is galling and infuriating and also, when I am able to step back for a moment and think about it, kind of wonderful. In the discus ring, the way is clear for her. I am nowhere to be found. She can use everything she's got to fling that thing, to empower herself.

In the discus ring—and outside of it too—I have come to think of Lizzie as a kind of teenaged Athena, the armed warrior goddess. I know Athena is all about wisdom, and I think Lizzie has some of that, much more to come later. But for now, it's about ferocity and skill, which is also what Athena was about. It is most certainly what discus is about. I already admire Lizzie for her technical skill, but the more I read about the sport during this eighth grade season, the more practices I attend, the more I listen in on the coaching she is getting, the more my admiration grows. Throwing is apparently much, much harder than it looks—and it already looks difficult. The act involves an astonishing complexity of large and small motor muscle movements, coordination, and balance. In fact, coaches say that the technique is so difficult to master and needs so much experience to get right that world-class throwers don't reach their peak until their thirties.

Enter my Athena, age thirteen, soon to be fourteen. No one has told her how hard this is. And that's just fine, because she doesn't have to, or want to, *know* first. She is a "just do it" kind of person. Among the many things I have learned about her as she's moved from babyhood to adolescence and into her teens is that she does not enjoy thinking through questions or ideas. She does very little strategizing. If you want to catapult her into a nasty mood, all you have to do is suggest that she plan out something, make a list, break down the problem, analyze its parts. This is how I go about life. This is not Lizzie's modus operandi.

Lizzie jumps in, makes something happen, figures it out later. The doing promotes the knowing. I've noticed that if she has a writing assignment at school, she doesn't think through what she wants to say or try to figure out the dimensions of the assignment. She just puts a character on the page and doesn't consider what will happen until she has to write the sentence in which that something happens. I find this maddening. And inefficient. It is one of the main reasons I can't ever seem to help her with her homework. It is also why she is so fearless.

Lizzie's goal for this, her third and last middle school track season, is to once again be the district champion, the best eighth grade girl. She's reasonably confident she can do this, given her past victories, but she doesn't want to seem *too* confident. She thinks it will jinx her. Also, she knows that some new kid could be in the mix this year, a girl she's never thrown against before, tough competition. The coach, Bud, is also walking the line between confidence and bluster. He knows Lizzie can do it, and he tells her so—"You have it in you," he says, often and with gusto—but he stresses that she will need to work harder this year than ever before. The goal that is in the back of both of their minds is for Lizzie to break the current thirty-three-year record of 106 feet set by an eighth grade girl. That is, as Lizzie says, a "monster throw." It's more than twenty-five feet longer than Lizzie has ever thrown. It is longer than many of the varsity high school girls are throwing.

• • •

On the first day of practice, Bud gathers the fifteen kids who have decided to go out for discus this year. I am delighted to note that seven of them are girls. It's true that track-and-field is the *only* sport offered in middle school in the spring, so it brings out any and all athletic-minded girls. It is also true that three-quarters of the girls on the school's track-and-field team have signed up for running events. But still—seven discus-throwing females! Just a generation or generation and a half ago, a girl was permitted to be rough and tumble, a grunter, a sweater, until maybe age nine or ten. But by thirteen or fourteen, most of the remaining female athletes (in school and in the professional sports world) were competing in girl-friendly activities like figure skating and gymnastics, the sports that emphasized cute, petite bodies and cute boy-centric outfits. What an amazing change to be living through.

But when I look at *Teen Vogue*, which is, unfortunately, coming into our house these days courtesy of a magazine drive fund-raiser, I see virtually no change from the images that warped me when I was Lizzie's age: the blemish-free, rail-thin girls in their perfect (perfect sporty, perfect boho, perfect whatever) outfits, the tousle-haired young men by their side, everyone laughing and having way more fun than any angst- or acne-ridden teen could ever dream of having. These media images are just as disconnected from real teens' lives as they ever were. Yet amid this, there are kids like Lizzie and the six other girls who came out for discus, teen girls who somehow manage to think it's cool, or at least okay, to participate in such an unfeminine sport.

Bud has the kids come up to a line painted on the gym floor in three groups of five. Lizzie is in the last group to go to the line. "Hit the stage, Liz!" Bud yells out. The stage is about seventy-five feet from the throw line. Lizzie's winning throw in seventh grade was seventy-nine feet. "Yeah . . . stage . . . stage . . . stage," a few of the other kids begin to chant in unison. It's her first throw of the first day, and Lizzie already has a rooting section. She steps to the line and adjusts her hand around the discus. Just a second before, she was lazing against the back wall talking trash with Jason, an eighth grade boy who seems to be taking an interest in her. Now she is all business.

It makes for an odd picture because, unlike everyone else, she has not dressed for practice. She's wearing her school clothes, what I have come to think of as her "uniform," almost the exact outfit she dressed me in for my "Come As Your Book" costume party: black Levis with a wide black and silver belt, a snug, black, short-sleeved T-shirt, and a thick silver necklace. Although I've given her two pairs of my old but still good Saucony running shoes, she is wearing black-and-white checked Vans slip-ons, cheap and flimsy, already filthy and stretched out. She doesn't look like an athlete.

And then, all of a sudden, she does. She stands on the line for a moment, her face a mask of concentration. She steadies her gaze, takes a breath. Then she bends her knees deeply while torquing her body to the right, her shoulder dropping, her discus hand almost touching the floor. She whips her arm around, her shoulder leading the way. Back and forth, back and forth, working up momentum until she lets the discus fly. This technique is called "scaling," which is a beginner's throw. It's hard to get a lot of footage out of it. Lizzie lets loose. The discus hits the floor about five feet shy of the stage, an amazing throw.

After another two rounds of scaling, Bud has them try spinning, the more sophisticated discus-throwing technique. The thrower takes an initial stance facing away from the direction of the throw, then spins around one and a half times to build momentum, then releases the throw. It can be beautiful to watch. Or it can be awkward and jerky. Each line of kids tries the throw. Most release either too soon or too late, the discus flying off left and right, hitting the sidewalls of the gym.

"Make a basket, Liz!" this one kid yells out when it's Lizzie's turn. The basketball hoop is suspended above the stage. Lizzie takes her time pacing back from the throwing line, measuring her turns. I've been watching discus videos, so I know what to look for. I can see that Lizzie is making her arm do more work than it should. She needs more back, more legs. I can see that she's hesitating on the follow-through. (Google makes know-it-alls out of the most ignorant among us.) On her next attempt, the discus flies on the stage, a solid seventy-five-foot throw. Bud hustles over and claps a hand on Lizzie's back, then gives me a thumbs-up.

I spend the next three weeks attending her after-school practice sessions. I try to make myself invisible, but sometimes pride gets the best of me, and I don't stay on the sidelines where I belong. One afternoon I walk over to Bud to quiz him about how Lizzie is progressing. Lizzie watches me, gives me a dirty look, and in the car on the way home, tells me to butt out.

"You're embarrassing me," she says.

"Embarrassing you?" I say, stupidly jumping to my own defense. "But we wrestled together in front of your whole team, remember? How could my just talking to your coach be embarrassing?" She sighs deeply and dramatically, inserts her earbuds and doesn't talk to me the rest of the way home.

Another day, after she's thrown the best I've seen yet, Bud motions me over. He wants to tell me that he's never worked with a kid who has so much talent. Lizzie watches us from across the field. I expect to pay for this moment in the car on the way home. But instead, she wants to know just what he said and beams when she hears it, and then, joyous and expansive, squeezes my arm and tells me how great it is that I am coming to all her practices. A year ago, this presto-chango act would have given me whiplash. Now, I smile and enjoy the moment.

It's the first track meet of the season, and the first day of sun after more than a week of steady rain. Lizzie's day began with jazz band practice at 7:30 a.m., then the full complement of classes, including two tests, then an hour of warming up with the team, followed by a twenty-minute bus ride to the track. It's five p.m. now. She's been on the go for nine and a half hours. I arrive with admiration and snacks—a vitamin water drink, a power bar, and a small bag of pretzels. Lizzie is standing by the discus ring with her teammates.

"Ya gotta win for us," one girl is saying to Lizzie.

"Yeah," says another. "Here's the plan: We wanna rule. You just come in first, and that'll get us started."

Lizzie takes several swigs of water in between jabbering with Starr, her teammate and casual friend. Two boys come over, then another two. This is an active social scene. Lizzie is talking fast, talking nonsense. I can see that she's nervous. She takes me aside and whispers that she's afraid of screwing up and making a fool of herself. Her team is expecting a lot from her, and she's expecting a lot from herself.

I give her a hug, say what I hope are the right words, and then move back, away from her and her friends. I want to be supportive, not intrusive. I am well aware of the phenomenon of the Spectator Parent from Hell, the parent who coaches from the sidelines when he or she (okay, he) is not bellowing at the actual coach or screaming at one or another official. That's not, and will never be, who I am.

Lizzie sees someone she knows from the opposite team, a girl who came in second at district last year. They high-five each other.

"Hey," Lizzie says, "when you're in that ring, like, I hate you. But when we're out here, you're my friend."

"That works for me," the girl says, grinning.

I ask Lizzie how far she'd like to throw, what would feel good for her this afternoon. "Anything over eighty," she whispers to me. There's a white line in the field that delineates eighty feet. She's staring at it. But she says out loud, sounding cocky but also self-mocking, "I can do this! I am the woman! Ninety feet has my name on it."

When it's Lizzie's turn, Julia, the girl who won second place in district last year, and Starr shout out encouragement. I struggle with negotiating that space between overly involved and supportive. I want to massage her shoulders, whisper encouragements in her ear, shout, clap. I rein myself in. "All right, Lizzie!" I yell once. Then I shut up and watch.

Lizzie has had one session with a university discus thrower, a young woman who now assists a high school coach, and I can tell immediately. She is doing something different with her body. She is, she tells me later, thinking of nothing other than what Nora has told her. She doesn't hear the shouts of her teammates, and she forgets about the boys who have come over to watch. Nora's voice is in her ears: Level shoulders. Block hip. Bend knees. Hop, big hop. Burst out. Release. Her spin is faster, more powerful than I remember. Also, more graceful. The discus sails through the air. When it lands, the guy who is helping at the ring, the volunteer, whistles.

"Whoa," he says to no one. "That's a winner." They pull out the tape measure. The other volunteer yells a number that I can't hear.

"What was that?" I shout over to the guy in the ring.

"That," he says, shaking his head, "was eighty-six feet eleven inches. Is she your daughter?" I am grinning. "Well, she just beat most of the boys as well as all of the girls." Lizzie hasn't heard the distance yet. I tell her, hugging her, whapping her on the back. First throw, first meet, and she has surpassed last year's district-winning throw by almost eight feet. She is glowing. She feels, she tells me later, like she could fly around the world.

"You know the number we're looking for," Bud says to me. We're standing behind the discus cage watching Lizzie's first throw. It's now the third meet of the season. The number Bud is referring to is not the number of feet Lizzie needs to throw to win this event. Whatever she throws, she will win the event. Her throws so far this season have been an astounding twenty-five feet farther than whoever takes second place. The number he's referring to, the number we're all eyeing, is that 106 feet set back in 1975.

Lizzie scales the first throw, as she always does. The basic technique, a bit of insurance. It soars across the eighty-foot chalk line on the field. Before the discus lands, she has her back turned to the field bending over to pick up the next discus. Her spins, all three, are quick, fluid, and graceful. She whips it. She has added the hop she saw on the YouTube video I found, the ten best throws set to *Rocky*-style music. At the release, she makes a noise that is something between a grunt and a yell. The discuses, each one of them, spin in low arcs across the field. Every one of the throws is over ninety feet, the longest being ninety-four feet five inches, a new personal best. She is buoyant. At home, she is suddenly Little Miss Perfect, volunteering to clean her bathroom, studying for a math test without my merciless nagging, even eating a few pieces of sautéed zucchini without complaint. I wish track season could last forever.

At subdistricts the next week, Lizzie—loose, laughing, flirting with the boys—comes up with yet another personal best: ninety-six feet six and three-quarters inches. She is less than ten feet away from breaking the record. "I *own* one hundred," she tells her teammate Starr. "One hundred is *mine*." At home she continues to be cooperative and downright chipper. I observe her actually hanging up a wet towel, a sighting as rare as coming upon an ivory-billed woodpecker. On the one hand, it feels a little scary, like I'm in a movie: *The Stepford Teen*. On the other hand, I could totally get used to this.

At the final practice the next week, Lizzie hurts her wrist. She's out on the field, standing apart from the rest of the team, crying, when I get there. I am late today, for the first time, and have missed most of the practice. She says she's not crying because her wrist hurts. She's crying because every one of her throws has been out-of-bounds, scratches. She's never had such a dismal practice before. Bud corrals the kids back to the gym for a pep talk. I want to get Lizzie back home, ice the wrist, get some ibuprofen in her, but Lizzie insists she's okay, and this is Bud's last chance to say those inspiring, coachlike things coaches say, so I stand off to the side and watch.

The boys are all sitting together, goofing off, elbowing each other, talking. One of the girls is fiddling with jewelry, another is texting, a third is rifling through her backpack. Lizzie, on the other hand, is staring straight at Bud, hanging on every word, more focused and intent than I have ever seen her. It makes me realize how little of her attention I actually have at other moments—and how little of this intensity I've seen from her in the classroom. This, here, is what passion is all about, the difference between doing what you have to do and doing what you love.

Bud is talking about blacking everything out but the throw. Lizzie is blacking out everything but Bud. When he dismisses the team, everyone but Lizzie rushes to the door. She seems still to be in a self-induced trance. Bud walks over to her, puts his hands on her shoulders. "In ten years, I've never had a thrower like you," he says. Lizzie looks proud and scared. She grabs for my hand.

Two days later, it's the district meet, the culmination of the season and, for Lizzie, the culmination of her middle school athletic career. The event is being held at the University of Oregon's Hayward Field, arguably one of the most famous track-and-field venues in the country: the site of four (soon to be five) Olympic track-and-field trials; the track where the very first pair of Nikes were worn in a race, back when Nikes were a one-of-a-kind experimental running shoe created by an obscure track coach in his garage with the help of his wife's waffle iron. This is the track running legend Steve Prefontaine (and two subsequent movies) made famous. This field has history, and it has gravitas. It is a big deal that the area kids are allowed to compete on this hallowed ground.

Lizzie's discus event is supposed to begin at 1:30, but when I arrive a half hour early, I discover that there's been a last-minute schedule change. Now, eighth grade girls' discus is the very last event of the day. We have at least three hours to kill, and by "we" I mean my two sons, their girl-friends, my husband, and I. We have all come to cheer her on. We stand out in the field watching the long jumpers, then the high jumpers. Runners are circling us. The air is hot and still. We are baking out here under a surprisingly forceful sun. In Oregon in midspring you don't know what to expect—rain, hail, sun, clouds—but one meteorological event you don't even consider is a cloudless ninety-degree day. Today is a cloudless ninety-degree day. There is no shade anywhere, and no one has thought to bring sunblock. Lizzie's shoulders and forearms are fast approaching crimson.

The afternoon seems endless. There is nothing quite so uninteresting as watching other people's children compete. Lizzie walks from event to event. She is nervous and bored, wired and tired, alternately sullen—the heat is making us all ill-tempered—and flirtatious, because track, regard-less of whatever else is going on, is still a great place to scope out the guys.

I try not to hover, but I have difficulty restraining myself. I pester her to find a little slice of shade behind a utility pole. I pester her to drink the purple electrolyte drink my husband has bought for her. Then pester her not to drink too quickly or too much. I ask, occasionally—on far too many occasions—how she's feeling, how her wrist is, if she's nervous, if she needs to stretch out. She shoots me dirty looks, walks away.

It's almost four p.m. when the last group of eighth grade girls starts throwing. Because Lizzie is the leader, the girl with the longest throw through the season, she is the last of the last. There is no wind, not a whiff of a breeze. A light breeze would be good. It can help carry the discus a few extra feet. Lizzie's hair is matted to her scalp. The skin on her shoulders is an angry red. Her body, she tells me later, feels heavy and awkward. She feels nauseated and jangly, her hands tingling, her head pounding. She is thinking: This is it. This is my last meet, my last chance to beat the record. She is thinking: Everyone is watching me, not just my parents and my brothers and their girlfriends, not just my discus teammates but my whole team.

The crowd around the discus ring is six or seven deep. All the other events are over. Bud is standing by Lizzie whispering to her. He is going to position himself (illegally, it turns out) on the field about one hundred feet from the ring. "Just try to hit me," he says as he jogs away. Lizzie nods, her face expressionless.

On her first throw, a practice, she releases too soon, and the discus flies out-of-bounds, a scratch. I am standing behind the throwing cage, my fists clenched. I know I shouldn't say anything, but I do anyway: "It's okay. No problem." She doesn't look up, but I can tell that she hears me, and I can tell she wishes I'd shut up. The next throw is in. I allow myself a breath.

After the round of practice throws comes the first round of real throws, five girls, two throws apiece. Lizzie is last in the rotation. Long minutes go by. Finally, it's her turn. Her spin is a little slow, but the form looks good, and the release comes at the right moment. The discus is in the air, dead center. But there's no wind to keep it aloft. The second throw looks just like the first, technically perfect but with little oomph. She is throwing in the seventy-foot range, more than twenty feet shy of what she threw at the last meet. She doesn't stay in the cage or near the ring to hear the exact measurements. She knows, looking out on the grassy field, that the throws are short. Again, we wait. The four other girls all take their two final throws. Everyone is having a tough day. No one is throwing even close to Lizzie's short throw.

I can tell by her body language that she's not just hot and tired, she's discouraged and disappointed. Every meet this season she has posted a new personal record. We've all come to take it for granted. Those successes have fueled her. But this afternoon, the tank seems empty. I want to be the voice inside her head, the "you can do it" voice. I spend a second debating whether a comment from me would be helpful or harmful, and I come to no conclusion. So, I do what I feel compelled to do. I walk over and grab her by the shoulders. They are more muscular than mine. We are almost the same height now. When the hell did that happen? "You own this event," I say, and look her in the eyes. I know she's thinking, Two more throws, and that's it. She's also thinking, she tells me later, that I should get out of her face.

She sets herself up and throws. Her form is lovely. The discuses fall within a few feet of each other. The spotter runs to put in the little yellow flags. Lizzie turns her back on the field and walks away. I can see the tears in her eyes. She knows she hasn't thrown near one hundred feet. I move in closer to the cage to hear. The spotter holds one end of the tape measure at the farthest flag. The woman in the cage pulls the tape taut and calls out a number. Lizzie's best throw of the afternoon is eighty-three feet, less than the shortest of her winning throws through the season. Still, she takes first place. That's how much better she is than her competition. Really, her only competition, all season long, has been herself. With the eighty-three-foot throw, she is once again the district champion. But she hasn't broken the magic one hundred mark and, of course, she hasn't broken the 106-foot record.

I run after her to tell her that she's won. "I don't give a fuck!" she yells. I have never heard her use the word *fuck*. "I want to go home." She's crying. I move to put my arm around her shoulder, and she shrugs it off. I watch her as she walks away. I have to go to a meeting, and as much as I hate meetings, I'm glad. I don't know what I'd say to Lizzie in the car, but whatever I'd say, it would be wrong. My husband takes her home. He tells her that he understands why she's so upset but to remember that she just won first place, that she is the district champ for the third year in a row.

"I hate track," she tells him. "I'm never going to throw again." If I had been in the car with her, what would I have done? Stupidly tried to argue her out of her funk? Been smart enough to shut up and turn on her favorite radio station? I don't know. I want to say—I want to believe—I would have been smart. My husband *is* smart. He keeps his mouth shut.

At home, she gets out of the car, grabs the practice discus that always sits on the porch, and goes out into the meadow in front of our house. She twirls and throws, twirls and throws, grace and power, anger and release. Her fourth throw sails across the meadow and lands behind the pear tree. Then she marches inside, turns on the Xbox 360, turns on the TV, turns on her controller, and plays Halo for the next three hours.

When I get home, the discus is still out there behind the tree. I grab a tape measure. She has thrown 101 feet.

I run in the house to tell her, interrupting the Halo game. She looks up, clear-eyed.

"Oh, I'll do better than that next year in high school when I'm on varsity," she says.

TWENTY-TWO

I t is June. There are just a few days left of classes, just a week until eighth grade graduation. Lizzie and I both know what this means: We have to go shopping. For a dress. My discus-throwing, singlet-wearing warrior girl needs something fancy to wear for the ceremony and the party that follows. The air is thick with anticipation, and not the good kind.

We have managed, since our ill-fated outing before the start of eighth grade, to shop successfully together, if success can be defined as buying an occasional flimsy T-shirt at Forever 21 or another pair of slip-on, skull-imprinted Vans, at Hot Topic. But a dress? Lizzie has not worn this particular item of clothing since the fifth grade when it was mandated female attire for the school's traditional, end-of-the-year sit-down dinner at a restaurant. (One of the teachers conducted a one-month, proactive etiquette class before the event so the fifth graders wouldn't embarrass the school.) Since fifth grade, Lizzie has managed birthday parties and holiday galas, *Nutcracker* Christmas performances and theater outings, all without a dress.

But dress shopping we must go. The trip at first unfolds as our shopping trips have unfolded in the past, with a spirited discussion of plans (after buying the dress, we'd get a latte, we'd shop for jewelry) that within a half hour devolves into stony silence. We both know the script. Macy's has nothing she will even consider. At the Gap, I grab three sundresses from the racks while she looks idly through the basket of lip gloss at the counter. She grudgingly agrees to try on one, which turns out to be—no big surprise here—"the ugliest dress in the world." At one of the other mall stores, the dresses all appear to be designed for ninety-five-pound prostitutes. At another, the look is Bollywood on acid. We are now not even talking to each other as we trudge miserably from one store to another. Finally, at the sixth store, we (and by "we" I mean "me") find four dresses worth trying on, three of which fit, don't make her look like a whore, and are affordable. I am beside myself with joy. Short-lived.

"Which one do you like best?" I ask in my perkiest voice. Each time she emerges from the dressing room, I—along with two twittering salesgirls—exclaim, "Really cool. You look great." But when I ask her which one, she gives me an icy stare and stalks right by me and out of the store. "I hate them all," she says when I catch up with her. "I hate dresses. I am not going to wear a dress, and I'm not going to go to graduation." It is that steep, breathless descent from particular to all-encompassing, that dizzying downward spiral I have witnessed so many times before: I hate this book, she would say when I asked how homework was going. Then, I hate to read. Followed by, I hate school. And then, I'm never going to school again. Of course, I should be used to this by now. Of course, I should not react. But I am tired and cranky, and I react. The good part is I catch myself reacting. The good part is I recognize the script. The bad part is I keep reading from it. She has her role: explosive child, mercurial teen, rebel girl. I have mine: anxious mother who needs to prove she's better than her own mother was, wounded mother who yearns to feel a bond with her daughter that she never felt with her own mother.

I am busy psychoanalyzing myself into a funk as I trail behind Lizzie. Then, somewhere between Wetzel's Pretzels and Victoria's Secret, I have an epiphany. I have *two* epiphanies. Epiphany number one: It's a dress, dummy, and sometimes a dress is just a dress. This dress, this shopping trip, *any* shopping trip doesn't have to have deep meaning. It doesn't have to mean there is an unbridgeable gulf between my daughter and me. It doesn't have to be symbolic. It could just be. It could just be a crappy experience, and that's all. Epiphany number two: This script I've been carrying around, the one I've been reading from since Lizzie hit tweenhood, I could choose to put it down and walk away from it. No one is forcing me to play the angry, wounded mother role. No one is forcing me to lug this thing around with me, to keep reading, to keep turning the pages.

Sure, my character in this play has a backstory. But *my* past doesn't have to determine *our* future. I can't change my own childhood. I can't change who my mother was and the experiences I had as a daughter. But I can change how I think about it all. I can decide, for example, to be a grown-up, to consider that my mother's shortcomings as a mother were her problem, not mine. In that lifelong standoff we had at the "She's Okay, I'm Not Okay Corral," maybe I was—am—actually okay. So what about if I just take that thick, dog-eared script out of my backpack, set it down somewhere—that bench in front of Orange Julius looks perfect— and walk away? I imagine doing just that. I picture the script. I feel its weight, then feel my own lightness as I remove it from my pack and set it on the bench. I seem to be standing a little taller. My shoulders are squared. Have I been hunching all this time? The sense of lightness is both liberating and scary. I know I've just stumbled on a life lesson. Am I smart enough to learn it?

"Hey," I say, grabbing Lizzie's arm conspiratorially. "Let's go see a movie." She doesn't know what to make of this quick turn of events. Now is when we are supposed to trudge through the mall, silent and angry, get into the car and drive home, silent and angry. I am veering from the script. But she is game. That's the great thing about her mercurial nature. The mercury rises fast, but it falls fast too. There is a multiplex theater at one end of the mall. We buy tickets for the new Adam Sandler movie and spend the next ninety or so minutes watching it and eating our way through a large bag of popcorn. When the movie is over, and we are walking back through the mall to the exit nearest the car, Lizzie turns to me. "Okay," she says brightly, "let's go buy that dress."

Two weeks later, on an otherwise cool mid-June evening, the temperature in the big gym at Spencer Butte Middle School is inching into the eighties, the inevitable result of cramming more than four hundred parents, grandparents, and bored-to-tears (literally) siblings into this cavern-

ous but windowless space. It's eighth grade graduation, the finale—to the
school year, to the middle school years, and to the year and a half I have
spent immersed in my daughter's life. Tonight, sitting in the bleachers,
I am glad it's over—all of it—and I am also sad.

This has been an intense, operatic, nearly psychosis-inducing time, one
of those life experiences that grabs you by the throat and won't let go until
you've learned, somehow, to breathe with hands around your neck. And
then, and only then, when the hands loosen their grip, does what seemed
like a stranglehold become almost a caress. I have hated and loved this
time—hated the emotional upheavals, the turmoil, the just plain *work* of
it all, but I have loved the shared moments, the unexpected humor, the
insights into her character and mine, the intimacy, the intimacy.

Tonight, I look at Lizzie in her new black and white strapless sundress,
sitting with her eighth grade classmates on folding chairs set in neat rows
on the gym floor, and I think about how proud I am. I am proud of Lizzie
for many things, but at this moment, I am most proud that she has made
it through the land mine of middle school with an unshakable sense of
self. I am proud that *we* made it through these years without engaging in
all-out warfare—although some of the skirmishes were mighty, and there's
no denying wounds were inflicted and suffered. She could have made it
through school with a few more As, with a few more appearances on the
honor roll, and the two of us could have made it through with a few more
cease-fires. But the important thing is, we avoided disaster. I know that
sounds as if I had set the bar awfully low, but I don't mean it that way.
Avoiding disaster is a major accomplishment. Avoiding disaster is cause
for celebration.

It hasn't been a slam dunk. Lizzie's penchant for sketchy friends, her
forays posing as a sixteen-year-old in cyber society, her Attitude with a
capital A, her volatility, her unpredictability have made these years a
major challenge. And then there's me with my heavy baggage and my
high expectations and my iron-willed desire to have everyone do as I tell
them. When I first began this immersion into Lizzie's life and was reading
everything about teen girls I could get my hands on, I read—and laughed
out loud about—this statement: The two worst times in a woman's life are
when she's thirteen and when her daughter is thirteen. It's a clever turn

of phrase, which makes it funny, which maybe robs it of its stone-cold truth. It has been impossible for me to be the mother of a teen without, in some important, necessary, and painful ways, processing my teenage self. It has been impossible for me to learn how to be the mother of a daughter without revisiting my own life as a daughter.

I am thinking all this as I gaze down at Lizzie sitting tall at the end of the row in a metal chair. She is, like everyone else in the room, sweating. Through the close-up lens on my camera, I can see the sheen on her forehead. Just as I focus, as if she could sense the camera's gaze, she looks up into the bleachers at me and smiles. And I think: Last week we celebrated her fourteenth birthday—and no one said anything about *fourteen* being the worst time in a woman's life. Maybe we're out of the woods.

At the very least we—and I mean Lizzie and me—are out of middle school, officially, as of this evening. And I couldn't be more relieved. Everyone says these are the most trying years, and everyone is right. The hothouse environment of middle school means exuberant, luxuriant physical and emotional growth but also heat and intensity, the stress that comes with change—the price one pays for such growth. Social development, the making and nurturing of friendships—the single most important aspect of middle school for girls—has been very hard to watch as it has played out in Lizzie's middle school life: the best friend she can't always depend on; the posse that, unpredictably, does not allow her to ride along; the friends with issues; the revolving door of boyfriends. Eating lunch alone is a close second to bleeding through your tampon on the list of Worst Things That Can Happen to a Middle School Girl. And it's happened to Lizzie. I've seen it, and I've felt her pain.

Tonight if Lizzie is not exactly buoyant, she is at least upbeat. She is smiling as she sits quietly, half listening to a student jazz trio play a long, meandering tune, as she occasionally looks over her shoulder to check out the audience and more than occasionally tugs at her new dress.

She is wearing the dress with a black strapless bra (my child, my little girl, in a black strapless bra) and a pair of my Spanx underneath. She's got silver bangles on her wrist and three silver hoops in her ears, one in the right, two in the left. Yesterday, as a surprise present for graduation,

I took her to High Priestess, the edgiest piercing and tattoo shop in town (which in this town is saying something), where she got a second piercing in her left ear—something she's been wanting since sixth grade—and, on the spur of the moment, I got a third hole in my right earlobe. Lizzie was thrilled, both for herself and for us. "I'm so glad we did this together," she said as we walked back to the car. "It makes it even more special." Now *this* is a script I like.

"Just think," I said, "when you're eighty, and I'm long gone . . ." She looked stricken for a moment. I put my arm around her shoulders. "When you're eighty, you'll look at that hole in your ear and remember this *exact* moment."

"Cool," she said. We drove back home in intimate silence.

Finally, after the jazz trio, a poem, and two speeches, the student emcee brings the principal to the podium, and we begin the meat-and-potatoes part of the evening, the parade of 144 kids across the width of the gym, each one called by name, each one walking solo with plenty of photo ops along the way. Last week the kids were all asked to write a sentence to be read aloud by one of their teachers as they walked to get their diplomas. They had three prompts: 1. "My most memorable moment in middle school was . . . " 2. "What I most look forward to in high school is . . . " and 3. "What I am most proud of is . . . " The hands-down most memorable moment appears to be the daylong field trip to the Shakespeare Festival in Ashland. Lest the English teachers get too excited, the two dozen kids who cite this as unforgettable make clear they are referring to the several hours they got to roam around town without a teacher trailing them. As for what these middle schoolers most look forward to, the winner is "getting my license." Was life ever that simple? One boy in a suit jacket too big for him has written that he looks forward to "taking many different, interesting classes in high school." The room is momentarily stunned into silence. Another boy, a sweet-faced child, has written that he is most proud of his parents who helped and supported him. I am betting that every parent including that kid's parents are wishing they could clone that boy. One girl says she's most proud of getting straight

As, and I (along with every parent other than hers, I'm betting) work hard to suppress a groan. Self-esteem is one thing. Public self-congratulation is another.

I watch the parade of kids, the girls in their slinky dresses, high heels, and full-on makeup, the boys in their baggy jeans or ill-fitting dress-up clothes. The girls move sinuously, gracefully (except for a few who totter on the high heels), as if they already understood and were comfortable with the power of their now adult bodies. The boys, many of them, slouch and stumble. They are gawky and ill at ease, even those who put on airs, like the guy who fashions himself a gangsta or the kid who is wearing, as he has worn every day for the past two years, a woolen ski hat with earflaps, or the boy who ambles up to the podium wearing a black sweatshirt with the hood pulled down over his eyes.

When it's Lizzie's turn, she shuffles across the room, courtesy of the newly purchased silver flip-flops slapping against her heels. She absolutely, resolutely refused to try on dress shoes, and I wasn't about to press the issue. Heels are an abomination, a crime against nature, and I hope she never wedges her feet into a pair, ever. She is smiling, swinging her arms as she walks, shooting glances up into the stands where we all sit. Then I hear the teacher read, "Elizabeth is most proud of how she did in discus all three years."

I am so glad she wrote this to be said aloud. It means that she really is at peace with her performance at the district meet. That was such a hard and important lesson for her. If she is to be a competitive athlete in high school, learning how to deal with off days, learning to play the mental as well as the physical game will be key. Nora, the college student who gave her a few discus lessons during the season, said Lizzie was good enough to be tapped immediately for the varsity team. My daughter, the varsity athlete. Lizzie has already signed up for all her ninth grade courses, and among them is a special athlete training class during her last period. Will my daughter be a track star? Will she shine through high school, set records, be recruited by college coaches? Turn pro? It is not hard to have goals for the future—I am an inveterate goal setter—but it is very difficult to actually imagine the future. What will happen in the next four years? Will Lizzie find a teacher who sparks her? A class that grabs her, like junior year English grabbed me? (Thank you, Mr. Hawkey, wherever you are.) A dependable best friend? A boyfriend who endures more than a month? Will she hold on to the strength of character and stubbornness that make her *her* but learn to modify (or maybe just outgrow) the moodiness, to keep that mercury in the temperate zone rather than zipping between arctic and equatorial? What sort of young woman will emerge in four years' time? And what sort of relationship will I have with her? Watching her now in her new dress, her pretty face flushed with heat and excitement, I am overcome with optimism.

The ceremony is finally over. Middle school is finally over. How can three years be simultaneously interminable and expeditious? How did nine months of eighth grade go by in what now seems like a matter of weeks? To me, that is. Not to Lizzie. To Lizzie, this year, these three years, have been endless. It was as if, she told me in the car on the way to the ceremony, she had *always* been in middle school and always would be. All that came before was fuzzy; all that would come after was unimaginable, or rather, unimagined. She didn't think ahead like that. When you're in the middle, as in *middle* school, you can see neither the beginning— those halcyon days of elementary school with two recesses and teachers who read books aloud and chocolate milk at lunch—nor the end—the way life opens up after high school is over, the person you will grow to be when you leave home. Sitting in the bleachers in the gym watching Lizzie shake the hand of her principal, I wrap my arms around the shoulders of my two sons who are seated on either side of me. Both of them are out of high school now. They have broad shoulders. They are six feet tall. And all I did was blink.

It takes a while for all of us to file out of the gym. The kids—the graduates— head to the cafeteria at the other end of the building for the last big dance. I follow, not seeing Lizzie yet, then hover at the cafeteria threshold and peek in the room. It has been decorated by a parent committee and looks like every room decorated by every parent committee since the beginning of time. The windows are blacked out with drapes. There's a disco ball, strobe lights, blaring music, and long tables with bowls of red licorice ropes, Oreos, Skittles, Hershey's Kisses, mini-Snickers bars, and a two-foot-high stack of greasy pizza boxes. The girls are huddled together in clumps. The boys are diving into the food. I scan the crowd again looking for Lizzie. I see Nattie. With her newly shaved head, she is hard to miss. I see Allie in a flouncy dress. The Hawks are standing together by the Snickers bowl snickering. The music has started, eardrum-rattling techno-crap, and the strobes are strobing. I lean against the door frame, watching as a few girls dance. Then, from behind, someone grabs me around the waist and gives me a hug. It's Lizzie. I turn around, and we smile at each other.

"You can go any time," she says.

ACKNOWLEDGMENTS

This book would not have been possible—or, probably, *necessary*—without Lizzie, my charming, alarming, disarming, mercurial, and totally miraculous daughter. My greatest debt is to her for agreeing to this project; for letting me into her life at a time when many girls want as little to do with their mothers as possible; for sharing her thoughts, ideas, and experiences; for being my guide and my teacher in all things teen; for her openness and honesty even when it hurt; for lattes sipped at The Bean and songs sung in transit—and for consistently, insistently, willfully being absolutely true to who she is. She has taught me more about motherhood than one would think I needed to learn the third time around. And she has, unknowingly, helped me to better understand the daughter I once was.

I owe a big debt to my friend Elizabeth Sarah Reis, a model mother (and daughter) who listened and gave counsel all along, and to her lovely and accomplished daughter Leah. The bar they set is mighty (and, sometimes, infuriatingly) high. More power to them! I thank the teen girl experts who shared their ideas and insights with me: Christina Armstrong, Joyce Baker, Myles Cooley, Eliza Kingsford, Dr. Catherine Kordesch, Kara Penniman, Elizabeth Remini, and Kinlen Wheeler. I thank the amazing and talented middle school teachers, coaches, and staff who live with grace and humor in the tween/teen world and helped me understand it: Ron Black, Steve Connelly, Kenny Cox (gentle soul, in memorium), Bud Kaufman, Mary Beth Pattyn, Bekke Reiman, Michael Roderick, Ellen Siegel, and

Olivia Stieber. I thank the good people at Camp Wilani for allowing me to be part of what they do—and believing I could do it. I thank Jean, Abby, Jessica, Megan, and the rest of the crew at Supreme Bean, my office-away-from-home, for hosting many of my interviews and providing a space for Lizzie and me to chill when we did, indeed, need chillin'. I thank (and celebrate) the scores of mothers I talked to, listened to, and eavesdropped on in restaurants and grocery stores, waiting rooms and airports, conferences and coffeehouses who, with honesty (weariness, pride, tears, et cetera) told their mother-daughter tales. I thank mothers Teresa Barker, Barbara Ehrenreich, Sarah Lowe, and Leslie Steeves for showing me the light at the end of the tunnel. I thank Perrie Patterson (who dodged the bullet by having sons), for believing in me, no matter what.

To my team at Viking—Molly Stern, Liz Van Hoose, Laura Tisdel, Dina Rubin—my deep appreciation for your commitment to my work, your passionate efforts, and your creative energy. To my agent David Black, who always, always has my back: What can I say? You rock my world. To my extraordinary husband, Tom Hager, who finds himself caught between two headstrong females, who has had to dance—and duck—and does so with equanimity and love: Thank you for seeing that I had to do this and for keeping me sane while I did. And grazie mille encore, Betts, with all my heart.